Errors of Judgement

Errors of Judgement

SOE's Disaster in the Netherlands,
1941-44

NICHOLAS KELSO

ROBERT HALE · LONDON

Robert Hale Limited
Clerkenwell House
Clerkenwell Green
London EC1R 0HT

British Library Cataloguing in Publication Data

Kelso, Nicholas
    Errors of judgement : SOE's disaster
in the Netherlands, 1914–44.
    1. Netherlands – Resistance movements. Role
of Great Britain, Army. Special Operations
Executive, 1941–1945
    I. Title
    940.54'86'41

ISBN 0-7090-3345-1

Photoset in North Wales by
Derek Doyle & Associates, Mold, Clwyd
Printed in Great Britain by
St Edmundsbury Press, Bury St Edmunds, Suffolk
Bound by WBC Bookbinders Limited

Contents

Part One

Part Two

Illustrations

Picture Credits

All illustrations supplied by kind permission of the
Netherlands War Institute

Preface

In recent years the successes – such as there were – of Britain's war-time Special Operations Executive have been given wide publicity in a number of books and documentaries. But there is another side to the coin. This book is the account of one of SOE's major disasters, which took place in the Netherlands between 1942 and 1944. It is a tale of courage and sacrifice, crass stupidity and frustration, and of some brilliant counter-espionage work. The inherent weaknesses in SOE's security are cruelly exposed, providing powerful ammunition for those who believe that SOE was counter-productive. The effect is one almost of farce, as N (Dutch) Section blunders from one catastrophe to another with appalling ineptitude. It is also a sobering thought that the personnel of Dutch Section, like their colleagues in F (French) Section, came close to providing the Germans with clues as to the timing of D-Day.

In the long run, the *Englandspiel* – as it was known to the German security staff – provides a good many lessons in the need for security. Most of this is common sense but very important common sense nonetheless. If there is one lesson that stands out above all else, it is that a country with an inefficient Secret Service is likely to do itself – and its allies – more damage than the enemy. As such SOE Dutch Section was a distinct liability to the Allied cause.

The book itself is divided into two main sections. The first part deals with the actual story of what happened, whilst the second part (p.179) is taken up with an analysis of SOE's mistakes.

German Secret Services and Security Forces

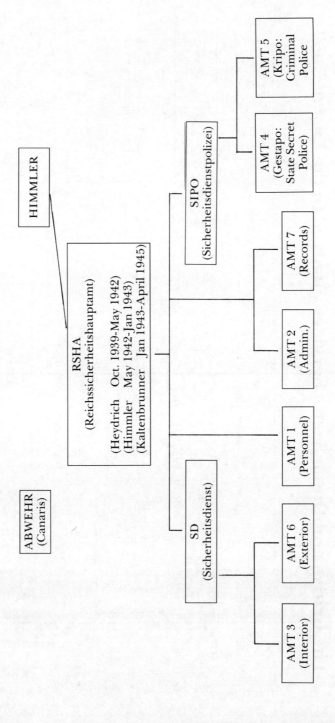

The British and Dutch Secret Services involved in the *Englandspiel*

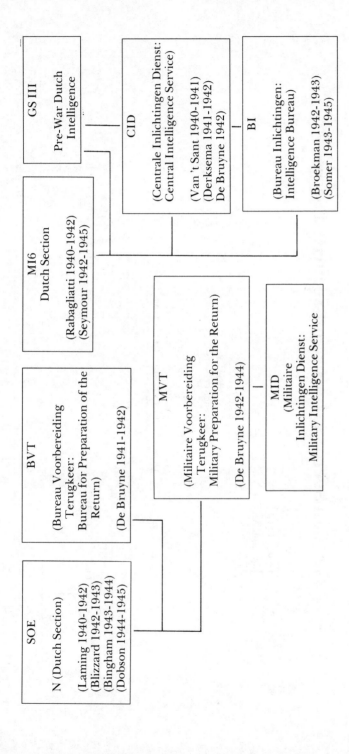

SOE
N (Dutch Section)

(Laming 1940-1942)
(Blizzard 1942-1943)
(Bingham 1943-1944)
(Dobson 1944-1945)

BVT

(Bureau Voorbereiding Terugkeer: Bureau for Preparation of the Return)

(De Bruyne 1941-1942)

MI6
Dutch Section

(Rabagliatti 1940-1942)
(Seymour 1942-1945)

MVT

(Militaire Voorbereiding Terugkeer: Military Preparation for the Return)

(De Bruyne 1942-1944)

GS III

Pre-War Dutch Intelligence

MID

(Militaire Inlichtingen Dienst: Military Intelligence Service)

CID

(Centrale Inlichtingen Dienst: Central Intelligence Service)

(Van 't Sant 1940-1941)
(Derksema 1941-1942)
(De Bruyne 1942)

BI

(Bureau Inlichtingen: Intelligence Bureau)

(Broekman 1942-1943)
(Somer 1943-1945)

Part One

THE NETHERLANDS

Key
Drop zones for British and Dutch agents
Country boundaries
Province boundaries
Rivers
Towns

North Sea

Waddenzee

GRONINGEN
Groningen

FRIESLAND

DRENTHE
Assen

Steenwijk

Zuidersee

THE NETHERLANDS

Zwolle
OVERIJSSEL

NOORD HOLLAND

Apeldoorn

GELDERLAND

Amsterdam
Haarlem
Hilversum

UTRECHT

Arnhem

Oude IJssel

Leiden (Leyden)
Utrecht

Waal

ZUID HOLLAND

Nijmegen

Maas

The Hague

Rotterdam
Lek
Waal

Maas

NOORD BRABANT

Eindhoven

LIMBURG

Maas

GERMANY

ZEELAND
Middelburg

ZEEUWS-VLAANDEREN

N

BELGIUM

Maastricht

0 10 20 30 40 miles
0 10 20 40 60 km

1 'An Oath of Silence'

The first British agent to be parachuted back into the German-occupied Netherlands during World War II was dropped during the night of 28 August 1940. Lodo Van Hamel, a twenty-five-year-old Dutch naval lieutenant, was dispatched by MI6 to set up some much-needed intelligence networks to provide information about the Germans' plans to invade Britain.

An officer of the highest calibre, Van Hamel was well suited to his task. In early May 1940, when the Germans had ruthlessly invaded the then neutral Netherlands, he had been responsible for guiding Allied shipping into the Dutch port of Ijmuiden. Then on 12 May he had supervised the escape of Princess Juliana, heiress to the Dutch throne, and her family as they fled to Britain with the rest of the royal family and most of the Government. Van Hamel had stayed on after their departure, but there was little he could do. Years of neglect had left the Dutch totally unprepared for Blitzkrieg, and their defences proved as mythical as the proverbial finger in the dyke. On 15 May 1940, after the bombing of Rotterdam and only five days after the German invasion, what remained of the Dutch Government surrendered. By then, however, the resourceful Van Hamel had escaped across the North Sea in a trawler.

Soon after arriving in Britain he had become heavily involved in the Dunkirk evacuation, and after the operation had officially come to an end, he had volunteered to return, in a vain attempt to rescue a British officer still fighting ashore. After Dunkirk he had felt the inactivity more than most. Officially he was due to become captain of a Dutch submarine but it was still in drydock undergoing repairs, leaving him with little to do. It was then that his life took a new twist. The Commander of the Dutch Navy in exile, Vice-Admiral Furstner, had lined up some of his younger officers, including Van Hamel, and asked for a volunteer to go to the Netherlands on a short mission. Van Hamel had stepped forward, casually saying, 'I don't mind doing it, I've nothing else to do at the moment anyway.' A tall and handsome man, he was one of the Dutch Navy's finest officers, courageous, capable and tough. During the following months these attributes would be severely tested.

The request for a volunteer for a secret mission to the Netherlands had officially come from the Dutch royal family. Only they commanded respect and loyalty from the Dutch politicians in exile. Amidst bickering and infighting about who should run what with whom, a new Dutch Secret Service had been set up in July 1940. CID (Centrale Inlichtingen Dienst) was headed by François Van't Sant, one of the most controversial characters in the Dutch community in London. Rumours about him abounded. Some likened his close working relationship with Queen Wilhelmina – he was her private secretary – to a Dutch Rasputin. Furthermore it was claimed that during World War I he had accepted money from the Germans and French as well as from the British Secret Service. These rumours were to be carefully exploited by the Germans, who often told captured agents they had been betrayed by Van't Sant, leaving such an impression that, despite his complete exoneration by a Dutch Parliamentary enquiry after the war, these suspicions were to follow him to his grave.

In 1940 Van't Sant was in his mid fifties and at the height of his powers and influence. He was the only senior Dutchman in London who had contacts with MI6, with whom he had been in touch since 1914; after the creation of CID he had visited MI6's Dutch section, to see if the British would be interested in co-operation. Van't Sant had been very persuasive, arguing that the Dutch would be best at evaluating and interpreting information from their own country. Nor did MI6 need much persuading. The 'Venlo Incident', in which the two most senior MI6 officers on the Continent had been kidnapped by the Germans, had led to the collapse of all MI6's networks in the Netherlands. The British, like the Dutch, would be making a completely fresh start. After some discussion MI6 had agreed to help, though their terms were tough. CID would recruit the agents and be allowed access to the messages they sent, but that was all. The British would remain in complete control of training, equipment and the planning of operations.

Despite the fact that MI6 had driven a hard bargain, this had still been a major breakthrough for CID. The pre-war Dutch Secret Service GSIII, whose members were now in official disgrace, had totally failed to organize a network of agents to operate should the Netherlands be overrun. As a result the Dutch Government in exile had no contacts with its own country and thus no means of discovering what was happening with regards to public opinion and German laws and behaviour. It was this veil of ignorance that Van Hamel was being sent to lift.

As part of his equipment he was given a radio transmitter, cleverly hidden inside a small suitcase. According to MI6, it would be untraceable by the Germans owing to a so-called 'swinging beam' which constantly changed the frequency of the transmission. There were, however, a number of serious flaws in Van Hamel's preparations. He was given a set of forged papers which gave his date of birth as 29 February 1915, a date any keen-eyed German would have realized did not exist! This incredible blunder might not have been so bad had the papers themselves been anything like decent forgeries, but this was not the case either. The MI6 forgery department had quite simply handed Van Hamel a potential death sentence. In addition he did not possess a security check for his transmitter code, so that in effect MI6/CID would have no way of knowing whether or not he was being forced to transmit for the Germans. Nevertheless, despite these mistakes, Van Hamel's mission may be seen as more than just a defiant gesture. Conceived when the Battle of Britain had reached a crucial stage and the survival of Britain itself hung in the balance, it represented an act of considerable foresight and optimism.

Van Hamel was dropped 'blind' (that is, without a reception committee) near Sassenheim and landed safely – something which, given the state of parachuting in 1940, should not be too readily assumed. After hiding until dawn he made his way to the university town of Leyden, where he contacted a medical student called Hans Hers. The two men had already met before the war at a party held by The Hague gliding club, and it was there in 1939 that Hers had been recruited to a pre-war MI6 network controlled by a certain 'Cumberlidge'. All this made Hers a valuable asset, and Van Hamel wasted no time in explaining his mission, adding that he had strict orders to confine recruiting to the ranks of pre-war Dutch intelligence officers.

It soon became apparent, however, that they would have to go beyond this instruction. Efforts to recruit ex-GSIII officers met with little success. Most of those approached claimed to have signed documents giving their word of honour that they would not act against the Germans – paradoxically, professional spies were suddenly holding their word as paramount. Eventually only two men were prepared to help. One of them, J.Allers, allowed Van Hamel to use his house for the dangerous task of transmitting. It was only now that a new problem came to light. The radio transmitter had not survived the drop intact and was in need of urgent repairs. Fortunately Allers' future son-in-law had been a radio operator in the Dutch Army and knew someone who would be capable of mending the set. His friend Ton Buys, an electronics student, was contacted by postcard, declared himself willing to help and within a few days had managed to repair the transmitter. Out of sheer gratitude, Van Hamel allowed him the honour of sending the first message back to MI6.

In London MI6/CID's period of uncertainty was over. Having had to wait helplessly as Van Hamel wrestled with his various problems, not knowing if he would ever contact them, they were now able to inform the politicians of their new link with the Netherlands. And the new link was soon paying dividends.

In marked contrast to the attitude of the older professionals, Van Hamel and Hers found few problems

in recruiting friends and acquaintances to their work.
Several networks started to spread, and information began
to come in at an ever-increasing rate. The manner in
which this intelligence was gathered varied considerably
from recording mere hearsay to real espionage. A good
example of the latter was the Luftwaffe mechanic whose
acquaintance Hers had cultivated. He had met the
German in 1936, when they had discussed their common
interest in aeroplanes. Over the years they had kept in
touch, and by sheer coincidence they had met the day after
the Dutch surrender. The German apologized for what his
country had done, adding, 'If ever I can help you, please
don't hesitate to ask.' Hers had subsequently reminded
him of this, and the mechanic declared himself willing to
help. Soon he was providing German papers, petrol and
even blueprints of Luftwaffe airfields.

For Van Hamel these were busy times. His transmitter
was on the air up to four times a day passing on this
information. Reports reached MI6 of shipping concentra-
tions in Dutch ports, of troop movements and of the
locations of German airfields. Added to these were little
titbits such as the news of the explosion of an ammunition
dump near Wageningen which killed at least seven
German officers.

By October 1940 the networks were operating smoothly,
and Van Hamel realized it was time to get out. He had
been extremely thorough. Everyone had cover-names and
operated on a 'need to know' basis only. He alone knew
how everything fitted together, the names, the addresses,
the meeting-places. To remain would merely risk
jeopardizing what had been achieved. However, MI6
showed little enthusiasm for collecting their agent, despite
the fact that before his departure they had promised to do
so; now they suggested he might make his own way back
via France and Spain. Hers knew better. He had witnessed
several MI6 pick-ups during his time with the 'Cumberlidge' network and now reminded the British of them.
No doubt this caused MI6 considerable embarrassment,
and a message was finally sent to Van Hamel asking him to
name places where a seaplane could land. Several
discussions ensued about possible pick-up spots before

MI6/CID decided to settle the matter by suggesting a lake called the Tjeukemeer. Neither Van Hamel nor Hers was happy with this choice. Lying in Friesland, a northern province of the Netherlands, the Tjeukemeer was territory totally unknown to both of them. Nor did they know where the local population's sympathies lay, in a province close to the German border, with a language and culture of its own. In any case, strangers in such a rural landscape were bound to stand out and be the subject of local gossip.

Despite these misgivings, the Dutch agents were soon presented with a *fait accompli*. The seaplane, it was announced, would arrive on the Tjeukemeer during the night of 13/14 October 1940, leaving Van Hamel only three days in which to make his plans. These were already considerably complicated by the fact that he had obtained permission for four others to accompany him – his girlfriend, Marion Smit, Hers, Jean Mesritz, (a student who had recognized Van Hamel on the street) and a certain Professor Becking. It was clearly going to be a conspicuous group.

The day before the seaplane was due to arrive, Hers travelled to Friesland for a reconnaissance of the area. Borrowing a relative's bicycle, he made his way round the lake, telling locals that he was preparing for a bird-watching expedition. He managed to hire a small boat and learned the disturbing news that a policeboat patrolled the lake at regular intervals. The next day the group met up at a hotel in Heerenveen. They were in high spirits. Among their belongings was a suitcase containing new maps of the Netherlands, ten blank passports, ration cards, German papers, lists of people who were pro-Nazi and many other valuable documents collected during the previous two months.

That night the 'bird-watchers' waited in the middle of the lake but to their dismay the seaplane failed to turn up. The following morning, almost suffering from exposure, they stepped ashore in Echtenburg. By then local suspicions had been aroused and a nosy farmer's wife rang the local policeman, who on hearing that the group were in a local coffee-house set out to check their papers. He was perfectly satisfied with their explanation that they were on a field trip and left soon after. Unfortunately a colleague who had also heard of the matter was less easily convinced. He insisted on ringing his boss in Leeuwaarden, to be told that he should investigate the strangers more thoroughly. Meanwhile, the company had already left the coffee-house for another 'excursion' onto the lake.

Hidden among the reeds, Van Hamel and his companions waited for darkness. It was to be another frustrating night. As midnight approached, a thick mist came down, covering the lake and obscuring its calm waters. To make matters worse, they heard the seaplane approaching and then circling overhead. The pilot made several attempts to land but was finally forced to give up the struggle and return home empty-handed. In doing so, he left the would-be escapers facing a dilemma. The noise of the engines had woken up the entire neighbourhood, and it was clear that, if the police caught up with them now, they would have a lot of explaining to do. Hers suggested to Van Hamel that the two of them should get out of the area as quickly as possible, but Van Hamel, reluctant to abandon Smit, Mesritz and Becking to their fate, would only consent to hide the suitcase, and did so on a small island in the middle of the lake.

Ashore the police were waiting for them. They were arrested as soon as they climbed out of their boat and taken to a local café, where they were searched and had their papers taken from them. They decided that their best chance was to be completely open and appeal to the policemen's sense of patriotism and loyalty to the Dutch royal family. The Netherlands were still at war with Germany, they argued, and they were official represen-tatives of the Dutch Government in London. They appreciated the difficult position the police were in and asked only for a few hours headstart. The chief constable remained unmoved. Angrily Hers told him, 'We are officers of the Dutch Army on a secret mission for our Government in London, a Government to which you too owe loyalty.' 'I have nothing to do with the Government in London. My boss is in Leeuwaarden,' replied the chief constable. In desperation Hers changed tactics, claiming to know his boss and asking to speak to him on the phone. It was only a slim chance, and his hopes were dashed when the man turned out to be pro-Nazi. Delighted by the arrests, he ordered them to be taken to the town hall at Joure, where he himself arrived later that afternoon accompanied by a large number of high-ranking intelligence officers. From now on they would be in German hands.

The Tjeukemeer was soon crawling with Dutch police, all hunting for the suitcase the prisoners were known to have returned without. Assuming that the mystery seaplane might attempt another landing that night, the Germans stationed two infantry battalions around the lake. Armed with anti-aircraft guns, they settled in to wait the night. The bait was to be the Dutch policeboat, which was equipped with a heavy machine-gun and Van Hamel's signal lamp.

Back in Britain the crew of the seaplane discussed whether or not to make another attempt. For the Dutch naval pilot, Lieutenant Schaper, the past forty-eight hours had been especially frustrating. On the first night set for the rendezvous bad weather had prevented his taking off, whilst the previous evening he had been thwarted by the groundmist and had hung around over the target so long that he knew the Germans might have been alerted. However, the urge to save their fellow-countrymen was strong, and the crew unanimously voted to try again.

Ironically, the weather was good for once, and they had no problem locating the Tjeukemeer where they received an ambiguous signal from below. The gunner thought it the correct code letter but Schaper was less certain and made sure the moon was behind him as they approached the policeboat. At a range of fifty metres the Germans opened fire. Schaper's gunner immediately returned fire and succeeded in knocking out the German machine-gun. Suddenly the whole lake erupted with gun fire as the seaplane was raked from all sides, whilst a searchlight clumsily attempted to pin-point its target. Schaper, reacting quickly, threw his plane into a zigzag course until he had gained sufficient speed to take off. Once airborne he wasted no time in heading for Britain. It had been a

close-run thing. The seaplane had been hit over forty
times, and two crew members were slightly wounded. Ten
German soldiers lay dead around the lake, victims of their
own crossfire.

The next day the Germans furiously searched the lake
for the hidden suitcase, eagerly assisted by the Dutch
police. A tracker dog was used to hunt among the reeds,
and finally the suitcase was found. The damning evidence
was handed over to German Intelligence, placing Van
Hamel and Hers in even greater trouble and endangering
the networks they had set up. A good many people's lives
now depended on Van Hamel's silence.

All the prisoners were taken to The Hague headquarters of Section IVE, the Gestapo's counter-espionage unit,
the Sicherheitsdienstpolizei, more generally known as
SIPO. Van Hamel and Hers were soon identified as the
ringleaders and were subjected to 'special treatment'. Both
were badly beaten up before their first interrogation, but
they refused to say anything.

Hers in fact soon gained a moral victory. He was sharp
enough to notice the captured suitcase tucked away
behind a cupboard in his interrogation room. When his
interrogator started off by screaming at him to say where
he had hidden the suitcase, Hers was able to reply calmly
that it was within a few feet of them. The German,
considerably taken aback, asked Hers sarcastically whether
he was always so observant. His interrogators soon realized
that they were dealing with a very tough young man.
Likewise Van Hamel. It was clear to the Germans that the
name 'Van Dalen' on his papers was false – not least
because of the date of birth – but they had great trouble
finding out who he really was. Eventually a Dutch Nazi
heard a rumour in The Hague about an officer called Van
Hamel who had just been arrested for spying. Even then
Van Hamel admitted who he was only after the SIPO had
threatened to put his entire family in a concentration
camp. This was the only thing he ever admitted. Despite
terrible threats he steadfastly refused to discuss his work.

For Joseph Schreieder, the man leading the investigation, the case had become a great embarrassment. For
several months, right under his nose, a Dutch agent had

been transmitting information back to London, and he had been completely unaware of what was going on. It was only by sheer chance that the man had been prevented from returning to Britain along with a lot of valuable information, and now he was proving impossible to break down. In near desperation Schreieder turned to the SS for inspiration. Rather uncharacteristically, the SS decided on a psychological approach. One night they entered Van Hamel's cell armed with a pen and paper and told him to write down the answers to their questions. On refusal he was told that he had twenty minutes in which to change his mind. If he did not, the SS promised to execute one of his fellow prisoners. This process would then be repeated every twenty minutes until either the questions had been answered or his colleagues were all dead. After twenty minutes the SS returned to find the paper untouched. They then left his cell door slightly ajar so that he could clearly hear an SS squad marching down the corridor, opening a cell door, marching a prisoner away and lining up in the courtyard. Soon after, the sound of shots rang out. This happened three more times in the next hour but still Van Hamel refused to give in. It was only much later that night that a Dutch prison warder was able to whisper that the Germans had been bluffing. What had been going on in his mind can only be guessed at.

The intensive interrogations of the others arrested along with Van Hamel produced nothing of importance for the SIPO. The only name that Schreieder was able to come up with was that of Allers, because he had been mentioned in a letter found in the suitcase. The letter also contained a good deal of anti-Nazi sentiment, and this goaded Schreieder in his efforts to track Allers down. Within a week the SIPO had found him. They raided his house, finding coded messages but not the radio transmitter they were looking for. The messages proved impossible to break without the special code 'bible', despite the attentions of many expert cryptologists, and for the moment the trail went cold.

Meanwhile, after three months of captivity Van Hamel had managed to block the lock on his cell door so that he could open and close it at will. He managed to tell Hers, who was in an opposite cell, how it was done. Around noon one day, in early February 1941 the two of them left their cells and marched down the corridor. The plan was simple. Van Hamel, who spoke fluent German, would impersonate a Gestapo officer, while Hers was to play his assistant. They managed to get the guards to open the doors to the courtyard and, crossing it, walked through the front gates. Here their luck ran out, for as they did so a car pulled up containing one of their interrogators. They were instantly recognized and recaptured within sight of freedom. A few minutes would have made all the difference.

The Germans were not slow to take revenge on their captives. For a month the two were chained to a cell floor, without daylight, and given only salted potatoes to eat – another subtle torture, which left them suffering greatly from thirst. They were forced to relieve themselves where they lay, and were allowed no change of clothes. After a month of this Hers was dragged from his cell. He was driven to an interrogation centre and asked the same questions about his contacts, which he again refused to answer. The questioning ended and he was led back out to the car. Here his interrogator claimed to have forgotten his car keys, and returned inside, leaving an astonished Hers alone. Suddenly there were no Germans to be seen, and Hers immediately thought of escape. Some sixth sense warned him not to. The situation was too obviously contrived. Either the SIPO would follow him to his contacts or they would use the opportunity to shoot him out of hand. Calmly he waited for the German, who arrived back twenty minutes later having finally 'found' his keys. His interrogator was unable to hide his disappoint-ment at finding Hers still there. Yet another of Schreieder's ploys had failed.

On 7 April 1941 the 'bird-watchers' were put on trial in front of a German military tribunal. The prosecutor started by publicly rebuking Schreieder for having failed to obtain information from the accused. This was a serious business. As far as the Germans were concerned, they were now none the wiser about the extent of Van Hamel's contacts than they had been five months before. Nor did they realize how close they had come. The SIPO had picked up a new trail, which led to Allers' future son-in-law being tracked down the day before he was due to go into hiding. He had heard of Van Hamel's arrest and had just hidden the radio transmitter when the Germans arrived on his doorstep. A search of the house revealed an envelope with Ton Buys' name on. Buys too was arrested and after two weeks admitted having repaired a radio transmitter.

Against this background Van Hamel was asked in court about the work he had done before his arrest. He told the tribunal: 'I took an assignment to serve my people, my country and the royal family. There are certain things that I cannot tell you because I have taken an oath of silence on those matters. I will not besmirch that oath.' Several German officers present saluted his words, though they could not prevent the judge from sentencing him to death – a verdict, incidentally, which so upset some officers present that they left the court-room in protest.

Van Hamel's resistance throughout torture and trial was remarkable. Though the war seemed hopelessly lost and any resistance futile, he did not crack. The same may be said of Hers, who was given a lighter sentence, life imprisonment, which he would probably not have received later in the war. In fact, Hers survived the war, emerging from Sachsenhausen to resume his medical career and to tend hundreds of surviving members of the Resistance. Allers' future son-in-law also got life, and he too survived the war, spending time in several concentration camps before returning to the Netherlands in 1945. Buys was sentenced to one year, and he too survived. The Germans never did find the radio transmitter he had repaired. Allers received ten years but died during his captivity, whilst the student Jean Mesritz, who had persuaded Van Hamel to take him back to Britain, was given three years. Both Professor Becking and Marion Smit were acquitted.

Strenuous efforts were made by the Dutch Government in exile to exchange Van Hamel and save him from his fate. A message was sent to Berlin via a Swiss delegation offering ten German prisoners of war in return for his release. The offer was turned down, and Van Hamel was shot on the morning of 16 June 1941. Shortly beforehand he had written his final letter to his parents in which he told them: ' ... I die in the conviction and the satisfying knowledge that my behaviour of late has been dictated by the way in which God and my conscience have appeared and ordered. You would never have wanted me to do otherwise, and that is a great comfort to me, in as far as we need comforting, for is it not almost to be envied that one may die in following such a beautiful duty? I have done everything that a human being could do ...'

The Van Hamel case had several major consequences for the future of resistance and counter-resistance efforts in the Netherlands. Sturmbannführer Joseph Schreieder, who had been openly reprimanded for his failure in the affair, was determined not to be caught off-guard again. In future the SIPO would be on its toes. MI6, for their part, viewed the treachery of the Dutch police as further evidence that the Dutch were, in general, unreliable and untrustworthy. From that moment on, MI6's operations in the Netherlands became more reserved, thus hindering future resistance work. This trend will soon become relevant to our story, for, as the professionals started to keep a lower profile, the amateurs were about to move in.

2 Early Setbacks

Major Herman Giskes of the Abwehrstelle Niederlande (German Military Intelligence), was posted to the Netherlands during the summer of 1941, to take up his new job as head of counter-espionage and save the military establishment from serious embarrassment.

Giskes had the 'right' sort of background for the Abwehr. Born in 1896, the son of a Krefeld tobacco merchant, he had served in the German Army during the 1914-18 war, after which he had joined the Freikorps. Having helped 'save Germany from Bolshevism', he had settled down to run his father's tobacco company. Then fate intervened. In 1939 Giskes was recruited into the Abwehr, the old-established German secret service, where he soon rose to the rank of major. His competence brought him to the notice of Admiral Canaris, head of the Abwehr, and he became one of the latter's protégés. After the fall of France in 1940, he was sent to Paris, where he acquitted himself brilliantly, establishing his reputation by uncovering a series of espionage cases involving the US embassy, fully justifying Canaris's hopes.

The situation into which Giskes arrived in the Netherlands was a complex one and stemmed from the bitter rivalry between the Abwehr and another intelligence bureau, the SIPO/SD. This rivalry had its origins long before the war, from the moment in 1933 when the then newly appointed Chancellor Adolf Hitler decided that the Abwehr should remain the dominant organization in counter-espionage. This position was soon under challenge from leading Nazi officials who wanted more room for their own fledgling, the Sicherheitsdienst (SD). In 1936 the SD came under the command of Reichsführer

Himmler and his second-in-command, Heydrich, and a year later Canaris and Heydrich had hammered out the so-called 'ten commandments' which defined the specific roles of all secret state organizations in relation to each other. It was determined that counter-espionage – the penetration of foreign intelligence services and the feeding of false or misleading information to them – would remain the domain of the Abwehr. The SD's task would be to collect 'political' intelligence, and both sides were required to hand information to each other if it concerned them.

At the outbreak of World War II Hitler had formed the RSHA, (the Reich Central Security Office), under the command of Heydrich. This consisted of two major organs, namely the Sicherheitspolizei (SIPO), incorporating the Gestapo and the Kripo (*kriminaal polizei*), the ordinary civilian police, and the SD, which was effectively the SS's Secret Service.

Not surprisingly, the 'ten commandments' almost never worked, because a military intelligence service is always in need of political information of its own whilst the question of counter-espionage is quite often linked to the exploitation of traitors. Both sides complained of abuses by the other, and it soon became clear to the Abwehr that the SIPO/SD were intent on pushing them out of the field. By 1941 Heydrich was openly arguing for a new deal and a stronger say for the RSHA. According to him, the situation of the war demanded it. It was against this background that Canaris read a very critical report about the Abwehr in the Netherlands which showed just how little it had achieved in comparison with the SIPO/SD. Well aware of how little criticism his organization could afford, he decided to send one of his most talented officers to redress the balance.

Despite an initial reluctance to leave Paris, Giskes threw himself enthusiastically into his new job as head of counter-espionage (Abwehrstelle III F). He was initially briefed by Oberst Hauswaldt, head of the Abwehr in the Netherlands, who warned him that the personnel under his command were of poor quality and that he should not expect too much too soon. Furthermore, unlike Paris, the

Netherlands were officially under a civilian as opposed to a military government. This meant that only the SIPO were empowered to make arrests and that Giskes would have to co-operate with them. Despite these problems, he remained confident he could continue his French successes.

Giskes found his new headquarters in a small, well-furnished house in Scheveningen. Only one of the officers there impressed him, a Lieutenant Wurr, who was able to give him a clear report on what had been happening in the Netherlands. Wurr pointed out that the Van Hamel affair proved that the British did have direct links with the newly forming resistance groups and that there was evidence of material being smuggled out to Britain. Their major problem, explained Wurr, was that they did not have any competent V-men (Dutch traitors) capable of infiltrating a resistance group. Those employed by Section III F were interested only in easy jobs with little or no personal risk. Giskes told Wurr to get rid of them all. His own style was to operate with only one or two highly skilled V-men, a technique which would stand him in good stead during the following years. He also forbade his section to act as *agents provocateurs*, realizing that a good many Dutchmen could be tempted into some form of underground work. Such arrests would only prove a political embarrassment and waste valuable time.

The next stage was a visit to the listening-post at Scheveningen. This was probably the most vital section under his command and would make all the difference between success and failure. In charge was Lieutenant Heinrich, who immediately endeared himself to Giskes by producing some Russian vodka. Even more attractive was the professional approach Heinrich took to his work. Giskes was proudly shown the new electronic surveillance equipment Heinrich had acquired, of which great things were expected.

The surveillance procedure was quite simple. Once a new transmission had been identified, Berlin was informed. At the next transmission a cross-check was taken of it, and the rough calculations were telexed through to Scheveningen. In this way Heinrich had discovered that there were two secret transmitters operating in the Netherlands. Somewhere in the triangular area between the cities of Utrecht, Zeist and Amersfort, there was an agent operating under the call sign UBX and transmitting on frequencies 6677 and 7787 KHZ at an average of five times a week. The other agent, according to Heinrich, was working within the Delft-Gouda-Noordwijk area under the call sign TBO. As yet he had not had time to take the detector-vans out after it.

The detector-vans were small and unremarkable-looking vehicles, but their insides were packed with the Third Reich's latest technical inventions which could pin-point a transmitter, given a little time, to within a hundred metres. This was well within the range of hand-carried detectors which could be carried under a coat and taken up a suspect street. Giskes realized that he now had the means to capture an enemy radio transmitter intact – the dream of every counter-espionage officer. Heinrich told him that it would take another two weeks to track down UBX, and he promised to keep his new boss well informed of his progress.

In fact, UBX was being operated from Bilthoven by the twenty-year-old Hans Zomer, who had been parachuted into the Netherlands in June 1941 along with his twenty-four-year-old companion Wiek Schrage. Both men had been sent by MI6, and their present address was the last in a long list they had been given in London. Both had good reason to doubt the claim that their radio set was untraceable by the Germans. At his first safe house, Zomer realized that he would need an outside aerial if his messages were to reach Britain. This proved conspicuous, and after a few transmissions he spotted several German police vans in the area. Wisely he had not waited to find out what they were looking for and had moved on immediately.

Schrage, a pre-war police inspector, had been setting up a new resistance organization and had linked it with several existing groups in the Arnhem area. But he also had a more specific task. Queen Wilhelmina wished to be surrounded by advisers who knew something of the real situation in the Netherlands, and Schrage had been sent to persuade these people to come to Britain. Most had been persuaded but, as the question of transport had not yet been arranged, the matter was left open.

All contact with MI6 went through Zomer, who by mid-August 1941 had moved into a large villa in Bilthoven owned by the parents of an old school friend, Jaap Sickenga, who was keen to help Zomer with his work. Together they decided that the best place for the transmitter was at the bottom of the garden in a large shed. As a precaution they rigged up an alarm system by which Sickenga's parents could warn them if anyone suspicious turned up at the front door. In the loft of the garden shed Zomer found a hiding-place for the transmitter and the small file of messages which he was forced to keep – an enormous risk made necessary because MI6 frequently referred back to previous messages. The only problem was the outside aerial, which they were forced to put on top of the shed roof. It was a matter about which very little could be done, and they could only hope that their luck would hold.

The strain of their work soon began to tell on the agents, and towards the end of August Zomer began to enquire when they could both return to Britain. It seemed clear to him that they had carried out their assignments in good time. Schrage had contacted the people he had been instructed to and had set up some hard-core resistance groups in Apeldoorn, Arnhem and Bilthoven. Gathered around him were colleagues continuously recruiting more resistance workers, who provided more and more information for him to transmit.

However, MI6 would not hear of its agents returning to Britain for a rest, and Zomer and Schrage were ordered to continue their work. The British might well have heard more about the matter had Schrage not suddenly become dangerously ill and confined to bed. Lying in a friend's attic, helpless and unable to move, he became increasingly worried by the danger of his situation. A doctor who was called proved to be mentally unbalanced and only increased Schrage's fears. He wanted to get out as soon as possible.

Schrage would have been even more distressed had he

known that Lieutenant Heinrich's surveillance unit was closing in on Zomer's transmitter. The original triangle between Utrecht-Zeist-Amersfoort had been narrowed down to a few houses in Bilthoven. Only at this stage did things become tricky for Heinrich. His surveillance van could not drive up and down the street without becoming too conspicuous, and the danger was that the agent might be alerted and move to another part of the Netherlands, thus ruining weeks of hard work. In order to get around this problem, he sent out a woman with a portable detector, and she was able to pin-point what she thought was the transmitter's position. Only now were the SIPO reluctantly called in. The raid was timed for 6 p.m. on 31 August 1941.

At 5.30 that evening, Zomer and Sickenga were in the loft of the garden shed encoding the messages to be sent that night. This was a time-consuming business requiring total concentration, so they failed to notice anything going on outside. A few streets away the raiding party gathered quietly alongside the surveillance van. They were under strict instructions not to move before Heinrich gave the signal.

Nervously Heinrich waited for six o'clock, only too conscious of the enormous responsibility on his shoulders. To his relief he heard the sound of transmitting start in his headphones, as Zomer tapped out his call-sign: 'UBX ... UBX ...'. After giving the signal, Heinrich followed the vans down the road and saw the SIPO storm the house. To his dismay the transmitting continued as before, and he became seriously alarmed at the possibility of having led everyone to the wrong house. It was left to Lieutenant Wurr to save the day. On hearing that the transmitting had not ceased, despite the fact that the house was now crawling with Germans, he pulled out his gun and ran into the garden, where he noticed the shed. Stealthily slipping inside he climbed the ladder leading to the loft, where he could just make out two figures hunched over a radio set, one dictating, the other transmitting. Wurr screamed at them to put their hands up.

With the tension gone and success assured, the Germans became better humoured. Both the SIPO and Abwehr had reason to be delighted by the outcome of the raid. Two men had been arrested and a good deal of spying materials found, including messages in both code and clear language which would make the unravelling of Zomer's code relatively easy. For Heinrich there was also a more personal satisfaction: for the first time he was able to inspect a British radio transmitter.

Giskes had not been present at the raid, having gone to Paris to recruit new personnel for his department. When he received an urgent telegram from Wurr telling him of their success, he quickly drove back. His initial excitement quickly disappeared when it became clear how little information the SIPO were passing on to his section. His chances of playing the radio transmitter back to MI6* – his sole concern – were becoming less as the days passed. In frustration he sent one of his officers to see what the SIPO were doing. The officer returned empty-handed, having been told to mind his own business. Giskes was furious and arranged to meet his Gestapo counterpart, Joseph Schreieder.

The SIPO meanwhile were having their own problems. Both Zomer and Sickenga were proving very difficult to break down, despite the use of violence and persuasion. Zomer, in particular, deeply conscious of his responsibility towards Schrage, still seriously ill in bed, was well aware of the fact that every hour he could remain quiet would increase his comrade's chances. Determined not to undo all the good work of the previous months, he remained silent on all but the most trivial matters.

The meeting between Giskes and Schreieder took place in a rather cool atmosphere. Giskes complained about the way the Abwehr had been treated and forcefully put his case for co-operation. It appeared, he claimed, that the SIPO had carried out only a normal police-style investigation without giving any thought to using the captured radio transmitter. There would, argued Giskes, be great advantages for both Schreieder's section and the Abwehr were they to succeed in playing a radio set back to

* Using the radio transmitter to send false messages while impersonating the agent concerned.

the British. Schreieder was diplomatic. He explained that, though he was interested in what Giskes was planning, little could be done until they had got Zomer to talk. At present all Zomer would say was that he had been put ashore by boat a couple of months before and had gone straight to Bilthoven. As for the other man, he appeared to be merely an acquaintance who had helped Zomer with his work. Schreieder assured Giskes that the minute they found out anything important he would let him know, and as a gesture handed him a file containing transcripts of all the interrogations so far.

Eventually the Abwehr did manage to get Zomer to transmit for them, and for the first time since his arrest he opened up contact with Britain. However, he managed to change his opening call-sign and his style of transmitting without the Germans noticing. MI6 did notice, and for the British Secret Service there could be no other conclusion than that yet another one of their agents had fallen into enemy hands.

The disastrous news of Zomer's arrest reached Schrage as he lay almost delirious in bed. He was in a desperate situation, being unable to move whilst his companion was being tortured into revealing his name and whereabouts. A friend decided that his first priority was to get well again and that, for this to be achieved, better medical attention was needed. When this was provided, Schrage slowly began to recover; soon he was able to apply himself to the problems in hand. MI6 had to be warned about Zomer, and something had to be done about the large amount of information which was still flooding in. Through contacts Schrage was able to get in touch with a group in Apeldoorn who were in radio contact with the British. He managed to persuade them to send a message for him, but despite its being correctly coded and containing a security check, there was no reply from MI6. Gradually it dawned on Schrage that the British knew of Zomer's capture and regarded him as also suspect. He was now on his own, with the Germans likely to arrest him at any moment and secret material continuing to pour in. Not surprisingly, as his health improved he lost no time in planning his escape back to Britain.

In April 1942 Hans Zomer and Jaap Sickenga were tried, along with twenty-two others, before a German military tribunal. All were found guilty and sentenced to death, a sentence which was carried out on 11 May 1942, probably in the sand dunes where so many were to be anonymously executed.

For Giskes and Scheieder, both intelligent men, the lessons were there to be learned. They would have to co-operate quickly in future after a radio operator had been captured and, unlike their superiors, both realized the advantages this could bring. The way ahead would soon be open for some of the most brilliant counter-espionage achievements of all time.

3   Enter SOE

SOE, Britain's Special Operations Executive, was officially set up in July 1940. Legend has created the false impression that the whole idea was dreamed up by Winston Churchill one afternoon when Britain faced her darkest hour. The true origins of SOE are to be found long before the war. It represented the coming together of various departments and strands of thought concerned with subversion and sabotage. Ironically it was Churchill's predecessor as Prime Minister, Neville Chamberlain, who had drafted what SOE always regarded as its founding charter – one of his last political acts before he died in November 1940. Ministerial control of the new organization was given to Hugh Dalton, who in turn appointed Sir Frank Nelson, a former politician with MI6 connections, to run it.

SOE was divided into three branches concerned with propaganda, planning and active operations. Under the latter came the sections which dealt with either one specific country or an area of operations. One of these sections, exclusively concerned with the Netherlands, was commanded by Major Richard Laming, a reluctant intelligence officer who, despite having spent many years in the Netherlands, felt little enthusiasm for his new job.

Dutch Section, in common with their counterparts in MI6 and CID, began with very little knowledge of what was happening across the North Sea. As early as August 1940 Laming had sent his first agent J. van Driel, by boat to the Dutch coast equipped with a radio transmitter, but he had disappeared without trace. (He had been picked up by the Germans before he could land; his rowing boat was set adrift too far out to sea. He managed to throw his transmitter overboard and succeeded in persuading his captors that he had deserted his ship in order to return to the Netherlands. Thereafter he remained at large but was unable to establish any contact with Laming.) During the winter of 1940/41 several more rushed attempts were made to land agents by sea but these all failed and Laming decided to wait until he had some fully trained agents before trying again.

Dutch Section's difficulties in getting started were mirrored throughout SOE. Very little was achieved during the first year, and by the time the resources were available and the first agents properly trained, it was the summer of 1941. It was now that Dutch Section decided to dispatch two more agents, 'Ab' Homburg and Cor Sporre, to make a general reconnaissance, after which they would return to Britain with a list of contacts and 'safe houses'. Originally it had been intended to land the two by motor boat but after three failures they were returned to a holding house outside London to await further orders. Realizing that his plans were falling way behind schedule, Laming finally did the sensible thing and had them sent on a parachute course at Ringway. All in all it had hardly been an auspicious beginning.

Dutch Section's unhappy start was soon compounded by a rebellion in its first group of trained agents. Of the original seven, one, Dessing had been sent to Scotland as a punishment for insubordination and was not expected to go abroad, whilst Jordaan had been sent to Beaulieu on a radio operators' course. The trouble started because Laming was unwise enough to allow Homburg and Sporre, who had been chosen for the mission, contact with the remaining agents after they had been briefed. Soon the rest knew of the vague orders they had been given, in which most things were being left entirely up to the agents' own initiative.

For Ter Haar, De Bruine and Hazelwinkel, this was not good enough, and it only confirmed their belief that Dutch Section was a poor organization. They had originally volunteered for Special Operations on condition that their mission was competently organized, but all had long since been critical of the faults in security which they noticed. There were several grievances in particular. First, none of their courses linked up, so that, when the men were given leave to visit London – and got drunk, they would inevitably start discussing the training they had just completed. Despite their having warned Laming about this, nothing was done. Then there was the problem of the cover-names. For security reasons none of the agents was supposed to know the others' real names. This was fair enough, but British officers would then come round handing out mail which was addressed to them in their real names, so that soon all of them knew each other's true identity. In addition to this, the clothing which they were to wear on their mission was simply bought in local shops and, though it was converted by sewing Dutch labels in, this was done in such a way that it was clear the labels had not been put in in the Netherlands.

The vagueness of Homburg and Sporre's assignment was the final straw as far as Ter Haar and his colleagues were concerned. In a typical display of Dutch stubbornness, they wrote a letter to Laming's superiors saying that they were prepared to go to the Netherlands but not under Laming's command. SOE vented its wrath on the men for such insubordination and had them transferred to a remote outpost in the wilds of Scotland, where they were denied any contact with the outside world. Here they remained until December 1941 when, under pressure from the Dutch Government in exile, a compromise of sorts was reached. The men were allowed to return to London having signed a piece of paper promising not to discuss what had happened. The mishandling of this affair, however, had not gone unnoticed by the Dutch politicians in London, and from that moment on SOE Dutch Section was regarded with suspicion.

By this time Homburg and Sporre were facing rather more acute problems. Having finally been dropped during the night of 6/7 September 1941, they had made their way to Haarlem, where Homburg's uncle, J. Martens, ran a tobacconist's shop – a place which was to play a significant role in the story of SOE's early efforts in the Netherlands.

Their mission suggests more confused and muddle-headed thinking. Officially they were to build up contacts and make a general reconnaissance, but this would be of relevance only if they could communicate the results of their efforts. Neither was given a radio set, not having been trained as operators, so Dutch Section decided that they should be collected by motor boat from the coast. Given that at this stage SOE had not even managed to put an agent ashore by sea, let alone pick one up, this decision was nothing if not highly optimistic!

Once installed in Haarlem, Homburg and Sporre set about recruiting people for future resistance work. They soon found two very useful contacts in Jo Buizer and Jan De Haas. Buizer had worked as a radio operator for the Dutch telephone service and would be a valuable asset, whilst De Haas was a tough young man with useful connections. Both were determined to return to Britain with Homburg and Sporre as soon as possible.

After a few weeks the pre-arranged message for the coastal pick-up was broadcast over the radio, and all four men travelled to the beach at Noordwijk. Unfortunately, despite their spending several nights waiting in the dunes, the motor boat failed to respond to their signals, and no contact was made. That these trips were not without risk for the young Dutchmen was demonstrated when on one occasion they had to spend several hours in the icy sea to avoid a German patrol. This was enough for Homburg, and he called it a day, realizing they would have to find another way of returning to Britain.

It is a reflection on how fast gossip travels, even in an underground organization, that by the end of September 1941 Wiek Schrage, the stranded MI6 organizer, had learned that two more agents had arrived. Rumour had it that they would be returning to Britain shortly, and this seemed to present an ideal way out of his troubles. Ignoring his strict orders not to contact any other agent, he quickly arranged a meeting through intermediaries and ironically recognized in Homburg an old acquaintance. The two had met in London before being sent to the Netherlands and knew each other quite well – another security slip-up which better co-operation between SOE and MI6 might have avoided. Schrage explained that he was sitting on a considerable amount of intelligence information which needed to be sent to Britain, and the three agents decided to look for ways to escape back across the North Sea.

About this time Homburg developed serious toothache and needed treatment. Not knowing any regular dentist he could trust, he remembered an old acquaintance from his National Service days before the war who had subsequently become a dentist and whom Homburg considered completely trustworthy. The dentist J. Vos, was very surprised to see on his doorstep a man whom he knew had gone to Britain but he quickly offered to treat Homburg and even asked to help with his secret work. On 6 October 1941 Homburg had just left the surgery when he was suddenly overpowered by a group of armed Dutch police. Taken to the local police station, he was soon handed over to the SIPO, who had him transferred to the infamous 'Orange Hotel' prison in Scheveningen. Schreieder himself, on hearing of the arrest, took on the case.

The news of Homburg's arrest quickly reached Sporre, who warned Martens at the tobacconist's to remove all traces of them. He was convinced that it would only be a matter of time before the Germans turned up for him. Schrage too was greatly troubled by the news. With both Homburg and Zomer being tortured, it seemed almost certain that somewhere along the line his name would come up.

In fact, during his interrogations, Homburg was able to mislead the SIPO completely. Psychologically he was well prepared for his ordeal, and this gave him a decisive advantage. He claimed to have only just arrived in the Netherlands and that he had not had time to make any contacts, thus pleasing Schreieder by giving the impression that his department was working efficiently. He answered his questions in a very slow, dull manner, successfully giving the German the impression that he was not very intelligent. As there was clearly no radio transmitter involved, Schreieder did not bother informing Giskes of his catch, and he quickly lost interest in the case. Soon the interrogations ceased.

The SIPO were in a hurry to deal with Homburg, and on 10 October 1941 – only four days after his arrest – he was sentenced to death without trial. The date for his execution was set for 26 October, leaving him an unpleasant fortnight's wait in his cell. Escape seemed impossible. There was only a small window high up the wall, with thick bars across it. Undaunted, Homburg managed to turn his spoon into a file and at night set to work on the window frame. He succeeded in cutting into the wood above the bars and was able to break the wood away from the wall. This had been a noisy process but his luck held and he was able to attack the foundations of the bars embedded in the stone wall. After several nights' work he managed to cut a hole which might be big enough if he bent one of the bars back. Making some string from his mattress, he tied it to the bar and pulled it back. However, despite many attempts to squeeze through, the hole was not big enough and on one occasion the string even broke, causing the bar to slam painfully into his back. He was forced to spend valuable time enlarging the hole.

The night before his execution, Homburg made his last attempt. Stripping naked, he was finally able, after a tremendous effort, to wriggle through and reach the prison roof. Here he scaled the high prison wall by climbing a small outhouse and dropping to the ground outside. Once in freedom he ran to the home of Jan de Haas, who lived nearby, and was quickly hidden. He was in the nick of time, for the Germans had already discovered his escape and had mounted a search.

Sporre had only just come to terms with the fact that Homburg had been arrested when he learned that he was once again a free man. When a message arrived asking him for a meeting, he was faced with a dilemma: had Homburg been deliberately released by the Germans in order to lead them to his companions, or had he been 'turned'? Sporre remembered his instructors in Britain telling him never to contact anyone who had been in enemy hands, as it could so easily be a trap. But in the end curiosity got the better of him. Besides, he had already broken a good few SOE guidelines and had suffered no ill effects. He had, for example, taken his girlfriend out to the cinema and had visited all his relatives, in addition to making contact with the MI6 man Schrage. One more broken rule did not seem that important. It is an interesting sidelight on the psychology of agents to note how even trained agents could have little feeling for security. On this occasion Sporre was to be lucky. The future would bring a good many examples of those who were not.

On hearing Homburg's story, Sporre felt his imagination being stretched to the limit. His escape seemed hardly credible, the only evidence for it being some scars on Homburg's back. Discreet enquiries meanwhile established that Homburg had not been officially released, implying that he had either escaped as he claimed or was working for the Germans. Though Sporre could not bring himself to believe that his comrade would betray them, he decided to inform their contacts of his doubts.

It was not long before rumour and gossip were building up their own case against Homburg. One story claimed that he had climbed over the main wall using a ladder, but it seemed unlikely the Germans would leave ladders lying around. Then a former prisoner claimed that there were only wooden spoons in the 'Orange Hotel', so that Homburg could not possibly have turned his into a file. Yet another stated that the cell windows were too high up to reach, yet alone climb out of. Before long Homburg's story was discredited and both Sporre and Schrage decided that, though there was no hard evidence, he could no longer be trusted and should be regarded as a security risk.

This was a serious matter, and the point was raised with Schrage's group in Apeldoorn. In a cruel twist of fate it was decided that Homburg should be 'liquidated' as soon as possible and that they themselves would do the job. Sporre, who had not been present at the meeting, went round to protest at the decision. He pleaded that Homburg should be allowed to make his way back to Britain, where he could explain himself to the SOE. This much, he argued emotionally, they owed Homburg for his good work earlier in the war, and concluded by adding that he himself would soon be returning to Britain, where he would draw up a report about the whole affair. After much discussion the death sentence was finally lifted, but all contact with Homburg was broken off.

In the meantime, Schrage had discovered a possible way

of returning to Britain. He had been offered an eight-metre boat for the price of 10,000 guilders and, although the boat had no cabin, it did possess a mast and two sails in addition to an outboard engine. He was able to borrow the money to buy it and from that moment he became determined to sail back across the North Sea. The problems were many. The boat would have to be transported by road to the Dutch province of Zeeland, where it would have to be launched into the strong surf, and beyond the beach there were minefields and coastal patrol crafts to contend with. Detection by the Germans at any stage would be fatal. Nonetheless, despite many warnings both Schrage and Sporre were determined to take their chances.

Though Homburg had been left in the dark about these matters, he soon began to hear whispers about the escape attempt. Until then he had always believed he would be returning to Britain with the others, but now it dawned on him for the first time that he was no longer trusted. This impression was confirmed after he had sent De Haas out to make enquiries. Most of his former contacts claimed not to know him and refused to give De Haas any information concerning the forthcoming escape attempt. But Homburg was not the sort of man to give up without a fight. He decided he would make his own way back to Britain.

Meanwhile his comrades' story ended tragically. On 13 November 1941 Wiek Schrage and Cor Sporre made their attempt to cross the North Sea, after telling friends to listen for a message on the radio to the effect that the beer was nice – a wry joke which would indicate that they had arrived safely. Their friends waited in vain. The message never arrived and it is assumed that both were drowned in the North Sea. So ended the lives of two gallant young Dutchmen.

4   The Foundations Are Laid

For Huub Lauwers, working in Manila in the Philippines in May 1940, the news that his homeland had been invaded came as a severe shock. Deciding it was his duty to return and help his fellow-countrymen, he booked the next available passage home. However, while his ship steamed slowly across the oceans, the fighting on the European mainland came to an end, and Lauwers was forced to recognize the fact that the Netherlands had been occupied by the Germans. He arrived at Liverpool on 20 August 1940 and immediately joined the Dutch Volunteers Legion, in which he served until May 1941.

Lauwers was soon deeply disillusioned with the part he was playing in the war. He had not come half way round the world just to peel potatoes and stand sentry duty, so when his unit was asked for volunteers for a 'parachute battalion' he quickly signed up. That the 'parachute battalion' was merely a recruiting campaign for the Dutch Intelligence Service (CID) became obvious when he was asked at his interview whether he would mind parachuting in civilian clothes. Lauwers did not mind. He wanted to get into action as quickly as possible and was not particularly bothered how. Summoned for a second interview at the London headquarters of CID, he was closely questioned about his background, but the Dutch Intelligence Service soon lost interest when they learned he had been out of the Netherlands for five years. As far as they were concerned, he did not have enough current contacts to be of much use.

At this stage he was passed on to SOE Dutch Section, who accepted him enthusiastically. Lauwers was questioned by a 'Lieutenant Dawson', to whom he explained

CID's objections. Was this not also a problem for the British? 'Dawson' merely shrugged his shoulders and said that he would be given contact addresses before he went to the Netherlands. In view of the fact that at this stage Dutch Section had no reliable Dutch addresses at all, this was a somewhat dubious promise, but Lauwers was taken in by the confident tone. Under the mistaken impression that he had joined the legendary British Secret Service (MI6), he was completely over-awed by all that he saw and heard.

His training strengthened this favourable impression. As part of Dutch Section's second training group, he had nothing but praise for the quality of his instructors, all of whom appeared to be professionals with a high degree of competence in their work and some practical experience of what they were teaching. The early courses dealt mainly with sabotage and the handling of weapons and explosives, the very meat and drink of SOE's brief. In addition all agents were given a course in morse code, so that they could double as radio operators in times of emergency. Those who were to specialize as such – this group included Lauwers – were sent to Beaulieu in the peaceful surroundings of the New Forest.

At Beaulieu Lauwers was on a tight schedule. He was given a code which, according to his instructors, was unbreakable, and he was taught how to translate it by means of a poem of his choosing which would be known only by himself and his controller. Lauwers chose a verse which he had learnt by heart at school before the war.

It was on the shore
Around our coast,
That I found alone
On a piece of stone
An elderly Navy man ...

The code was equipped with a security check so that, in the event of Lauwers' capture SOE would know he was no longer operating in freedom. The security check entailed a pre-arranged signal to be repeated in every message. In Lauwers' case it involved making a deliberate spelling mistake in every sixteenth letter or multiple of sixteen –

thirty-two or sixty-four. His security check was his only
way of letting Dutch Section know that he had not fallen
into enemy hands.

Lauwers was also taught what to do were he ever to fall
into the hands of the SIPO. It was obvious, he was told,
that the Germans would ask for his code, and after a
'reasonable' length of time he should give it to them. The
reasoning behind this was sound. The Germans were
likely to find out by torturing him and in the process might
learn a lot that they had not initially been looking for. The
code was useless without the accompanying security check,
and it was this, above all else, that he should never hand
over. It is probable that Lauwers was also told that, if the
Germans got hold of him, they would ask him to transmit
for them. He was told that, if such a situation arose he
should agree to co-operate. Again the reasoning appeared
good: as long as he remained useful he would not be
executed, and the time gained would improve his chances
of escape. As far as SOE were concerned, all he had to do
was to omit his security check and they would be warned.
It might then be possible to play a triple-cross with the
Germans. This training was not lost on Lauwers. For him,
his security check became a cornerstone, a sacred symbol
which he would never forget, a secret agreement with his
headquarters which he determined to take to the grave
with him – if necessary.

Lauwers' training finished in October 1941, after which
he was summoned to London to be briefed on his mission.
By this stage, after the rebellion of the first training group,
Laming had been forced to look to his second, and now
that Homburg and Sporre had failed to turn up at their
rendezvous, he was preparing to send another two agents
to the Netherlands. Lauwers' companion was to be Thys
Taconis, a tall young man who had been trained alongside
him at Winterford. Taconis had escaped from the
Netherlands in 1940, in a fishing boat, and was now keen
to go back. The two men had developed a high regard for
one another which would make for a harmonious working
relationship.

Their orders were deceptively simple. First they were to
find out what had become of Homburg and Sporre, after

which Taconis was to set up several networks and train them in the art of sabotage. Once these groups had been trained, Dutch Section would begin dropping weapons and explosives. Lauwers' task was to set up a small intelligence organization and be the link man with Britain. The only problem was that the disappearance of Homburg and Sporre had left Dutch Section without any up-to-date safe addresses in the Netherlands the very thing Lauwers had been warned about before his training. Eventually three addresses, of dubious quality, were procured from recent arrivals in Britain – a highly unsatisfactory state of affairs, which led Taconis to tell Lauwers to forget all about them. He himself knew scores of people in The Hague who were absolutely trustworthy. Most, like him, had been in the Nationaal Jongeren Verbond, a pre-war patriotic organization which had argued for more defence spending and which, not surprisingly, had been the first organization the Germans outlawed when they occupied the Netherlands.

The two agents were told they would leave on 2 November 1941, in spite of the fact that their forged papers had not been completed. At the last moment the trip was cancelled, due to bad weather. Whilst they were held isolated in a 'holding school', SOE worked on their papers. These were not 'finished' until 6 November, just in time for their next attempt. Producing the papers, Laming asked them to sign them. Lauwers was not satisfied and asked to see a copy of the originals. Understandably, if he was going to risk his life with them, he wanted to see that they had been competently forged. At first Laming claimed not to have a copy of the originals but when Lauwers remained adamant he suddenly produced them from his pocket. The reason for his earlier reluctance was obvious. The forgeries were much darker than the original. The lion in the genuine document showed up clearly in great detail, whilst in his papers it reminded Lauwers of a packhorse. With only a few hours before they were due to depart, this was no laughing matter, and Laming, after admitting the forgeries were very poor, told them they did not have to go if they did not want to. But by this stage the parachutes were almost literally on their backs, and they decided to go ahead with the operation. Once in the Netherlands they would attempt to obtain genuine papers.

Their equipment, already packed and waiting, included handguns, ammunition, knives, compasses, emergency rations and a spade with which to bury their parachutes. A bicycle was to be dropped to act as emergency transport, and they were given 12,000 guilders, of which Taconis, who was to do a lot of travelling, received the lion's share. For the first time Lauwers was shown his most important piece of equipment, the radio transmitter fitted tightly into the usual MI6 suitcase. He wanted to test it but was prevented from doing so and told that it had been thoroughly checked. He was also reminded – though there was by now clear evidence to the contrary – that it was untraceable by the Germans.

Before he went, Lauwers wanted to make one last confirmation concerning his security check. He had heard a rumour about a Frenchman sent to France by SOE who had never bothered to use his security check. It had finally been decided that the man was still operating in freedom, and it was this decision that had preyed on Lauwers' mind. He told 'Lieutenant Dawson' that, if he ever left out his own check, there should be no doubt as to what had happened to him. Characteristically, he was told not to worry about it.

Having said their goodbyes to Laming and 'Dawson', both agents climbed into their bomber accompanied by a jumpmaster. Surprisingly, considering the pressure they were under, both fell asleep during their flight across the North Sea and had to be woken up shortly after crossing the Dutch coast. In the dim light Lauwers watched the jumpmaster hooking up their static lines and checking their parachutes. Then the door was opened and several bundles of leaflets disappeared into the slipstream – these were to serve as the aircraft's official cover story, and the bomber would continue on to Germany so as to avert suspicion.

As the light above the door turned red, both men prepared themselves mentally for the jump, fighting off the sickening thoughts they were experiencing. They were warned to be careful of smashing their heads against the side of the plane, and with that their jumpmaster wished them good luck. The light turned green, and Lauwers disappeared through the door. The wind was far stronger than he had expected and after a short descent he hit the ground very hard indeed. Rolling in the prescribed manner, he was dragged by his inflated canopy through a field of turnips, only just missing a post in the ground. Finally managing to deflate his canopy, he undid his harness and, picking up the suitcase containing his radio set, went looking for Taconis and the bicycle. The two men met up quite quickly but there was no sign of their bicycle, and they soon gave up the search, opting instead for some rest before daybreak.

The next morning they awoke to find their drop zone covered with the propaganda leaflets. What had formerly seemed like a good idea now appeared to be placing them in great danger, and they wasted no time in leaving the area.

As they walked towards the nearest station, Lauwers was able to reflect, for the first time, on his position. He realized that no amount of training could have prepared him for his feelings at that moment. The knowledge that one wrong move could cost him his life, that the badly forged papers in his pocket were unlikely to get him through any checks, that the gun in his pocket was a death sentence in itself if he were caught; all brought home to him the seriousness of what he was doing. Suddenly, to his horror, he realized that he and Taconis were wearing identical clothing. In fact, they looked like twins with their matching shirts, ties, raincoats and briefcases. In retrospect it seems quite incredible that they could have been sent to the Netherlands looking like that. (Dutch Section had added to its growing catalogue of major errors.) After a few minutes of worried discussion they decided that as soon as they reached civilization one of them would change.

Despite one scare when a policeman walked past, they reached the town of Marienburg at ten that morning and decided to visit a café. They did not stay long because the locals started staring at them suspiciously. When Taconis went to pay the café owner for their drinks, using some coins he had been given by SOE, the bar-tender looked at him in utter amazement. Unbeknown to Dutch Section, these coins had long since been taken out of circulation. Taconis decided to bluff his way out, uttering that where he came from they still used this kind of money, and the bar-tender, no doubt a little confused, handed him some small change.

Once outside they examined the coins they had been given, which appeared to have been made of zinc. Realizing that, if the Germans had changed the banknotes as well, they would be in serious trouble, they made their way to the station. Taconis went up to the kiosk and ordered two single tickets to Amsterdam, whilst Lauwers stood back and carefully watched the ticket-seller's reaction to the 10 guilder note he was offered. To their relief, the man handed over the tickets and change without even looking up.

They arrived in Amsterdam at 7.30 that evening but did not go to any of the addresses SOE had given them. Taconis was convinced that the father of one of his friends, a fanatical ex-army colonel, would help them. On their arriving at his house, Taconis told Lauwers to take a walk and return in half an hour whilst he arranged things. On his return Lauwers found Taconis waiting for him with bad news. The Colonel had not wanted to listen and had even threatened to call the police. It was their first experience of a common reaction in the early part of the war. Very few Dutch people were willing to risk their lives at this stage.

Fortunately they had planned for this eventuality and spent the night at the home of an uncle of Taconis, who welcomed them with open arms. The following day they made their way to The Hague, where Taconis wanted to look up an old friend.

This would be a sentimental reunion. Directly after the Dutch surrender in 1940 Taconis had managed to obtain a place on a trawler for himself and his friend Frits Bouma. Under the impression they would not be leaving for a few hours, Taconis told Bouma that he had time to collect some things from his home nearby, but circumstances changed and the trawler was forced to set sail early, leaving Bouma stranded. Taconis not only wanted to apologize for what had happened; he wanted Bouma for his sabotage team.

They succeeded in contacting Bouma and another friend, Wil Van der Hilst. Both proved keen to help. That evening the four men had a long and serious discussion about the work ahead. An organization had to be set up, comprising trustworthy people who were willing to risk their lives for the Allied cause. Recruits would have to be trained in the use of weapons and explosives. In addition they would need to find a number of safe houses for themselves and the radio transmitter. Bouma knew a family in Oosterbeek near Arnhem who would help, and Lauwers decided to use this as his transmitting base.

On 13 November 1941 he attempted to open contact with SOE but to his dismay his transmitter refused to work. Recalling how he had been told on departure that the set had been properly tested, he concluded it must have been damaged on landing. There was nothing for it but to start looking for a technician.

It took two weeks to find a contact who could repair the transmitter. When the set was stripped down, it was discovered that the problem was due to a manufacturing fault, making a mockery of Dutch Section's claim to have tested the set.

Lauwers' faith in SOE was further shaken when he discovered that he could not contact Britain with an inside aerial. After more problems with a large and dangerously conspicuous outside aerial, they decided to try transmitting nearer to Britain and moved back to The Hague. Here Lauwers came into contact with Wout Teller, who showed great enthusiasm for the problem and agreed to let Lauwers transmit from his attic. Together they constructed an aerial, and finally, on 3 January 1942, Lauwers was ready to transmit. Nervously he tapped out his call sign 'RLS ... RLS ...'. To his immense relief he heard SOE answer. After two long and frustrating months, contact had at last been established.

One of Lauwers' first requests was for more information about Homburg and Sporre, who were still missing. Dutch

Section gave him the address of Martens, the tobacconist in Haarlem, and told him to make enquiries there. Convinced the risk was worth taking, Taconis went round to the shop and learned from Martens where Homburg was to be found. A meeting was quickly arranged. Homburg was delighted to be in contact with his own organization again and talked for a long time of his arrest, his interrogations, his escape and the sudden mistrust of his colleagues. He had investigated the matter of his arrest, and it appeared that he had been betrayed by his old friend J. Vos, the dentist. Proof of this had been delivered when Homburg's friend Jo Buizer had telephoned Vos, impersonating the Dutch policeman who had arrested Homburg. Buizer had asked Vos if he had any further news about Homburg, to which the dentist replied that he thought he was back in Britain, adding that if the police ever needed his help again they had only to ask.

Taconis was in favour of liquidating the traitor there and then, but Homburg asked him to wait until he, Homburg, was definitely back in Britain and could get official permission for the execution. If this was forthcoming, he would arrange for a message to be sent concerning a fox in sheep's clothing. (The name Vos in Dutch means fox.) Meanwhile Lauwers informed SOE of Sporre's attempt to cross the North Sea the previous November along with Schrage. Dutch Section replied saying that neither had arrived and that it was now imperative that Homburg should return safely. By this stage, however, Laming had finally become sceptical about coastal pick-ups, and Homburg was told to find another way of getting back to Britain. It was in effect an admission of defeat. Dutch Section had renounced its responsibility for getting its men back.

Fortunately for them, its men were not short of initiative. Homburg travelled to the port of Ijmuiden, where he came into contact with a trawler captain who was persuaded to try to make a dash for Britain, on condition that financial arrangements be made for the families of those seamen who would sail with them. Lauwers consulted SOE who gave their approval. The plan was for

Homburg and his two would-be agent friends, Buizer and De Haas, to be smuggled aboard and hidden in the fish holds. Once the trawler was well out to sea, they would emerge and force the crew at gun point to sail to Britain. Only the captain was to know of the plan beforehand, so as to maximize security. The date of the attempt was set for 15 February 1942.

Homburg made some final arrangements and took his leave of Lauwers and Taconis. (It was the last time they would ever see each other.) He left them with a promise that Radio Orange, the Free Dutch station in London, would announce his safe arrival with the cheerful message 'Keep Smiling'.

On 15 February the trawler *Beatrice* left Ijmuiden in heavy seas with its three stowaways safely on board. However, a combination of severe sea-sickness and the stench of the fish holds left them all very ill, and when the time came for them to emerge and take over the trawler they were so weak they could hardly stand up. It was hardly the stuff that glamorous legends are made of, but fortunately for them the captain managed to persuade the crew to sail for Britain anyway, and the following day the *Beatrice* arrived safely in Portsmouth.

Dutch Section were able to question Homburg very closely on the situation in the Netherlands, and both Buizer and De Haas were found suitable for immediate training. After his debriefing Homburg declined to remain with SOE and joined the RAF. In time he married a girl whom he had met during his first period in Britain and went on to become a successful fighter pilot. He was killed a month before the final German surrender in April 1945, when his Spitfire was shot down over the Netherlands.

Lauwers and Taconis heard the message 'Keep Smiling' and knew they had successfully completed the first part of their mission. The second part – to set up sabotage groups and wage an underground war against the Germans – would not prove nearly so easy.

5   'North Pole', Act I

Both CID and SOE Dutch Section underwent changes in leadership during the winter of 1941-2. As early as August 1941 François Van't Sant had been outmanœuvred by his many enemies in the Dutch Government. Told that he could no longer remain as both head of CID and Queen Wilhelmina's private secretary, he chose to retain his real power base, his position with the Queen. He was succeeded at CID by Captain Derksema, whose rank alone made him totally unsuited for the job. Colonel Rabagliatti, unable to accept the fact that a mere captain could be running his country's Secret Service, deliberately set out to make his life very difficult. By February 1942 Derksema had had enough and resigned. He was succeeded by Colonel de Bruyne, a professional soldier and also Commander in Chief of the Dutch Marines.

At Dutch Section Laming had also been replaced. This was due partly to the rebellion of the first training group, partly to the fact that he had disclosed the embarrassing information that MI6 had paid Van't Sant £25,000 for his services during World War I. In any event, as he made clear to the Dutch after the war, he was not sad to be going. His successor was Major Charles Blizzard, a professional soldier, who took over in February 1942. Blizzard was in a hurry to get on with the task of setting the Netherlands ablaze, and he sent his two agents in the field a message telling them to prepare a drop zone for a consignment of weapons and explosives.

Out in the field, Lauwers' perception of the situation differed somewhat. It seemed clear to him that Dutch Section did not fully understand the situation in the Netherlands. His agents were not yet ready for weapons and explosives; there were as yet no trained sabotage groups to use them, nor was there an organization to arrange the hiding and distribution of these supplies. So far most of their efforts had gone into getting the transmitter working and finding safe houses to operate from. By rushing things, it seemed to Lauwers, Dutch Section were risking infiltration and catastrophe.

It was not going to be easy to build up the organizations required. This had already become clear to Taconis as he travelled up and down the country trying to recruit old friends and colleagues. Most refused to have anything to do with him and the dangerous work he was offering. A born idealist, Taconis found this hard to accept. He had actively warned against the Germans long before the war and now felt that events had more than justified his arguments. To his mind there was only one thing a Dutch patriot could do: actively resist the Germans. In early 1942, with German war fortunes approaching their peak, this was a point of view with which few Dutchmen agreed.

Another major problem which Dutch Section did not seem to appreciate, in Lauwers' eyes, was the way people gossiped about things which ought to have remained secret. Many onlookers delighted in telling stories about the new secret agents they had met, completely unaware of the security implications involved. Lauwers himself frequently upset people by refusing to give them his address, and he could only hope that there were no traitors amongst them. Unfortunately traitors were never in short supply in occupied countries during the war.

Despite these problems Lauwers and Taconis set to work carrying out Blizzard's orders. As early as November 1941 Lauwers had been in contact with a certain Captain Van den Bergh who had useful contacts with another resistance group. Unbeknown to both Lauwers and Van den Bergh, this group had been infiltrated by one George Ridderhof, an alcoholic diamond-smuggler with a nose for a quick profit. Ridderhof decided to contact the Germans, to see if they would be interested in paying for the stories he was beginning to hear about two British agents recently parachuted into the Netherlands.

Ridderhof timed to perfection his arrival – late in

November 1941 – at Abwehr Section III F. Giskes had just finished a thorough shake-out of his organization and had told his V-man recruiter Willy Kupp to go and find him a high-quality traitor, capable of infiltrating a resistance group. Ridderhof met Kupp and whetted the Germans' appetite with some information about the resistance group he was involved in. Kupp reported to Giskes, who was sceptical but finally consented to allow Ridderhof 500 guilders to see what he could come up with. During the following weeks the results would surprise him.

The search for a suitable drop zone proved more difficult than expected, not least because of the high standards it had to satisfy. For instance, it had to be big enough for a plane to find at night, in a rural area and within easy reach by car; there should be no Germans in the vicinity or suspect locals, and there should be safe houses nearby. Not surprisingly, in such a densely populated country as the Netherlands, such locations were few and far between. Finally Captain Van den Bergh was enlisted for advice and he claimed to know a perfect site, in the east of the country, where he also had many trustworthy contacts. In the course of making preparations, he alerted several colleagues, including Ridderhof, to be on standby to help out with the drop.

Giskes soon learned of this news via Ridderhof and Kupp. According to Kupp's report, a newly formed resistance organization was preparing for a weapons drop which would enable it to launch a campaign of sabotage. Initially Giskes did not believe a word of it, and he became angry at the thought that Ridderhof had duped him out of some money. Quickly scribbling a footnote under the report – 'Gehen Sie zum Nordpol mit dieser Geschicte' ('Run to the North Pole with your story') – he gave Ridderhof three days to come up with some evidence for his claims. Ridderhof insisted he was telling the truth, and finally Giskes began to have more faith in him. By now there was also some independent evidence.

Heinrich's surveillance team had been aware since the first week in January that a new transmitter was operating under the call sign RLS and being answered by station USL. Measurements of the co-ordinates showed that USL was operating from somewhere north of London, whilst RLS had been narrowed down to The Hague area. This tallied with Ridderhof's description of the two agents, one of whom was thought to be in The Hague. Further reports had been received from the SIPO in Arnhem stating that one of their V-men had managed to infiltrate a secret organization which was thought to be run by a British agent. More details would be made available as soon as possible.

Giskes received Kupp's second report from Ridderhof, which stated that his organization was looking for transport for the weapons drop. It was agreed that Ridderhof should be provided with a lorry. Giskes had already concluded that the two agents in the reports were linked. Now with a bit of luck he might be able to capture both with one move.

During February 1942 Lauwers' transmitter became increasingly busy. Details of the weapons drop, along with the normal flow of intelligence, meant that he was spending dangerously long periods on the air. Dutch Section had warned him against using one of the addresses they had given him: it had subsequently been discovered that the owner was a Dutch Nazi, and Lauwers was intensely grateful they had decided to use their own initiative instead of relying on SOE. So far at least there had been no hint the Germans knew what was going on.

Blizzard finally set the date for the drop between 26 and 28 February, and this information soon reached Giskes via Lauwers, Van den Bergh, Ridderhof and Kupp. In his office in Scheveningen Giskes went through the details of the reports. Slowly but surely, thanks to Ridderhof's efforts, a clear picture had emerged of what was going on. The British Secret Service had sent two agents to the Netherlands. The first was in general command and was to instruct in the art of sabotage. He was living in the Arnhem area. The second was the radio operator who, according to Heinrich, was operating from The Hague and who would be pin-pointed within the week. Both agents were known to be in contact with a Captain Van den Bergh, whose home address Ridderhof had also revealed. Van den Bergh had been tailed and Giskes had descriptions of seven men thought to be connected with his work. It seemed probable that the two agents were among them. Within a few days there was to be a weapons drop in Eastern Holland, at a site whose location was known – again due to Ridderhof's efforts.

Giskes' plan was to let the drop go ahead and wait until all the leads were followed up. The Abwehr, in reluctant co-operation with the SIPO, would then strike at the radio operator before he could warn SOE, after which an attempt would be made to play his transmitter back to the British.

On 28 February a coded message on Radio Orange confirmed that the drop would be that night. Giskes spent the evening at a Luftwaffe radar station. This was to be Ridderhof's first real test, and Giskes was prepared to get very tough were he to fail it. As things turned out, however, he need not have worried. Around midnight a radar operator came up to inform him that a single aircraft, a bomber, was being tracked across the Netherlands. During the next hour Giskes could only pray that a night fighter would not get to the bomber before it had the chance to drop its cargo.

On the drop zone the reception committee switched on their torches as soon as they heard the plane approaching. Taconis and Van den Bergh had placed their men to form a wide arc of light for the pilot to see. Recognition signals were exchanged and a few minutes later two canisters were floating earthwards. Unfortunately the wind was strong and the parachutes overshot the DZ by a considerable distance. The first was found not far off, deeply imbedded in the earth, but the second had disappeared without trace, and Taconis soon gave up the search on the assumption that it had fallen into a nearby canal. Within minutes of this decision the DZ was deserted.

The following day Ridderhof reported the fact that only one of the canisters had been recovered. Giskes, realizing that he could not allow weapons and explosives to lie around in a field, contacted the Wehrmacht. Two days later German Army trucks drove into the drop-zone area and cordoned it off. Officially this exercise was part of manœuvres but even the Army did not know the real reason for their presence. They had been told they were looking for a canister containing top-secret Luftwaffe equipment, and for several days groups of soldiers dutifully combed the area. Nothing was found and eventually Giskes was forced to conclude, as had Taconis, that the canister must have landed in the nearby canal.

On 4 March 1942 Lauwers transmitted the disturbing news that a few days after the drop a German battalion had cordoned off the area around the DZ. To him it seemed his luck was still holding good. Little did he know that at that very moment Heinrich's surveillance team had pin-pointed his block of flats. From previous transmission times the Germans knew that the next transmission would be at 6.30 p.m. that Friday, 6 March. Giskes determined to strike then.

For the first time during the whole operation the SIPO were now informed of what was happening. Armed with a detailed report, Giskes went to see Schreieder. If he could get the latter's support, the operation might well bring rich rewards. He had also anticipated an outcry from the Nazi Party hierarchy, and that is what he got. Schreieder's boss, Sturmbannführer Hugo Wolf, in particular, was incensed; he warned Giskes that if any of the weapons in the recovered canister were used against the Germans, he personally would be held responsible. Irked by the young SS man, Giskes stood his ground, claimed that the case involved a radio transmitter and pointed out that it was his job to track them down. In spite of the general outrage, Giskes eventually got what he wanted. Schreieder, shrewd enough to see the possibilities on offer, quietly told him he would go along with the plan, and set off to arrange the details.

Giskes knew that, if everything went according to plan during the next few weeks, his section would be in for a busy time. His aims were clear, as was his plan of action. After the radio operator had been taken alive, and his set captured intact, he would have to be forced into handing over his code as soon as possible. Then, having obtained his security check, Giskes would have to persuade the agent to transmit for him, because it had to be assumed that the British had taped Lauwers' morse code 'fingerprint' and would instantly notice if he were not behind the set himself. This seemed likely to prove the most difficult challenge of all, and it was not something that Giskes relished. He did, however, have some levers, and he was determined to use them to the full when the time came. Throughout the whole operation speed would be of the essence. Time was the one commodity that Giskes lacked, for if Lauwers was off the air for more than a week, SOE could not help but get suspicious.

In an attempt to break Lauwers' code, the Abwehr came up with a very neat little trick. Giskes handed a message to Ridderhof to give to Van den Bergh, who in turn passed it on to Lauwers. The message ran: 'THE BATTLE CRUISER PRINZ EUGEN HAS JUST ARRIVED IN SCHIEDAM'. Van den Bergh was tailed delivering it, allowing the SIPO to confirm exactly which flat to storm.

Friday 6 March 1942 was a cold day, and the streets and pavements were covered in ice and snow, making all movement very difficult. Lauwers arrived at the Tellers' house around midday and set to work encoding the evening's messages. This was a slow job – it had taken him half an hour to encode the latest message from Van den Bergh, concerning the *Prinz Eugen*. Finally, after much thought, he decided to put in his security check – that is, to make a deliberate spelling mistake in the middle of the word 'stop'. By coincidence, in one of the other two messages he was to send the sixteenth letter had also fallen into the middle of the word 'stop'. Having prepared his messages, Lauwers burned all the paper he had used for his calculations – part of standard security procedure – and settled back to await 6.30 p.m.

Out of sight, around the corner, the SIPO were also waiting, in their vans. The procedure was similar to that used in the arrest of Zomer: they would act only when Lieutenant Heinrich gave the signal that the messages had started. However, just as Lauwers was warming up for his transmission, Teller burst in to say that some of his friends had spotted a German raiding van parked down a side street. Lauwers automatically switched off his transmitter and decided to go on a short walk of the area to see for himself. Before he went he gave Mrs Teller hurried instructions that, should the SIPO raid the flat, she should throw his transmitter out of the window, so that it would not fall into German hands intact. Nevertheless, this was just a precaution, for Lauwers was not unduly worried, remembering being told by SOE that his transmitter was untraceable. On the strength of this he decided not to destroy the encoded messages – they had taken such a long time to encode, and he put them in his pocket. Then, putting on his coat and shoes, he went out and started to walk down the street, accompanied by Wout Teller.

Further down the street, Giskes had quickly realized that all was not well. Heinrich's surveillance van had just pulled up to inform him that the transmitter had gone off the air. Seemingly the operator had just been warned of their presence. Giskes wasted no time and ran over to the raiding vans, jumped into the front of the nearest one and ordered the driver to step on it. They soon came across Willy Kupp, the V-man recruiter, in a state of considerable excitement, pointing towards two men, apparently in deep conversation, a few hundred metres ahead of them. Arresting them, Giskes foresaw, might well be difficult because of the ice and snow which prevented the vans from being able to drive onto the pavement. Praying the two suspects were not armed or fanatical, he ordered the vans to draw level with the men and then stop. Moments later the SIPO, guns waving, were pouring out of the vans across the ice towards the two men. Neither Lauwers nor Teller offered any resistance, and they were roughly pushed up against a wall and searched.

By this time the block of flats had been deluged with Germans, who were nevertheless unable to prevent Mrs Teller's hoisting the radio transmitter over the balcony. Unfortunately her brave action was in vain. The transmitter caught in several washing lines, which broke its fall, and when the SIPO retrieved it from below, it was found to be intact. Mrs Teller, despite being pregnant, was tied into a chair and watched as Lauwers was brought in and pushed into a separate room. A table and some chairs were brought in for the first interrogation.

Once over the immediate shock of his capture, Lauwers was surprised to find that he was still able to analyse calmly the position in which he found himself. It was obvious that, with the radio transmitter intact and with the messages found in his pockets, he could not deny being a British agent. He recalled the main points of his SOE preparation for such an eventuality – that he should play for time, so as to warn SOE and give himself more chance to escape; that he should not give up his code until the last possible moment, and that under no circumstances should he give up his security check. He remembered what Ab Homburg – who had also been in this situation – had told him, and he knew that escape was possible. The Germans would need him to transmit for them and were therefore unlikely to torture him. It was this knowledge in particular that strengthened his grim resolve not to give in to the enemy, and he felt there was still a long way to go before he faced a firing squad. In fact, Lauwers' handling of his interrogations would be masterly.

6   Act II – The Tragedy Begins

Lauwers' first ploy was to pretend he did not understand German, thus gaining some extra thinking time because an interpreter had to be used. As expected, he was immediately asked for his code, and he politely but firmly refused to hand it over. He did, however, admit to having come from Britain. It would have been pointless to deny this, given the evidence – when Giskes inspected his forged papers, he had all but laughed.

Many of his other possessions, Lauwers knew, were probably safe. He had given his gun to Van den Bergh, whilst his suicide pill, along with the rest of his belongings, was at his digs nearby, where he also kept his file of messages, stuck between the pages of some old newspapers in his landlord's loft. Lauwers was quite confident that these would survive a search and that Mr Nakken, his landlord, would destroy them, along with his other belongings, as soon as he heard of the arrests. Together they had already arranged a cover story. All the Nakkens 'knew' about him was that he was a traveller from the Dutch East Indies who had needed digs.

After some fifteen minutes of questioning Heinrich came into the interrogation room and began to ask Lauwers about his code and transmitting procedure. He pointed out that, by always transmitting on the same wavelength at the same time, SOE had made it very easy for the Germans to monitor Lauwers' transmissions. Silently, Lauwers could only agree. He himself had put forward proposals to SOE for a change in procedure which would have tightened up security considerably but the British had not been interested. (These proposals were adopted later in the war.) Heinrich went on to list the

Lodo Van Hamel, the first MI6 agent to be dispatched to the Netherlands and (*above*) the seaplane which failed to pick him up in October 1940

Gestapo chief Joseph Schreieder

Han Jordaan, the captured
SOE agent who was told to
use his security check by
Dutch section. He died in
Mauthausen concentration
camp in May 1945

Hans Zomer, MI6 agent
executed in May 1942

George Ridderhof, the
Dutch traitor who
penetrated SOE's first
network, executed 1947

Martin Slagter and Leo Poos, Dutch policemen who worked for
Schreieder and were sentenced to life imprisonment after the war

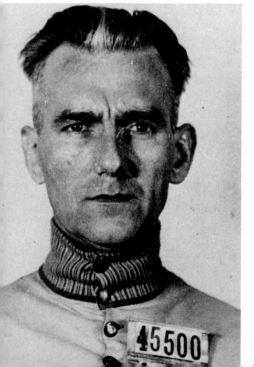

Anton Van der Waals, Holland's No.1 traitor

Officially listed as missing, Ernst De Jonge was another MI6 agent caught up in the *Englandspiel*

Jan De Haas, an SOE agent who escaped to England with Homburg. He was recaptured shortly after his return to the Netherlands and died on 7 September 1944 at Mauthausen

Barend Klooss, dispatched as part of SOE's second network in Holland and murdered at Mauthausen on 6 September 1944

Evert Radema (*above*), George Ruseler (*below left*) and Willem
Niermayer. Ruseler was an SOE agent, whilst Niermayer and
Radema both belonged to MI6. Captured in the *Englandspiel*, they
were all murdered at Mauthausen, 6-7 September 1944

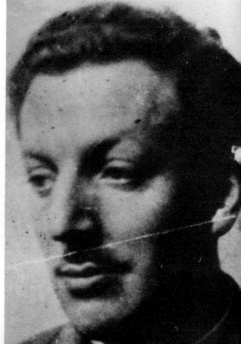

Jacob Bakker, an SOE agent dispatched on 27 October 1942 as part of the Plan for Holland and officially listed as missing

details: call signs, wavelengths, times of transmission, average length of transmission, and the type of code being used. With all this information, he boasted, along with the captured messages found in Lauwers' coat pocket, it would be a simple matter to break his code. Lauwers, addressed throughout as 'Lieutenant', was told that his interrogator had a great deal of respect for his courage but that he would be shot if he did not co-operate. This was not, Heinrich added, his own wish, but a fact of war, in which the penalty for spying was death, on all sides. By telling the Germans his code, Lauwers would only be saving them a bit of work and would help to save his own life.

Several thoughts flashed through Lauwers' mind. First and most importantly, he was convinced the German was bluffing. Without his code poem, he knew, it would take many months to break the coded messages. Secondly he knew he had to hold on to his code as long as possible in order to gain time. He had already missed one transmission time. If he could miss the next one as well, Dutch Section ought to become suspicious.

Heinrich repeated his claim to be able to break his code and, irritated by the obvious ploy, Lauwers told the German that, if he could crack the coded messages, he would hand over his code. Heinrich accepted the challenge with a grin and quickly left the room, saying that he would be back in twenty minutes. Once next door he exchanged impressions of Lauwers with Giskes. Without his knowing it, Lauwers' technique was already succeeding. Both Germans were completely puzzled by their prisoner.

Meanwhile the SIPO quickly followed up some of the leads they had found in the Tellers' flat. One of these took them to the Nakkens' home where Lauwers had been staying. On opening the door Mrs Nakken was roughly pushed aside, and the Germans stormed into the kitchen only to be confronted by the sight of Mr Nakken innocently washing his feet. Fortunately for Lauwers, the ensuing search failed to reveal his file of old messages hidden in a pile of newspapers in the loft. Mr Nakken, instantly realizing what had happened, waited until the Germans had left before he set about burning the papers.

With this done he set out to warn his colleagues of Lauwers' arrest.

At the Tellers' flat Lauwers had been further questioned by Willy Kupp, for just over a quarter of an hour, when Heinrich came running back into the room. Smiling broadly at Lauwers, he said, 'I see the *Prinz Eugen* has arrived in Schiedam', before placing a paper and pencil in front of him. Lauwers', unable to hide his amazement and frustration, was completely at a loss to understand what had happened. Fifteen minutes earlier he had not expected to see Heinrich again, but now the German appeared to have done the impossible. New thoughts crossed Lauwers' mind. It seemed clear that the Germans could break his code without help and that it was now his task to gain the trust of his interrogators so that he could improve his chances of escaping. By giving up his code he would not be betraying anything crucial – nothing that had not already been written into his interrogation scenario by SOE. Slowly, with a lot of prompting from Heinrich, he wrote:

> It was on a shore
> Around our coast
> That I found alone
> On a piece of stone
> An elderly Navy man ...

For Lauwers there was no going back.

Outside in the hall Giskes was delighted to hear from Willy Kupp that the trick with the *Prinz Eugen* had succeeded and that the agent was at that very moment writing down his entire code. Once this had been completed, he could hand Lauwers over to the SIPO for more questioning and thus placate Schreieder, who was getting impatient. All the Abwehr had to do now was to discover the security check and persuade their prisoner to transmit for them.

Before the SIPO sank their teeth into him, Lauwers was taken, along with Wout Teller and his pregnant wife, to the 'Orange Hotel', where he was isolated from the others and questioned about his contacts. Instructions had already gone out that all the suspects tailed during the previous weeks should be picked up, and Schreieder was confident that the second agent would be among them.

It did not take Lauwers long to realize he was better off inventing a story for the Germans than attempting to remain silent. If nothing else, it would keep his mind occupied and ensure that his interrogation was over quicker.

Lauwers' work before the war had been good training for his present situation. Then, as a salesman, it had been his job to keep irate customers happy, to twist the truth, to avoid difficult questions and, most importantly, to think on his feet under pressure. Using all the techniques he had acquired as a salesman, he began to tell the SIPO of his 'adventures' in the occupied Netherlands. He had, he said, been put ashore by a British motor-boat near Nordwijk, even going as far as to point out the precise location on a map. He had arrived in the Netherlands on New Year's Eve and had been contacted by a stranger who had taken him straight to the Nakkens' home in The Hague. Every now and then Lauwers would be forced to 'remind' himself of dates by looking in the diary of his interrogator, and he padded out his tale with harmless but true graphic descriptions of places he had visited and things he had seen. In this way he was able to paint a convincing picture, and his interrogator seemed quite happy. Lauwers went on to explain that the Nakkens knew nothing about his work and that his only contact had been a man he used to meet in a café in Amsterdam. He did not know his contact's name and had recognized him only because he wore a flower in his top buttonhole. It was through this contact that he received his messages for Britain.

Lauwers had kept it short and sweet, and his interrogator finally appeared satisfied. As he stood up to leave, Lauwers suddenly noticed that the German had carelessly left his gun holster lying on the table. Rapidly he calculated the time necessary to get the gun out. It did not seem feasible. The building outside the room was swarming with armed Germans, and he decided to return his thoughts to his interrogation. This was not the right time or place to try to escape.

Whilst Lauwers had been carefully spinning his yarn, Schreieder was facing some difficult and unexpected problems. Initially he had been told that the second agent had been arrested but two hours later he was informed that the interrogators appeared to have the wrong man. Whoever he was, he was not a British agent, because he had never been to Britain in his life and could apparently prove it. Nonetheless, the surveillance teams were certain he was the man they had been trailing for the past week, and they were convinced he had been closely connected with Lauwers' work. In fact, the stranger turned out to be no small catch for the SIPO: Johan van Hattem, who had taken over control of the major network set up by Lodo van Hamel back in 1940, had been a leading Dutch resistance commander. At the time this success was lost on Schreieder. He desperately needed to arrest the second agent before he could warn SOE. To make matters worse, his men had already picked up Van den Bergh, leaving the Abwehr without a source of intelligence. His only chance was to follow up the Arnhem clue, which suggested that the local SIPO were onto the trail of a suspected agent.

The men who could have told Schreieder Taconis' whereabouts were at that moment meeting in secret to discuss what had happened. Mr Nakken had managed to contact Frits Bouma and Wil Van Dijk, neither of whom had been arrested, and had told them of the evening's events. All three agreed that Taconis should be warned immediately, but it was too late to go that night because of the curfew. When Bouma arrived at Taconis' house in Oosterbeek the following morning, he found to his relief that Taconis was still safe and totally unaware of what had happened. On learning what had happened, Taconis refused to go into hiding, claiming that he had some very important meetings coming up for his sabotage group and, despite much pleading from Bouma, he remained adamant. He would only agree to return to The Hague after the meetings on condition that Bouma would find him a safe house.

The SIPO report from Arnhem had been accurate. The Dutch traitor Johnny Den Droog, whom Taconis had thought a useful contact, had slowly managed to discover most of the people connected with the new sabotage group. The net was quickly drawn tight around Taconis, and on Monday 9 March 1942, whilst he was visiting a friend, there was a knock on the door. In came two of Schreieder's V-men, Leo Poos and Martin Slagter, posing as Dutch policemen, and they asked Taconis if he was called Timmer. Taconis denied this, said his papers would prove it and pulled out his gun. As he pulled the trigger, however, the gun jammed and, after recovering from their shock, Poos and Slagter quickly overpowered him and he was taken to a waiting van. This time the Germans were careful to check they had the right man. Once recognized as the British agent by Den Droog, he was taken to The Hague, where his companion had just spent a very uncomfortable weekend.

Lauwers had been fighting a lonely battle. By that Monday afternoon he had been interrogated non-stop since his arrest the previous Friday evening. He had been over his story numerous times and had reached a stage where he was almost ready to believe it himself. His main aim was to lead the Germans away from Taconis and to preserve the organization they had set up. Taconis was the hope he had clung to during these difficult hours, the one person who might save something from the wreckage.

Finally the SIPO decided that enough was enough and escorted Lauwers out of the interrogation room to his cell. Despite his long ordeal he felt quite awake and glanced down the corridor ahead. There to his horror he saw Taconis being led away handcuffed between two guards. Lauwers felt his hopes of the previous two days shatter, and for the first time since his arrest he was overwhelmed with despair.

Taconis had been on his way to his first interrogation, and his interrogators soon discovered he was a very awkward customer. There were no politely told fabrications, no apparent willingness to help, only a very hostile silence and a refusal to answer any questions. The SIPO were not surprised by this reaction. They knew from experience that prisoners often started off in this defiant manner only to weaken later. Nor were they in any hurry. The interrogator calmly sat back in his chair and offered

Taconis a bottle of beer. This turned out to be a big
mistake for the German. As quick as a flash Taconis
grabbed the bottle, broke its head on the table and took a
swipe at his interrogator's throat. Considerably shaken,
the German only just had time to let himself fall over
backwards, narrowly avoiding the jagged edge. Then
Taconis was smothered in guards and beaten up. They
demanded his name but he refused to talk. After many
hours he was confronted with it in the national census, and
only then did he speak for the first time, proudly
confirming that he was indeed Lieutenant Thijs Taconis.
His German interrogators soon nicknamed him 'The
Tiger'.

In his cell Lauwers was unable to sleep until he had
sorted out the implications of Taconis' arrest. It seemed
probable that the Germans had also captured Bouma and
Van den Bergh and would torture them. If so and if they
were to break, their confessions would contradict all that
he had just about got the SIPO to believe. Then, of course,
Taconis himself might be forced to contradict Lauwers'
statements – but here at least he could see some
possibilities. The Germans did not know he had seen
Taconis, so that if he told them voluntarily that he had a
companion he might be able to improve his credibility.
This might make all the difference to his future chances of
escape. Comforted by this thought, Lauwers fell into a
deep sleep, his first for almost four days.

Giskes spent the weekend preparing his approach to
Lauwers. If his intended double-cross were to succeed, he
would have to get Lauwers on the air within the next few
days. However, when he first asked Lauwers to transmit
for the Abwehr, he was told politely but firmly that this
was out of the question and that his prisoner had no wish
to be a traitor. Giskes impressed upon Lauwers the fact
that it would be the only way in which he could save his
life, and perhaps the lives of others, but Lauwers
remained adamant in his refusal. Giskes almost pleaded,
saying that he wanted him to transmit only those messages
which had been found on him at his arrest and that
nobody could regard him as a traitor for doing that.
Finally Giskes concluded that Lauwers had no wish to

survive without Taconis, and he played his trump card, offering both agents their lives if Lauwers would just transmit the three messages.

Lauwers was prepared for Giskes' approach and, with a salesman's nose for bargains, he knew he could gain a lot better than the present offer. He also knew from his training that he would be allowed to transmit for the Germans as long as he left his security check out of any messages he sent, and so he continued to frustrate Giskes by his refusal. Seeing he was getting nowhere, Giskes pulled up a chair and tried a different tack. He started to talk to Lauwers, telling him in confidence that he himself was anti-Nazi and in particular anti-SIPO/SD. He greatly admired Lauwers' courage but unfortunately there was a war on, and this meant that if Lauwers ever came in front of a military tribunal he would be shot. This was, of course, not Giskes' wish. He knew that Lauwers was a British officer carrying out his orders and that in a similar position he would do the same. According to Giskes, the Abwehr might be prepared to overlook the evidence of Lauwers' involvement with sabotage groups. Giskes then went on to question the ethics of conducting a sabotage campaign in a small country with such a dense population of people as the Netherlands. It would achieve very little and would only provoke massive reprisals by the SS against innocent civilians.

Although he did not show it, Lauwers recognized that Giskes had a good point. The Netherlands *were* small and densely populated. Any sabotage action would put innocent bystanders at risk. In short, the country was not suited to an SOE-style sabotage campaign.

However, Giskes soon threw away his temporary advantage by changing his angle of attack, and Lauwers began to recognize the rhetoric for which his training had prepared him. The people who had sent him to the Netherlands, Giskes argued, deserved no respect. They themselves ran no risks, yet expected others to die rather than talk, even under torture. They played war-games from behind their desks, dropping fanatics into the Netherlands armed with weapons and explosives, regardless of possible reprisals against innocent bystanders.

Giskes told Lauwers that he saw his task as preventing this from happening and that, in order to do this, he needed his help. This was not, Giskes readily conceded, of decisive importance, because sooner or later SOE were bound to find out what was happening, and then the whole process of tracking an agent down would have to begin again. Clearly the war was madness, and after it was over both sides would need each other, which meant they would have to be capable of looking each other in the face. If Lauwers would help in this matter, he would respect him as a fellow officer.

Lauwers' training had left him unmoved by this torrent, and he recognized that Giskes was under time pressure. His next transmission time was coming up and, if he missed it, the chances of a double-cross succeeding would be minimal. Lauwers knew that with this ace up his sleeve he could obtain quite a few concessions from Giskes, and he began to reel off his demands: that Mr and Mrs Nakken should be left alone by the SIPO, that Mrs Teller should also be left alone to have her child in liberty, and that Wout Teller should not be tried by a military tribunal but treated as a prisoner of war; in addition both Taconis and himself should be treated as ordinary prisoners. Giskes consulted his superiors, and they agreed to the demands. In the years that followed, Giskes would keep to this bargain.

In fact, the Nakkens were left alone for the rest of the war, as was Mrs Teller, who gave birth to a son in June 1942. Wout Teller was not prosecuted for his part in the affair but stood trial later in connection with other resistance activities, along with Van Dijk, Bouma and Van den Bergh. All were sent to concentration camps under the infamous 'Nacht und Nebel Haftlinge'*, and none returned after the war. Johan van Hattem, who had been mistakenly arrested in place of Taconis, was executed, along with fifteen colleagues, in July 1943.

---

* 'Night and cloud treatment'. This meant that there was no official acknowledgement of the prisoner's existence. He or she received and sent no mail, and did not have their death recorded. Most of these prisoners simply disappeared.

Lauwers knew that he would be asked to continue transmitting after the first three messages. This did not worry him unduly. He knew that by omitting his security check he would instantly warn Dutch Section of his capture and that the messages he was to send could do little harm, as they were genuine anyway. In return for this he had managed to save his own life and that of Taconis, and had gained time in which to plan an escape.

7 A Fox in Sheep's Clothing

Lauwers had been in German hands for some five days when he was faced with a desperate problem. In a casual conversation Giskes had asked him for his security check. The effect was completely devastating. To his horror Lauwers realized the Germans were fully aware of his security link with SOE. It was only instinct which led him to play for time by pretending not to know what Giskes was talking about. Giskes left Lauwers in no doubt that he was risking his life.

Back in his cell he did some quick and urgent thinking. At first sight, things seemed utterly hopeless. The Germans had his three encoded messages containing his real security check, making it impossible for him to claim anything that was not already contained in these. With his code also in their hands, it was clear they would be able to analyse the mistakes made in these messages, and it seemed unlikely that his security check would survive such scrutiny. Then there was an even greater problem: that the Germans had probably monitored his transmissions from the start and, with his code, would be able to work out all his previous messages. If this was done, his security check would stand out like a beacon.

Somehow, despite his anguish, Lauwers managed to focus on the crucial points. Ignoring the last possibility – which was completely out of his hands – he started thinking about his last three messages. Recalling the difficulty he had had placing the security check that last afternoon, he remembered putting it in the middle of the word 'stop', which he had conveniently changed to 'stip'. Coincidentally he had done this in two of the three messages, and he decided to try to convince Giskes that his security check involved changing the letter 'o' into an 'i' or 'a'. As for the third message, he would say that it was not necessary for every message to contain a check. The whole thing, Lauwers knew, was extremely tenuous but it was the best he could do. He was also well aware that, if the Germans were not convinced, he would be facing a firing squad after all. Again he fell into an uneasy sleep.

The following day, 12 March 1942, Lauwers took his place behind his transmitter for the first time since his arrest. He was surrounded by a large group of Germans who had taken the wise precaution of rigging up a switch so that the electricity supply could be cut off should he do anything suspicious. Lauwers transmitted the three messages without a hint of emotion, despite the fact that he could literally feel the Germans breathing down his neck. Giskes, for his part, sighed with relief as the event passed without incident and as SOE responded to Lauwers' signal. The Abwehr had crossed another barrier.

Lauwers' personal barrier was also soon crossed. As expected, he was asked about his security check and shown a file containing copies of his previous broadcasts which Heinrich and his section had monitored. To his delight, he noticed that the messages were all incomplete, with large chunks missing out of each sentence, making a thorough analysis of his check impossible. Now all that remained was to convince Giskes of his ploy. Fortunately for Lauwers, at that moment Giskes was more interested in persuading him to continue transmitting for the Abwehr and was so delighted when Lauwers consented that he quite readily accepted his claim that his security check consisted of changing the word 'stop' into 'stip' or 'stap'. In fact, he contented himself with a cursory check that this had indeed been in the three messages captured on Lauwers. With this, Lauwers felt an enormous weight fall from his shoulders. It was one of the few mistakes Giskes would make.

Lauwers had good reason to wish to continue transmitting. It was necessary to prevent the Germans' sending a message containing his true security check by accident. In order to build up trust, he volunteered to do the coding of the new messages, claiming that he was the most experienced at it and likely to do the best job. Giskes, pleased at such co-operation, let him go ahead, though he made sure that what Lauwers had done was thoroughly checked.

After finishing the coding, Lauwers took his place behind the transmitter. Again the room was crowded with Germans and, to their excitement, Dutch Section answered the message with one of their own. As the Germans busied themselves decoding this message, Lauwers reflected that this was probably the last he would ever receive. SOE would notice his security check was missing and break off all contact. When this happened, he was under no illusions as to what might happen to him.

The message from SOE ran: '*NEW AGENT, CODE-NAME ABOR, WILL BE SENT TO HELP WITH WORK*'. Giskes was delighted and Lauwers used the moment to obtain another important concession from him: that any agents captured in future by the double-cross should not be executed but treated as ordinary prisoners. Not that he expected for one moment that 'Abor' would be dropped, but it was better to be on the safe side, and it might be useful one day.

At his next transmission time Lauwers was surprised to receive another message from Dutch Section, but all soon became clear to him. The message stated that 'Abor' had become ill and could not come, although the second weapon drop would go ahead as planned. To Lauwers it felt as if he was being guarded by an invisible friend and that, by keeping in radio contact with him, Dutch Section were trying to give him more time in which to escape. Back in his cell he was able to relax for the first time since his capture. He had successfully omitted his security check and, in so doing, had done his duty.

Unlikely bedfellows as they were, the Abwehr and SIPO prepared jointly, in their new-found spirit of co-operation, for their first arms catch of the double-cross, now officially code-named 'Operation North Pole'. For Giskes it would provide further evidence of Lauwers' trustworthiness, for he was still not entirely convinced, feeling there was something odd about Lauwers' willingness to co-operate. He dared not let one of his own operators take over the work because he was still assuming that the British had taped Lauwers' style of transmitting, and with the possibility of another agent falling into his hands he was unwilling to take any chances. In future, he decided, he would not allow Lauwers to see the decoded messages from London.

Meanwhile Lauwers had been facing his furious interrogator, who had discovered that the story he had told was full of lies and fabrications. He was threatened with torture, a threat which had little effect as Lauwers knew that as a special prisoner he was needed for transmitting. From what his interrogator told him, he was able to deduce that both Van den Bergh and Bouma had been arrested. Both men had been badly tortured and had said enough to contradict Lauwers' claim to have operated alone. Calmly Lauwers invented a new 'story', incorporating Van den Bergh, Bouma and Taconis. He had, he continually claimed, observed the golden rule of security and had not learnt anything that was of no concern to him. The German started to veer the conversation away towards British parachute techniques, and Lauwers realized he had got away with it again.

Though it was not apparent, there was method in this new line of questioning. Unbeknown to Lauwers, Dutch Section had already informed Giskes that the 'Abor' drop would go ahead as planned on the night of 27/28 March 1942. The night before, the drop was confirmed by a message on Radio Orange, and Giskes and Schreieder set about organizing the 'welcoming party'. Everyone involved met early in the evening, in The Hague, including the Germans' most successful V-men, Ridderhof, Poos and Slagter, who were to provide the early reception committee. The plan was that they would meet 'Abor', posing as his resistance contacts, and take him to a car nearby where they would attempt to elicit as much information as possible before he became suspicious and had to be arrested. This would take place only when Ridderhof gave the signal to the waiting SIPO, hidden outside. It had been agreed that Schreieder would be in charge of the arrest and have first interrogation rights, whilst Giskes was to be in charge of the DZ.

It took the party three hours to reach the drop zone near Steenwijk, and on arrival Giskes met the local Wehrmacht commander, who was to provide anti-aircraft cover. A detachment of 88mm guns was placed around the field, in case the RAF came and blasted the DZ. (This precaution was necessary as in France the British had once bombed a drop zone, killing twenty Germans.) Strict instructions were given to the reception committee: they were not to smoke, talk or make any noise; it seemed probable that, if 'Abor' heard any German being spoken he would not be captured alive.

Just after one o'clock that morning, the men on the drop zone heard the approach of an aircraft. Giskes sprinted around the field, making last-minute checks, and was furious to discover that Ridderhof had been secretly drinking and was now almost incapable of walking unaided. It was, however, too late to do anything about it, and after the correct torch signals had been exchanged several parachutes were observed drifting earthwards. Ridderhof staggered towards the one descending man, who was presumably 'Abor', and brought him back to the car. Once inside, the newly arrived agent spent almost an hour in unsuspecting conversation with the three V-men. Outside the Germans were jubilant, and Schreieder walked over to Giskes to shake hands.

Finally Ridderhof gave the signal, and 'Abor' was asked to get out of the car on the pretext of burying his parachute and flying-jacket. When he had half taken off the jacket, he felt a gun being jammed into his back and his arms being pinned from behind. At the same moment the Germans emerged from nearby bushes, and within seconds 'Abor' had been handcuffed. When, after a few seconds, it sank in that he had fallen into enemy hands, 'Abor' broke down and begged to be shot there and then. However, after all the trouble they had gone through to catch him alive, the SIPO had no intention of granting this request. 'Abor' was marched away.

Within an hour the DZ was deserted. Schreieder took his prisoner to Scheveningen, whilst Giskes and his section stayed on in Steenwijk to debrief Ridderhof. But the Abwehr were to learn very little that night. Ridderhof was so drunk that he could remember hardly anything of what had been said in the car, and Giskes could only hope that Poos and Slagter would be able to produce a clear report. In the meantime he was forced to wait for a report on 'Abor's' interrogation.

Back in The Hague, the SIPO wasted no time in pressurizing their prisoner, and 'Abor's' resistance was quickly broken. Schreieder played all his trumps, acquired from previous interrogations, asking after the health of Major Blizzard and 'Lieutenant Dawson' and telling 'Abor' that he had been betrayed in London. There was no point in remaining silent, he said, as the Germans knew everything anyway, and by talking he could save his own life, as Lauwers and Taconis had already done. Schreieder's onslaught was successful, and a shattered 'Abor' began to tell him everything he knew. It was to be a turning-point for the Germans. For the first time, the SIPO had completely broken an agent, and they were soon learning about SOE's training methods, the names of instructors, the location of buildings and the names of the commanding officers. With this information, Schreieder was able to build up a very comprehensive picture of Dutch Section. No longer would the Germans be working in the dark. The effects on future interrogations would be marked. It was a totally broken 'Abor' who was led away to the cells at the 'Orange Hotel'.

As a reward for what the Abwehr considered was his complete co-operation, Lauwers was taken to see some of the contents of the weapons containers dropped along with 'Abor'. He was led into a shed where he saw a few weapons, an insignificant amount of explosives and several piles of propaganda leaflets printed in French. On seeing this small haul, he became even more convinced that the British were aware of what was going on.

The 'Orange Hotel' was one of the Netherlands' most infamous prisons during the Second World War, housing hundreds of captured resistance workers, and by the spring of 1942 it was filling up rapidly. In his cell, Lauwers had almost become accustomed to the many noises of the prison, the heavy boots walking down corridors, the rattling of keys, the screams and shouts of other prisoners, but one evening when he was sitting alone in his cell he heard the sound of singing. Suddenly he recognized the song, and the voice as being that of a colleague who had been on the same training course as he. Realizing that the man must only just have been sent to the Netherlands, he was struck by the thought that his colleague might be 'Abor'. Had Dutch Section still sent their agent despite his warnings?

That night Lauwers attempted to analyse what was happening. He knew he had left out his security check, thus warning SOE. He was furthermore still convinced – despite obvious evidence to the contrary – that the British were the best in the world at secret intelligence work and would not make elementary mistakes. The only conclusion he could come up with was that SOE were playing a triple-cross with the Germans, which necessitated the sacrifice of an agent. Nevertheless, just to make sure the British knew he had been captured, he decided to place another hidden warning in his next message.

With 'Abor's' capture and the information he had provided, the Germans began to treat Lauwers with more respect. Giskes was by now convinced that his new radio operator was genuinely co-operating and he allowed him showers and new clothes and even provided him with a radio. This in turn gave Lauwers the strength to set about his new warning to SOE. He needed a word which he could insert into a message and which would leave no doubt as to what had happened. He thought of 'arrested', but realized it was too long, and then came up with 'caught'. This could be conveniently halved into 'cau' and 'ght' and, with a bit of luck, he might be able to slip them into a message without the Germans noticing.

The next message he was asked to transmit involved letting Dutch Section know that both 'Abor' and the weapons canisters had arrived safely and that 'Abor' was ready to help Taconis with his work. As usual Lauwers did the coding himself, and he mentally noted the best places to insert his warning. When he finally got down to transmitting, he was well prepared. He managed to slip 'ght' in without any bother and went on to finish the message before enquiring whether there was anything else the Germans wanted sending. On receiving a negative reply he announced he was signing off. Normally this involved the letters 'qru' but, taking advantage of the Germans' relaxation, he quickly substituted the last part of his warning, 'cau', and then leaned back in his chair.

He was half expecting to feel a blow to the back of his head but nothing happened and to his relief he realized that he had got away with it. The Germans meanwhile were fascinated by the cryptic message which Dutch Section had sent them concerning 'A fox masquerading in sheep's clothing'. To Giskes it meant nothing, but Lauwers recognized it as confirmation of the pre-arranged message with Homburg about the liquidation of the traitor J. Vos. He was soon asked about it but, having no intention of helping Giskes, claimed as seriously as he could that it meant the double-cross was over. He was being accused of treachery by the British – as a fox in sheep's clothing – and that they would probably try to liquidate him. He succeeded in looking so upset that Giskes momentarily forgot his worries and began to laugh. He told Lauwers not to worry. The Abwehr would make sure that no one would be allowed to shoot him.

Having got round another awkward problem, Lauwers was in a confident mood. He knew his warnings would be received by Dutch Section. Not only had he omitted his security check again but the letters 'ght' and 'cau' would be sticking out of the message like a sore thumb, and it would be a simple exercise to turn these into the word 'caught'. Now, surely, he felt, SOE would stop using his radio link to send agents and supplies over, and the flow of messages would cease.

Giskes was feeling considerably less confident, and with good reason. If he could not discover the meaning of this latest message, his whole double-cross could be in danger, and just at a time when things seemed to be going so nicely.

8 Dutch Section's Second Network

Shortly after the capture of 'Abor', the Germans discovered the dead body of another British agent. The man had died of severe headwounds apparently sustained after a heavy landing. Reports stated that a single aircraft had flown over the area during the night of 29/30 March 1942, two nights after 'Abor' had been dropped, and a search of the area revealed two hastily buried parachutes alongside a broken radio transmitter. It was clear that at least one British agent was on the loose, and Giskes knew how vital it was that he should be tracked down before he tried to contact Lauwers, Taconis or 'Abor'. The Germans seemed to have only one advantage in their search: without his radio transmitter the agent would be unable to contact SOE.

In fact, Dutch Section had been very busy that spring. During the night of 29/30 March 1942 they had dropped two more pairs of agents, 'blind', in different parts of the Netherlands. The first two were the twenty-four-year-old Jan Molenaar and a twenty-eight-year-old priest in training, Leo Andringa. Both men had decided to jump in spite of the fact that the wind was stronger than expected; no doubt the thought of another cancellation was too much to contemplate. For Molenaar it was to be a fatal decision. On landing he was dragged into a concrete post which crushed his skull, knocking him immediately unconscious. He was found by Andringa, who carried him out of the cold wind and into shelter but could do little more for his companion than cradle him until daybreak. Finally Andringa, realizing that Molenaar was going to die anyway, administered him his suicide capsule. Having buried the parachutes along with the smashed radio transmitter, Andringa dragged Molenaar's body into some bushes and set off for Amsterdam.

The other pair of SOE agents dropped that night met with better fortune. Both landed safely, despite the strong winds, and even their radio transmitter survived intact. For twenty-three-year-old Han Jordaan this was his first-ever experience of the German-occupied Netherlands. He had been studying in Britain at the outbreak of war and had volunteered for the Dutch Army in exile. His companion was twenty-seven-year-old Gosse Ras, a former textile merchant, who had left the Netherlands the day before the nation capitulated and a week before he was to have been married. The two agents travelled to the home of Jordaan's brother, where they were under orders to spend a week acclimatizing to life under the Germans, a sensible precaution given the circumstances.

A week later, during the night of 5/6 April 1942, Dutch Section sent a third pair of agents, dropped 'blind' into the Veluwe, (a rich agricultural province of the Netherlands just north of the great rivers). After a safe landing the agents made their way to their contact address in Hengelo. They were twenty-three-year-old Henk Sebes and twenty-nine-year-old Barend Klooss. Sebes had fought with the Dutch Army in May 1940 and had escaped to Britain via Dunkirk. Klooss had been working in Saigon (in what is now Vietnam) before the war and, like Lauwers, had decided to return to Europe to fight. He had been out of the Netherlands for over six years and would urgently need his acclimatization. Neither man carried a radio transmitter.

Three days later Dutch Section sent in yet another agent, this time by sea. A British MTB sneaked in between the German coastal defences and put Jan De Haas ashore near Castricum – the same De Haas who had escaped to Britain a few months previously with Ab Homburg in the trawler *Beatrice*. Once in Britain he had put a very ambitious plan to SOE. According to him it would be possible to lay an underwater telephone line between Britain and the Netherlands, thus providing a round-the-clock link. Dutch Section had not been interested and instead had sent De Haas back across the North Sea, armed with the latest in radio transmitting technology, the 'S' phone. This operated on a shortwave frequency and could be used to talk to aircraft and motor boats operating off the Dutch coast. It was almost impossible to track down unless the tracker could get within a couple of miles. At last SOE had come up with a device which fulfilled its promises.

De Haas's mission was to relieve Lauwers and Taconis, who had been 'operating' for six months and were presumed to be in need of rest. He did not envisage any problem in finding them, as he had already met them when planning for his escape in February with Homburg. Optimistically he set off for the tobacconist in Haarlem.

A few weeks later the five surviving agents who had been parachuted into the Netherlands met up in a café in Utrecht for a pre-arranged rendezvous where they were to discuss their progress. Andringa had very little to report. After the death of his companion Molenaar, he had been left without contacts – a situation which Dutch Section ought to have foreseen. Having tried several addresses in vain, he had spent the last few weeks living like a tramp in the open. Badly suited to SOE work, he should never have been sent, having agreed to go only because of the constant persuasion of some of the officers at Dutch Section. Now he was forced to ask his colleagues for help.

Ras and Jordaan had experienced no such troubles. At the home of Jordaan's brother they had spent a week getting used to their new way of life. During this time they had decided that it would be too risky to remain together in the same house, so Jordaan contacted a friend, Daan Burg, who was only too willing to help out. Though clearly aware of the risks involved, he offered Jordaan the free use of his flat.

Klooss and Sebes had had an eventful time. Welcomed at their safe address in Hengelo, they discovered what all early SOE men discovered sooner or later: that their personal papers were badly forged and unlikely to get them through any checks. In an attempt to alleviate the problem, their contacts gave them some genuine plastic covers, to help conceal the poor quality of the documents.

After a period of acclimatization, the two set off to meet up with contacts in Western Holland. Klooss went to his former boss in Rotterdam, whilst Sebes met up with his brother-in-law in Dordrecht. His sister was amazed to see him. It was a social comment on the times that she had only just received a long-overdue Red Cross postcard from him in Britain stating that he had arrived there safely and was engaged to a British girl. This, he was able to tell her, was old news. He had long since been married, and his wife was now expecting their first child.

Klooss and Sebes arranged to meet every day at a restaurant in Rotterdam to discuss their work and make plans. One day Klooss did not turn up. He had been stopped by a papers check and been arrested by Dutch police who were not taken in by his forgeries. On his way to the police station, however, he used his SOE training to knock out the policeman accompanying him and managed to escape into the crowd.

The following day Klooss turned up as usual at the restaurant and told a worried Sebes what had happened. It was clear to both of them that they would have to try to obtain genuine papers as soon as possible. As they left, their worst fears became reality. After walking only a few hundred metres, they were challenged by two Germans. After a count of three, they took the Germans by surprise and succeeded in knocking them out. As onlookers stood back in amazement, Klooss pulled out his gun and ran over to a lorry which happened to be driving slowly up the street. Forcing the vehicle to stop, both agents climbed into the cab and told the driver to step on it. The lorry quickly took them to South Rotterdam, and to their relief they noted that they had not been followed. After thanking the lorry-driver for his help, they made their way to the home of Sebes' aunt, where they managed to change their clothes.

Both men realized it was time to get out of the Rotterdam area. Their descriptions would soon be circulating, and they desperately needed to change their papers. Fortunately they had the address of a member of the Pijnacker local council who, it was thought, might be able to obtain new identity papers for them. As Sebes returned to Hengelo, Klooss decided to follow up this lead.

Koert Bolle had helped four Dutchmen escape to Britain in the autumn of 1941, and this information had ended up at Dutch Section. Unbeknown to them, MI6 had also learned of Bolle's aid and had already sent an agent, Jan Emmer, to the same address, for the same reason. Bolle was naturally very suspicious when a second agent arrived on his doorstep unannounced, claiming to have come from Britain and it took him some time to accept Klooss as genuine. Ironically he was finally convinced by the forged papers he was shown. Dutch Section's information for once had been accurate, and within a few days Bolle had managed to supply Klooss with genuine papers.

At their meeting in the Utrecht café, the five agents determined their priorities. With Molenaar dead, it was decided that Jordaan would have to act as radio operator for the whole group. He gave the others a telephone number where he could be contacted. The question of what Andringa should do would be left up to SOE. In the meantime he was sent to Koert Bolle in Pijnacker to see if he could acquire new papers for the rest of the group. Before leaving, they decided to meet again in a fortnight's time, on 1 May 1942, at the same café.

Dutch Section instructed Andringa to help De Haas in The Hague. His search for Lauwers and Taconis had run into problems, and it seemed to De Haas as if both men had disappeared off the face of the earth. Through Andringa and Jordaan, De Haas – who had not yet managed to contact SOE – was able to ask SOE for additional information about Lauwers' whereabouts. This request was transmitted on 26 April 1942, along with the news that Jordaan had found a new operator who would take over the transmissions, freeing him for more important work. These transmissions were monitored by the Germans, and Heinrich was able to inform Giskes that the new transmitter was operating somewhere in the Utrecht area.

On 27 April 1942 Dutch Section sent 'Lauwers' the following message: '*GO TO THE TOBACCONISTS IN*

HAARLEM – ASK FOR ARROW – CLAIM TO HAVE BEEN SENT BY BOW.' Giskes took the message to Lauwers, who was genuinely perplexed by its meaning, although it struck him as strange that Dutch Section should be breaking its own security guidelines by sending him to make contact with an agent from a different network.

The message left Giskes feeling gloomy. Problems were piling up. The messages that Dutch Section had been sending over Lauwers' link were trivial and almost meaningless. Nor did they appear much interested in the 'chickenfeed' he was sending them in return. Now, with a new group operating behind his back, the danger was that they would try to contact Lauwers and Taconis. If this happened, the prospects for his double-cross were poor.

In desperation Giskes turned to Schreieder for help. The SIPO quickly threw themselves into the task of tracking down the man code-named 'Arrow'. Before long they succeeded in tricking Taconis, of all people, into mentioning the name Martens. A quick search of the telephone directory revealed that a certain Jan Martens ran a tobacconist's at 26 Oostvest Street, Haarlem. This was more than enough for Schreieder, who sent his V-man Leo Poos round to the shop to ask after 'Arrow'. Poos introduced himself to Martens as 'Dick', an agent newly arrived from Britain who had a message for 'Arrow' sent from 'Bow'. Martens, suspecting nothing, took 'Dick' into his living-room and introduced him to Andringa, saying he would be able to put him in touch with 'Arrow'. 'Dick' quickly ingratiated himself with Andringa and was told to return the next day, when he would be taken to see 'Arrow'.

The following morning Poos returned to the tobacconist's. He had been well briefed by Schreieder. Together with Andringa, he was to meet up with 'Arrow' and then take him to the Paul Kruger Square in The Hague, which was where Schreieder had decided to strike, arresting all three men, so as to maintain Poos's credibility. In case of any unforeseen mishaps, the SIPO would trail them, but these seemed unlikely as neither Andringa nor Martens suspected anything.

In the event, the plan worked perfectly. Andringa took 'Dick' to meet 'Arrow' at his safe house, and 'Arrow' turned out to be none other than De Haas. The three men set out to walk to the Paul Kruger Square nearby, where they were swiftly overpowered and taken to the 'Orange Hotel'. Schreieder telephoned Giskes to inform him of what had happened and urged him to send Dutch Section the following message: '*CONTACT MADE WITH ARROW AND AKKI*' (Andringa's cover-name). The spoils of capture were quickly divided up. The Abwehr got De Haas and were particularly interested in the new 'S' phone which had been found among his possessions, whilst the SIPO set about interrogating Andringa.

For the first time, the information supplied by 'Abor' was put to good use. Andringa was told that he had been betrayed in London and that silence was pointless and would only lead to execution. To support this point, Schreieder presented his prisoner with a detailed picture of SOE's activities, covering every detail of his training down to the personal characteristics of the men who had sent him. The effect of this information was dramatic, a detail not lost on Schreieder. Genuinely convinced that there was nothing left to hide, Andringa let slip details of the forthcoming meeting in the Utrecht café.

On 1 May 1942 Andringa was forced into the café at gunpoint by Leo Poos. He had been told that, if he did not co-operate, the SIPO would be forced to storm the café and that a blood-bath would probably ensue, leading to a lot of innocent deaths. Poos was under instructions to look out for anyone who more than glanced at them. In an attempt to warn his comrades, Andringa decided to stare straight ahead as he walked to the bar. As he did so, Jordaan glanced at him in surprise. He was sitting with Sebes and Daan Burg at one table, whilst the others, Ras, Klooss and their friend Evers, were opposite on the other side of the café. Jordaan instantly noted the stranger following Andringa, keeping his hand deep in his coat pocket, and suddenly realized something was wrong. At the same time Klooss beckoned Andringa over from the other table, and Poos took him over to sit down. Making use of this distraction, Jordaan, Sebes and Daan Burg slipped out of the café unnoticed. Outside they saw several German vans, and it became obvious that their comrades were caught in a trap. Jordaan set off to warn SOE immediately.

Shortly after Andringa had sat down with his three comrades, the Germans stormed in and overpowered them all. Schreieder, waiting outside, noticed that only three men had been arrested. At least one agent was still missing. The captives were taken to the Orange Hotel, where it quickly became clear that they had missed at least two agents, the third man arrested being merely a friend of the other two. That evening Jordaan transmitted to SOE the news that Andringa, Klooss and Ras were missing and had probably been arrested, adding that he would give more details when he got them. Dutch Section regretted what had happened and told him to take over Ras's assignment. This would enable Jordaan's new radio operator to take over the transmitting.

Schreieder knew that he would have to move fast before the radio operator could warn SOE of what had happened. He had one important lead, a telephone number found in the pocket of one of the captured men. After torture the man revealed that it was the radio operator's contact number. Further enquiries from Giskes showed that the radio operator had transmitted several messages the previous evening and that the area to which Heinrich had narrowed him down corresponded with that of the phone number. Schreieder decided to try to lure Jordaan into the open. To do this he proposed to use his most successful V-man, the infamous Anton Van der Waals.

Van der Waals was born in Rotterdam in October 1912. In his youth he had trained as a house painter but soon got bored with the job. He discovered he was technically minded and during the 1930s had done a lot of scientific research, making some important innovations in the field of motors. In 1934 he had joined the NSB, the Dutch Nazi Party, and had married for the first time. During the following years he discovered a liking for women, and by the summer of 1940 he was well into his third marriage. His dealings with women helped him develop 'a way with words', and he was able to deceive people very easily. After the Dutch surrender in 1940 he soon realized he could use these skills to great profit by working for the Germans as a V-man. In April 1941 he had approached Schreieder with information concerning a man wanted for shooting a German soldier, and from that moment on he had rapidly established himself as the single most dangerous threat to the Dutch resistance movement.

Van der Waals started off by telephoning Jordaan, claiming to be 'Ton', a friend of Ras. He told Jordaan that Ras had managed to escape from the café and was now in hiding, from where he had sent his colleague (Van der Waals) to make contact with Jordaan again. Jordaan, relieved at hearing this, agreed to meet Van der Waals by the banks of a lake in Laren. On reflection, however, Jordaan became suspicious. Had Ras really escaped from the SIPO, whose vans he had seen parked outside the café? It seemed more likely that the Germans had tortured Ras into handing over his telephone number. Deciding to play safe, he sent his friend Daan Burg to make a thorough reconnaissance of the area before the meeting. Burg reported back that he had seen nothing suspicious and, despite his worries, Jordaan decided to go ahead with the meeting.

Whilst Burg covered him with a gun, Jordaan approached the stranger standing at the lakeside. The two men talked for some ten minutes before joining Burg. Jordaan introduced him to 'Ton', a fellow agent sent from Britain. The three of them went to a café for a drink and a talk. 'Ton' gave more 'details' of Ras's escape but refused to disclose his present hiding-place. He suggested that Jordaan go into hiding for a while, until the storm blew over. They discussed their training in Britain, and slowly but surely Jordaan's suspicions dissolved. Using information obtained from 'Abor', confirmed by Andringa, Van der Waals was able to give a detailed account of places, names and courses. It was enough to convince Jordaan that he was indeed talking to an SOE's colleague. In fact, given his present difficulties, 'Ton' appeared nothing short of a godsend.

The first priority, according to 'Ton', was to find

Jordaan a new safe house. This would be a simple matter as he had many friends and contacts in Rotterdam, and the two men decided to meet up the following day at Delft railway station. At the pre-arranged time the unsuspecting Jordaan found 'Ton' waiting for him, and together they walked to the city's Hofplein Square. He had good news for Jordaan, having found him some safe accommodation, and suggested that, if everything was satisfactory, he should go and collect his radio transmitter or, better still, let one of 'Ton's' contacts bring it over. Jordaan agreed to this and told his new 'colleague' where the transmitter was hidden. And there was one other matter. 'Ton' had 'forgotten' Sebes' telephone number in Hengelo and thought it important that he too should be warned. By now, completely trusting his 'colleague', Jordaan gave him the number. On receiving this, 'Ton' excused himself, saying he would telephone Sebes there and then, and he suggested to Jordaan that, if he walked on a bit, he would soon catch him up again. In fact, Jordaan's walk continued for only another four or five paces before it was cut short by the SIPO.

As soon as his latest victim had been taken away Van der Waals made his way to the address where the radio transmitter was hidden. Introducing himself to the landlady as a friend of Jordaan's, he told her he had come to collect all the latter's belongings, including his radio set and the papers which went with it. The landlady was very helpful and unsuspectingly set about the task of collecting the things together.

The Germans had good reason to be delighted with the material that had fallen into their hands. Giskes was able to show Jordaan the piles of his old messages and the code calculations and claimed that with these it would be only a matter of time before his code was broken. The same methods of persuasion were used as had been on Lauwers. There was no point in his trying to conceal something the Germans would soon find out anyway, and by handing over his code he would save himself from a firing squad. There was also the precedent of Lauwers, who, according to Giskes, was co-operating nicely. Understandably, remembering what SOE had told him, Jordaan soon handed over his code to Giskes. However, he succeeded in persuading the Germans that he did not have a security check.

Giskes was even more pleased to discover, from Jordaan's previous messages which the Abwehr had managed to decode, that another radio operator was due to take over the work shortly. This meant that he could avoid the nervous tension and risk of having to let Jordaan transmit for him, by using one of his own men, posing as the new operator.

Meanwhile Van der Waals was turning his attention to some more unfinished business. He travelled to Hengelo, where he introduced himself to Sebes, again posing as a fellow SOE agent. Having quickly won his confidence, he persuaded Sebes that his present address was too unsafe (the Germans were unwilling to arrest him at his present house for fear of the news leaking out and reaching Britain) and that he should move to a new safe house in Rotterdam. Sebes, suspecting nothing, made the journey, having told friends in Hengelo that he would be operating in the west for some time. With no one likely to miss him, the SIPO moved in and picked him up as he arrived at his 'new home'. With Sebes' arrest SOE's second network had been completely wiped out, not least because of Dutch Section's own ineptness. Worse was to follow.

Having sorted out the intricacies of Jordaan's position, Giskes sent a message to SOE, using his own operator, explaining that he was taking over the work from Jordaan. The message did not contain a security check – the first time the Jordaan link had omitted the check. All this was unknown to the Germans as they decoded the reply received from Dutch Section. The message ran: '*FOR TRUMPET [Jordaan's code-name]. INSTRUCT NEW OPERATOR IN THE USE OF SECURITY CHECK.*'

Realizing he had been very lucky Giskes quickly confronted Jordaan with the message. The news had a shattering effect on the young Dutchman. Before long he was forced to hand over his real security check.

From that moment on, the Germans were aware that every captured operator would possess a check of some sort. Crass stupidity of this nature made SOE's Dutch

Section a real threat to the growing numbers of resistance workers in the Netherlands. People's lives were being needlessly thrown away. It was in sad contrast to the professionalism being shown by their opposite numbers across the North Sea.

9 MI6 Threaten 'North Pole'

The story of twenty-one-year-old Aart Alblas demonstrates clearly what could have been achieved in the
Netherlands during the early part of the war, if an agent
was lucky enough to remain at large.

It was Alblas' transmitter, operating under the call sign
TBO, onto which Giskes had set his surveillance team at
the same time as the Zomer affair. By the summer of 1942,
however, Alblas was still at large, despite the furious
attentions of both the Abwehr and SIPO, and he had
begun to present a serious threat to 'Operation North
Pole' itself.

Alblas' strength was his character. A strongly developed
sense of honour and loyalty, a serious nature and an
innate sense of duty – all this made him a good agent. He
loved the sea and had trained as a merchant seaman
before the war and had later transferred to the Dutch
Navy. Involved with resistance work from the very
beginning, he had succeeded in escaping across the North
Sea in April 1941. In Britain, when one of his fellow
escapers had fallen under a cloud of suspicion Alblas was
asked if he would spy on the man: it was typical of Alblas
that he refused even to entertain the suggestion. He
volunteered for duty at sea but MI6 got to him first and
persuaded him that he would best aid the war effort by
returning to the Netherlands with a radio transmitter.
Reluctantly he had agreed, giving up his intention of
sailing on convoy duty. After a short but intensive training
course he was parachuted back into the Netherlands by
MI6 during the night of 5/6 July 1941.

Alblas' first few days on Dutch soil were interesting, to
say the least. On landing he discovered he had been

dropped in the wrong place, some 400 metres from the German border. That evening he ran into a papers check and was immediately arrested by the Dutch police. Evidently the MI6 forging department had not changed much since the experience of Lodo van Hamel, nine months previous. Deciding – as Van Hamel and Hers had done earlier – that his best chance was to be completely open, he explained to the Chief Inspector that he had been sent on a mission for Queen Wilhelmina. He was lucky. The Chief Inspector was a true patriot and even offered to help Alblas with his work. He astounded his former prisoner by saying he could personally sabotage the telephone system between the Netherlands and Germany. Furthermore, he insisted that Alblas ask MI6 to get the RAF to bomb the busy Nieuwschans-Germany rail link.

On release, Alblas contacted Jacques Batenburg, an old friend who lived in Rotterdam. Batenburg put him in touch with another resistance worker, Jan Idema, who offered him accommodation and a place from which to transmit. When the radio transmitter, which had been buried on landing, was retrieved, Alblas, like all the early agents, discovered he could not reach Britain without a large outside aerial. As this was out of the question at Idema's flat, Batenburg suggested a move to the home of his fiancée, Gre Hoogervorst, who lived with her parents and two sisters. The house turned out to be ideal, standing next to a church which could provide excellent cover for the aerial.

The family Hoogervorst gave their consent, and Alblas moved in, finding that he could rig up an outside aerial out of sight from the street below. With this done, he succeeded in making contact with MI6 and was able to set about his mission, which involved reporting information about German coastal convoys and the location of shipping in Dutch ports. The work was soon proceeding well, with Idema using his contacts to collect the necessary information and Ablas, in the background, keeping MI6 well informed. So efficiently did they operate that the RAF would often attack coastal shipping only a few hours after it had been reported.

During this period the Abwehr's radio surveillance units had been monitoring Alblas' transmissions and after two months' hard work were able to pin-point the new operator. This was in late August 1941, at a time when Giskes had only just taken over his new job and before there was any question of close co-operation between the Abwehr and SIPO. In the prevailing atmosphere of the time, Giskes decided to have a go at capturing the radio operator single-handed, without calling in the SIPO, as official policy demanded. It was a brave decision. He was only too well aware of the row that would ensue should he fail.

This monitoring had not gone unnoticed by those protecting Alblas. Both Idema and Batenburg were convinced the Germans had been closing in on his transmitter, and whenever Alblas was on the air they would go out on bicycles and ride round the area looking for anything suspicious. On one of these trips they observed two white vans with small antennae on their roofs. They warned Alblas but he refused to believe them. The British, he said, had assured him his transmitter was impossible to trace.

On the morning of 28 August 1941 a man rang the front door bell at the family Hoogervorst's house and claimed to have come to check the gas meter. Batenburg, who had opened the door, was instantly suspicious and sent his girlfriend out into the street to have a look around. She returned almost immediately, saying the Germans were setting up a road block at the end of the street, and ran upstairs to warn Alblas. The Hoogervorsts, who had often rehearsed for this moment, all knew exactly what to do. Gre Hoogervorst was to take care of the transmitter: putting it into a suitcase, she tied it on the back of her bicycle, then she went outside and started cycling down the street. On approaching the road block she ignored the cries of 'Halt!' and carried on through, disappearing around the corner.

Giskes, seeing his plans going awry, decided to follow the girl in his car. During all this excitement, the Germans failed to notice a small figure walk slowly down the side of the street and slip through the road block unhindered. It did not take Giskes long to catch up with the girl on the bicycle but he was unable to force her to stop. Ignoring his waving, she pulled up outside the local supermarket and disappeared inside, carrying the suitcase. Once inside she handed the suitcase containing the transmitter to the cloakroom attendant, saying that it would be collected very soon. Minutes later Alblas turned up carrying an identical-looking suitcase containing some old papers. The switch was made just in time, and he quickly disappeared into the streets outside.

Meanwhile Batenburg having also escaped through the road block, made his way to the local hairdresser's. This too was part of the pre-arranged plan. He now knew that, were the plan to have any chance of succeeding, he would have to return innocently to the Hoogervorsts' house and face whatever was awaiting him. The temptation to disappear into hiding was overwhelming but somehow he managed to resist it. Back at the Hoogervorsts' he was met by some of Giskes' men, who told him he was under arrest for treason. Batenburg remained calm and denied everything, claiming that the long aerial up the side of the church was for his old radio set to improve its reception. (Commercial radio sets had not yet been banned by the Germans at this stage). Mrs Hoogervorst had also played her part, managing to dispose of Alblas' files and papers by flushing them down the toilet. All that the Abwehr were left with was circumstantial evidence.

At the supermarket, Giskes sent three men in to seek Gre Hoogervorst. On finding her, they were sarcastically asked whether three men were needed to arrest one girl. She was questioned about her suitcase and, after a few moments stalling, declared that she had left it in the cloakroom. It was quickly retrieved and the Germans were furious to find that it contained only some old papers. In spite of the fact that they had no evidence against her, Gre Hoogervorst was arrested and taken to the 'Orange Hotel'.

Giskes kept his men in the Hoogervorsts' house for a further twenty-four hours, in the hope that Alblas might return, but he knew he was stabbing in the dark. By now he was embroiled in a conflict with the SIPO, who had got to hear of the matter. As a result, Giskes was strongly reprimanded by his superiors, and the case was handed over to Schreieder. The SIPO investigated the affair with considerably more thoroughness than had Giskes. Schreieder had the entire Hoogervorst family arrested, along with Batenburg and taken to the 'Orange Hotel'. The house was thoroughly searched, and at the bottom of one of the dustbins the SIPO found a piece of paper containing part of Alblas' code poem. It was an extract from Goethe:

Wer reitet so spät dürch Nacht und Wind?
Es ist der Vater mit seinem Kind

(Who rides so late through the night and wind?
It is the father with his child.)

Schreieder confronted the entire family with the poem and asked whether it was part of a secret code. They all claimed never to have heard of it, except the youngest sister, who annoyed Schreieder by quoting a parody of it:

Wer fliegt so spät dürch Nacht und Wind?
Es ist der Tommy, der kommt geschwind.

(Who flies so late through the night and wind?
It is the Tommy, who's coming quick.)

When asked about the stranger who had been staying at their house, the family replied that the youngest sister had met him one day at the beach and had invited him home. They claimed to have been deceived by the man and had no idea that he was a spy. They were all sincerely sorry. Knowing that he did not have enough evidence for a prosecution, Schreieder finally decided to release the Hoogervorsts on the understanding that, should any further evidence be discovered linking them to the radio operator, they would all be shot.

As they arrived home, Batenburg had the sense to warn the family against talking about Alblas, as the Germans might easily have installed microphones to trap them. At first they refused to believe it and started to make fun of

him by loudly praising their treatment at the hands of the
Germans. Shortly afterwards, however, Batenburg
unearthed a microphone which had been hidden in the
wall. There was complete silence. The entire family had
narrowly escaped a firing squad.

Schreieder refused to give up. Having failed with the
microphones, he had the Hoogervorsts followed each day
and set Van der Waals onto Batenburg. Fortunately for
them, the family were soon aware of what was happening
and made sure they did nothing remotely suspicious. As
for Batenburg, he was initially taken in by Van der Waals'
talk about the British Secret Service and was saved only by
Gre's pointing out that nothing that Van der Waals had
said was likely to be unknown to the Germans. Coming to
his senses, Batenburg decided to break off contact with
Van der Waals and in doing so became one of the few
people to escape the latter's attentions.

After this narrow escape, Alblas went to Idema's flat in
Rotterdam. Slowly, as the news filtered through that the
Hoogervorsts had not talked, his confidence returned. By
mid October 1941 he had started transmitting again, and
in his first message he warned MI6 that the Germans had
tracked down his transmitter, despite their assurances to
the contrary. He received a reply: '*CONGRATULATIONS
ON YOUR ESCAPE*', but nothing was said about the
transmitter. But Alblas was not slow to learn his lesson. In
future he determined never to transmit from the same
place for more than a week at a time.

During the autumn of 1941 Alblas was, in fact, the only
radio link with Britain and as a consequence he soon
became overworked. Contact was established with Siegfried
Vaz Dias, a journalist who had worked for the pre-war
Dutch Secret Service GS III, and before long Alblas found
himself at the heart of Dutch resistance activities.

Alblas remained both passionate and intense about the
work he was doing, and quite often this led him into
danger. An example of this was an occasion when he was
travelling with Idema in a railway carriage full of German
soldiers, when they were carrying the transmitter with
them in a suitcase. The soldiers started discussing
Rotterdam and began to complain that it was a horrible

place with nothing to do – even the women were unpleasant. Rotterdam – having been bombed by the Luftwaffe – was an emotional issue for the Dutch. Alblas burst out in fury, telling the Germans exactly why it was that the women shunned their company. There was a stunned silence in the carriage but Alblas, charmed as he seemed to be, got away with it. Idema was less than happy about the whole incident.

In early 1942 Alblas was contacted by two MI6 colleagues, Wim Van der Reyden and Jo Ter Laak. Van der Reyden bought him a new code, on MI6's instructions, because the old one had to be regarded as suspect after the arrest of the Hoogervorsts.

Alblas continued to be pursued by the SIPO. On one occasion he was transmitting from a farmhouse when he noticed a suspicious plane circling overhead. Becoming worried, he immediately left the farmhouse and had only just reached the main road when he saw the German raiding vans racing up. Time and time again he was forced to move house, remaining only one step ahead of the Germans throughout, and the strain began to tell as more and more of his colleagues were arrested.

In February 1942 Van der Reyden was picked up by the SIPO, having proved totally unsuited to intelligence work, and before long he had told the Germans of the code he had passed to Alblas. From that moment on, Schreieder was able to monitor his messages. Slowly he began to close in on Alblas.

Things became increasingly difficult. It was clear to Alblas that by now the Germans had a detailed description of him, and this limited his opportunities to go out and relax. Time and time again he would voice his suspicion that there was a major traitor operating at the heart of the Dutch Resistance. Those around him began to notice his deterioration. For almost a year he had worked in the knowledge that any slip-up would leave him facing a firing squad. As his exhaustion increased, he became more careless.

By the early summer of 1942 Schreieder had learned from a local V-man that Alblas had become very friendly with a nurse called Pim Hueting and that he would occasionally visit her. In fact, Alblas had established close connections with the whole Hueting family. Both Pim's father, an ex-army captain, and her brother Gerard were involved in his secret work. For a time Schreieder was content to leave him alone as a control check on what the OD had learned. Then things changed suddenly. In early July 1942 Alblas sent MI6 a warning to the effect that an agent from Britain had failed to turn up – more about this later (p.120). Overnight Alblas had become a major threat to the Germans' 'North Pole' bluff, and his capture became imperative.

Schreieder decided to use the girl as bait. She was arrested, wrapped up in bandages and confined to her own bed at home, guarded by a young German typist posing as a nurse. A story was spread about the area that Pim had suffered concussion after having been knocked off her bicycle. This news soon reached Alblas, who was naturally concerned about what had happened to his new girlfriend. Idema persuaded him to check things out first by sending his aunt round to visit. The aunt met the 'nurse' and was told that Pim was too ill to speak, though she was allowed a glimpse through a half-opened door. Returning to Alblas, the aunt explained that she was far from satisfied with the situation, but Alblas suddenly became adamant about going. As a compromise he agreed to remove everything from his pockets. He was aware of the risk he was taking but was beyond caring. The SIPO waited until he was well inside the house before overpowering him.

On learning of Alblas' arrest, Idema went straight to the safe house where the radio transmitter was hidden, only to discover that the Germans had beaten him to it. A few hours earlier Poos and Slagter had turned up, claiming to have been sent by Alblas to collect his things.

As for Alblas, he was badly tortured but held out for the three days he had promised Idema and his other colleagues. After this he agreed to talk on condition the Huetings were not prosecuted. His fate will be described later (p.237).

The SIPO did not keep to this agreement. Captain Hueting, who had helped Alblas with his work, was executed on 25 September 1942. His wife, son Gerard and daughter Pim were released in December 1942, and all survived the war. Around this time the younger Hoogervorst sister was re-arrested for her part in the affair and was sentenced to sixteen months imprisonment. In February 1943 both Jacques Batenburg and his fiancée Gre Hoogervorst were tipped off to make themselves scarce and succeeded in reaching Switzerland. They too survived the war. Jan Idema would prove a remarkable survivor, continuing his underground work right through to the liberation of the Netherlands in 1945.

The Abwehr failed in its attempt to play back Alblas' transmitter: Yet again MI6 was instantly aware that something had gone wrong. The Germans could, however, console themselves with the thought that they had removed another threat to 'North Pole'.

10   Worked ... by Jerry

During the first half of 1942 the various German counter-espionage organizations in the Netherlands had reason to be satisfied with their efforts. By mid-May 1942 Giskes and Schreieder had removed most of the major obstacles to their double-cross. By co-operating effectively, they had obtained some excellent results, including the capture of three radio links and nine agents, some of whom had given detailed descriptions of SOE's methods and training. For Canaris, his decision almost a year earlier had paid handsome dividends. All that remained was to reap the benefits.

To Giskes' mind, it had all been made possible because of Lauwers' 'co-operation', and he ensured that Lauwers received the best possible treatment, given the circumstances. Lauwers, for his part, was confused. Each time he felt convinced Dutch Section knew what was going on, something happened to make him reconsider the matter. It had become clear that both De Haas and 'Akki' (Andringa) had been arrested as a result of messages sent via his radio link. If SOE was engaged in a triple-cross, the stakes were clearly very high indeed. Furthermore, it seemed likely that many others had also been picked up, including Jan Martens, the tobacconist, and Lauwers could not rid himself of the thought that his warnings might have gone unheeded. To set his mind at rest, he decided to attempt a really blatant warning as soon as the opportunity arose.

This happened sooner than expected. As he set about encoding his next message – which involved his putting letters into groups of five – he noticed that one of these groups read as 'cargs'. To his excitement, Lauwers realized this was very similar to the word 'caught' and on the spur of the moment decided to try to transmit this 'by mistake'. It seemed worth a try. He had already persuaded the Germans that his link with Britain was so weak that he needed to repeat each message twice so as to be sure that it arrived intact. This in itself ought to have warned SOE, because it entailed his transmitting for far longer than the maximum ten minutes, something which Lauwers had never done before his capture. Now it had the added advantage of giving him a chance to double his mistake warning.

On reaching the 'cargs' letter group, he quickly tapped out 'caugh t', followed by the mistake signal. There was no reaction from the German operator sitting next to him, so Lauwers decided to try again. He tapped out another 'caugh t' followed by the mistake signal. Still the German seemed to suspect nothing, and Lauwers determined to push his luck by repeating the trick a third time. This done, he swore softly and proceeded to tap out 'cargs'. The German operator smiled, recognizing that Lauwers had finally got it right, apparently unaware of what had really gone on.

The SOE operator, who by now had the following written down, '*PLRSN. CAUGH. T GR2, CAUGH. T. GR2. CAUGH. T. GRS. CARGS*', responded by acknowledging Lauwers' message with a good ten to fifteen 'R' signals ('Received') instead of the usual one or two. Lauwers felt certain his warning had been received.

In the meantime Dutch Section sent a message destined for Andringa: '*THE CITY WHERE YOU FIRST ARRIVED HAS A SQUARE NAMED AFTER THE CITY WHERE YOU WENT TO SCHOOL. THERE IS A CAFE THERE WITH THE SAME NAME. WAIT THERE ON WEDNESDAY FOR GEORGE.*'

Again Giskes was confused. Who was George? Where had Andringa first arrived? This time even Lauwers did not understand the message, nor did he understand why Dutch Section continued to link him with other agents and networks against all the rules of security. The message was passed on to the SIPO, who closely questioned Andringa about the details. Schreieder soon concluded that the meeting would take place in Amsterdam and set about working out who 'George' was and in which café he was to meet Andringa.

'George' was in fact one of the cover-names used by the thirty-two-year-old SOE agent George Dessing. Before the war he had been an accountant in South Africa but as soon as hostilities broke out he had made his way to Britain to volunteer for active service. Dutch Section had snapped him up, and he had been part of Laming's first training group. Unfortunately he got on badly with his colleagues, and his disdain for authority was such that it soon led to his being sent to Scotland on a disciplinary charge. Here he probably would have remained had not half the first group rebelled, leaving Dutch Section desperately short of trained agents. His rehabilitation followed soon after and he was dropped into the Netherlands during the night of 27/28 February 1942. After an initial scare when he found he had been dropped literally into an SS training camp – it is reported that he walked out saluting the sentries – he made contact with the organization of the Dutch Socialist politician Koos Vorrink, about whom more later (p.126). His mission was to persuade Vorrink to go to Britain and to help arrange this for him.

These bare facts hid an uncomfortable truth. Of all the agents SOE sent to the Netherlands during the war, Dessing was probably the least suitable candidate. He should never have been recruited by Dutch Section, let alone sent anywhere. He spoke Dutch with an appalling British accent and his mannerisms, even after his training, clearly showed him up as British. The people around Vorrink who came into contact with him were instantly suspicious, and he was thoroughly checked out before anyone would have anything to do with him. In the end he was accepted as genuine for reasons which reflected little credit on Dutch Section: quite simply, no one could bring himself to believe the Germans would be so stupid as to send such a suspicious character to act as a stoolpigeon. In the spring of 1942 Dessing appeared an obvious victim for the SIPO.

Once established, Dessing was taken to see Vorrink in hiding, who told him that he had no intention of going to

Britain. He was, however, in desperate need of a means of communication with the Dutch Government in London. For this, Dessing needed his radio operator, who was not due to be dropped until a month later. Unfortunately, as we have already seen, the operator, Jan Molenaar, was killed on landing, and it was a month before a message from Dutch Section reached Dessing telling him to contact a fellow agent in a café in Amsterdam. The two months wait had been a frustrating period for both Vorrink and Dessing. Now at last it seemed they would have an indirect link with Dutch Section.

Schreieder's questioning of Andringa revealed that the two had known each other in Britain and had a pre-arranged meeting in a café called the 'Roode Leeuw' ('Red Lion'). Unfortunately for Andringa, Schreieder knew this was a lie. The information in the message suggested that the meeting-place had to be a café called the 'Leidsche Poort' ('Door of Leyden').

To get at the truth, the Germans decided to use the same technique as had been employed for the arrests in the Utrecht restaurant which had led to the capture of Andringa's colleagues. After some initial hesitation, Andringa went along with the plan. He realized, as Schreieder did not neglect to point out, that the SIPO could simply hold an identity check at the café. Dessing's forgeries – there was no reason to suppose these were any different from those handed to the other agents – were certain to stand out a mile. On the other hand, if Andringa went personally, he might be able to warn 'George' as he had Jordaan and Sebes before.

The Leidsche Poort was quite busy when Andringa entered, followed closely by Poos. He immediately spotted Dessing in a corner and walked straight to the bar on the other side of the café. Dessing, who had been expecting Molenaar, did not react either. Informing Poos that 'George' had not yet turned up, Andringa went and sat at a table as far away from Dessing as possible. Twenty minutes later Dessing had still not moved, and Andringa was able to persuade Poos that their contact would not be turning up. Outside the café, however, Schreieder had other ideas and ordered the two men back inside. To

Andringa's consternation, Dessing was still seated in the same place.

In fact, Dessing had recognized Andringa. Realizing something was amiss, he had stayed out of curiosity! Finally he received a signal from Andringa to go to the toilets. Andringa followed and, with Poos just out of earshot, was able to whisper 'Gestapo. Go away'. This time Dessing got the message and left.

Andringa had barely time to feel pleased with Dessing's escape before he was faced with another dilemma. Schreieder had convinced him that the only way to save the tobacconist Jan Martens from arrest was if he did not suspect anything was wrong. To this end he needed Andringa, accompanied by Poos, to visit Martens regularly. Andringa had consented but, try as he might no amount of eye movements could alert Martens to the fact that he had been captured. In spite of his warnings, Andringa and Poos were introduced to Piet Homburg, whose brother Ab had escaped to Britain earlier that year. Homburg told Andringa and his companion that he was going to attempt the same trick as his brother, accompanied by a somewhat larger number of friends. Poos listened carefully to what was said and reported back to Schreieder.

A net was soon cast over the attempt. On 18 May 1942 ten men were arrested in Ijmuiden. In their possession was found a strip of microfilm which led the SIPO to Rotterdam, where they got onto the trail of a man of Indian appearance who had apparently been sent from Britain. The Germans finally raided a flat in Rotterdam, arresting three men, including the agent they had been looking for. He turned out to be the MI6 man Ernst Willem De Jonge, who had been put ashore by motor boat as part of Eric Hazelhoff Roelfzema's project 'Contact Holland' in February 1942, (about which more later, see p.114)

An attempt to play back De Jonge's transmitter failed. MI6 were again instantly aware that something had gone wrong, and their suspicions were soon confirmed by a message which reached them via Sweden. De Jonge was found to have a set of genuine papers, and the evidence suggested that they had been obtained in Pijnacker. Again Schreieder forced Andringa out of his cell and took him to Pijnacker, where he was made to introduce himself to the secretary of the town. It so happened that the secretary knew the whereabouts of another MI6 agent, Jan Emmer. Emmer was picked up a few days later, after Poos had tricked him into a meeting.

At about the same time further information led to the capture of two more MI6 radio operators, Felix Ortt and his colleague Evert Radema. (Attempts were made to play back both transmitters but MI6 would have nothing to do with it.) Dutch Section's blundering had left a devastating trail across the Netherlands.

These were busy days for Giskes and Schreieder. Their double-cross continued to bring them dividends far beyond their initial expectations. During the spring of 1942 they had arrested fifteen agents, all of whom had been taken alive (Terlaak, Lauwers, Taconis, Baatsen, Andringa, De Haas, Ras, Klooss, Jordaan, Sebes, Ortt, Radema, Emmer, De Jonge and Van der Reyden). From information provided by these men, V-men had been able to infiltrate many resistance groups, and arrests were being made almost daily. Nor had the results obtained gone unnoticed by the Nazi hierarchy. In May 1942 both Himmler and Goebbels paid Schreieder a visit. They were shown the increasing amounts of weapons and explosives which had been captured. Himmler requested to be shown a captured agent. The SIPO chose to parade Jordaan, who was asked by Himmler why such a Germanic-looking young man should want to fight against the Third Reich. Jordaan refused to answer and gave Himmler a look of such hatred that he was quickly led away.

Shortly after this visit, it was announced via the Jordaan link that two more agents would be dropped, along with more weapons and explosives. One of them would bring a radio transmitter to help with the setting up sabotage groups in Eastern Holland. They were also to try to find out what had happened to Andringa because by now Dutch Section actually suspected that all might not be well with him. All was not well for the two new agents, Herman Parlevliet and Toon van Steen either, after their encounter with and arrest by their German reception committee.

It had been another good night's work for the Germans. Not only had they captured two more agents and subsequently a fourth radio link but they recovered a new electronic beacon, the Eureka, which could be traced from an aircraft to provide pin-point accuracy whatever the weather. This would be a great help in future reception work, for it remained the Germans' greatest fear that agents might miss their reception points or be dropped blind. In fact, the beacon was so secret that it had been equipped with an explosive charge to prevent its falling into German hands.

Sitting in his cell, with endless hours for contemplation, Lauwers began to realize that the stakes had started to rise even more dramatically. Every week he could hear more and more prisoners marched down the corridors to their cells, and he correctly identified them as fellow SOE agents. Nonetheless, he remained convinced that the British were in control of the situation. It was inconceivable to Lauwers that the renowned British Secret Service – of which he still mistakenly believed he was part – would make such simplistic mistakes. These had to be necessary sacrifices.

At about this time the Germans decided that it was too dangerous to keep their 'North Pole' agents in the 'Orange Hotel'. The danger of news of their presence leaking out via other prisoners had become too great, and Schreieder had them moved *en masse* to Haaren prison, a former priests' training college in the province of North Brabant. Only Lauwers and Jordaan were kept in Scheveningen, the former to transmit, the latter because Giskes felt Lauwers deserved some company in his cell. It was several weeks before the two men came to trust each other but after the ice had broken they began to analyse what had happened.

Lauwers argued that everything pointed to the fact that the British were playing a triple-cross. SOE had wanted him to be captured. They had sent him and Taconis wearing identical clothing, had marked their drop zone with leaflets, had given them outdated money and had provided them with useless papers. Furthermore their contact addresses had turned out to be very dubious, and his radio transmitter appeared to have been tampered with before his departure, thus necessitating that outsiders be brought in to mend it. Then it had appeared that his transmitter was unable to reach Britain without a dangerous outside aerial, and he had been falsely assured it was untraceable. As Lauwers reasoned it, when, after all this, they had still not been arrested, SOE decided to overburden them by dropping weapons and explosives long before they were needed. Only then, he claimed, could they get on with the *real* task of misleading the Germans. Yet despite these confident assertions, Lauwers was unable to rid himself of one lingering doubt. Was it really necessary to sacrifice so many good agents?

During the night of 22/23 June 1942 two more SOE agents, along with radio transmitter and codes, were dropped straight into German hands. The agents were Jan Van Rietschoten, who was to train sabotage groups, and his radio operator Jo Buizer – the same Buizer who had accompanied Ab Homburg across the North Sea in February 1942. Now he had fallen into German hands after all. Using his transmitter, Giskes was able to set up a fifth link with SOE.

In early July 1942 Dutch Section sent a transmitter to be used by a locally recruited Dutch operator. This man – supposedly recruited by Parlevliet and Van Steen – was sent orders to examine the docks on the Wilhelmina Canal for a possible sabotage attack. Giskes did his best to dissuade SOE by sending a pessimistic report and succeeded in stalling the matter until the spring of 1943. In May 1943, however, Dutch Section sent the explosives needed for the job. At this stage there was only one thing the Germans could do. A message arrived in London shortly afterwards from 'Andringa', claiming that both Van Steen and Parlevliet had gone missing. It was a classic trick, which by then Giskes had used far too often for his own liking.

In mid-July 1942 the Abwehr received another message over the Lauwers link, telling them to prepare for the arrival of Gerard Jan Van Hemert (see p.195). His arrival

provided Giskes with another problem. On him were
found orders for Taconis, to blow up a large aerial mast at
Kootwijk, with which the German Navy were directing
U-boat operations in the North Atlantic. The attack was to
take place on the evening of 8 August 1942.

The Germans had no choice but to stage the 'attack'. For
fifteen minutes that night they fired off blank cartridges as
the SOE men were 'beaten off'. The following day all the
official Dutch newspapers printed the following
statement:

> The commander of the Wehrmacht in Holland, General
> Christiansen, announces the following: recently criminal
> elements attempted to sabotage an aerial mast in Holland.
> Because of pre-arranged security and the involvement of
> armed guards, the sabotage was prevented. Several of the
> attackers were, after some resistance overwhelmed and
> arrested. They will stand trial. Material found in the
> attackers' possession was of foreign origin. Should it
> appear that, despite repeated warnings against helping the
> enemy, some civilians have co-operated with them, several
> hostages will be taken in the area concerned and will be
> forced to pay for the deed.

That day Dutch Section received the following message
from 'Lauwers': '*ATTACK KOOTWIJK FAILED. PART OF
GROUP NOT RETURNED. POSSIBLY KILLED OR
WOUNDED BY LANDMINES. THIJS [Taconis] AND HIS
ASSISTANT FRED SAFE.*' Blizzard wanted to know more
about the landmines but Giskes was able to reply that
increased German security after the attack had made any
further reconnaissance impossible. The British understood and warned Lauwers and Taconis to break off any
dubious connections. Giskes sighed with relief. The
Abwehr had skilfully negotiated yet another awkward
situation.

The next message for Lauwers – much to the Germans'
amusement – announced that Taconis had been awarded
the Military Medal. Back in their cell, Lauwers and
Jordaan decided the whole thing was getting out of hand.
They determined to make one last blatant attempt to warn
SOE so that they could be completely certain that the

British knew they were prisoners.

Things had become a lot easier for them since the early days of their capture. Both men had managed to win Giskes' trust. They had caused no trouble, and with the way the double-cross was developing the Germans could not but believe they were holding nothing back. As time went by, the guard on them when transmitting – Jordaan was allowed to help Lauwers with his coding – dwindled to two men. These odds improved further still when they were taken to a sea-front house and one of their guards got into the habit of sitting out in the sun on the terrace. Both men saw their chance. If Jordaan could knock out the German watching them, Lauwers could warn SOE in plain language, after which they could overpower the German outside and escape in the guards' car. For three nights they discussed the plan before deciding against it. Their reasoning had a perverse logic to it. If, as seemed probable to them, SOE were playing a triple-cross, their escape would ruin everything and render the sacrifice of their comrades in vain. Better to make use of the laxer security to try to warn Dutch Section again.

They came up with a warning which could be split in two: 'WORKED BY JERRY SINCE MARCH SIXTH, JEFFERS [Jordaan's code name] MAY THIRD.' Together they practised the way they would slip it into the text, with Jordaan reading out the ciphers whilst Lauwers trans-mitted them. Unfortunately the day before they were to carry the plan out a new German operator was appointed to watch over them. Lauwers managed to slip in 'WORKED BY ... JERRY SINCE' but was unable to complete the warning because the German became suspicious. In any case the warning seemed clear enough.

The new operator reported his suspicions to Giskes, who decided it was time to have Lauwers replaced. Informing Dutch Section that Lauwers needed a rest – he had been 'operating' for almost a year, Giskes sent word that a newly recruited local operator would take over from him. Dutch Section were not impressed. They demanded that Lauwers continue with his work. Giskes was equally stubborn. He kept his own man behind the set and to his surprise heard no more about the matter.

In November 1942 Lauwers and Jordaan were finally transferred to Haaren, where the other victims of 'North Pole' were being held. Despite all Lauwers' efforts to warn SOE, the double-cross was by now in full swing.

And the stakes *had* risen dramatically. Ever since the summer of 1942, the Germans had been involved in work which might well have had a significant impact on the course of the war, for on 26 June 1942 SOE Dutch Section became a very serious liability, not only to its own agents, to the aircrews who flew them and to the Dutch underground they were to serve but to the Allied war effort as a whole.

11 'The Plan For Holland'

During the spring and summer of 1942, hostility between the British and Dutch Secret Services reached a crisis point. Co-operation between MI6 and CID all but ceased amid accusations of double-crossing and unreliability. MI6 regarded the head of CID, Colonel De Bruyne, as totally unsuited to intelligence work – De Bruyne, by training a professional soldier, was a straightforward man who was outraged by the underhand methods employed almost as second nature by the British. The crisis came to a head with the strange affair of 'Contact Holland'.

'Contact Holland' was a link with the occupied Netherlands which had been set up and organized by Eric Hazelhoff Roelfzema, a young Dutch law student who had escaped to Britain in the summer of 1941. His project had received backing from the head of MI6 Dutch Section, Colonel Euan Rabagliatti and the deposed head of CID, Van't Sant, who still maintained considerable influence in the Dutch community in London and as Queen Wilhelmina's private secretary had access to all official Dutch Government business. These men had always got on well and regarded 'Contact Holland' as very much their own private operation.

Hazelhoff Roelfzema was given an MTB and crew by the Royal Navy and, after initial difficulties, succeeded in landing some seven agents on Dutch beaches, including Pieter Tazelaar, De Jonge, Van de Reyden and Emmer. Problems arose when De Bruyne learned about 'Contact Holland' and demanded that, in view of the fact that Hazelhoff Roelfzema was technically a CID officer, the whole venture should be placed under his command. MI6 were horrified and, with the help of Van't Sant, set out to discredit De Bruyne.

With this quarrel raging around him, Hazelhoff Roelfzema found himself caught in an impossible position. Officially under De Bruyne's command, his job as liaison officer between MI6 and CID nevertheless led to his working closely with the British, and he made no bones of the fact that his sympathies lay with MI6. The final straw came when he blatantly disregarded De Bruyne's orders – at MI6's request – by taking the newly arrived escapers Gerard Dogger and Pieter Tazelaar to be debriefed by the British first. De Bruyne was furious and sacked Hazelhoff Roelfzema immediately, threatening him with a court martial. Shortly after this snub by the British De Bruyne resigned his command of CID in order to concentrate wholly on the running of the new Dutch organization MVT (Militaire Voorbereiding Terugkeer: military preparation for the return). CID itself did not outlive him by long, being disbanded in June 1942 after less than two years. With it disappeared 'Contact Holland'.

MVT, originally BVT (Bureau Voorbereiding Terugkeer), had been set up in December 1941; the change of name had taken place in July 1942. For a while both Dutch Secret Services, CID and BVT were run by the same man, De Bruyne. In April 1942 the future head of SOE, Major-General Colin Gubbins, approached BVT with a proposal to co-operate with a new British plan, known simply as 'The Plan for Holland'. This was to represent Dutch Section's contribution to the still-distant Allied invasion of Western Europe and involved the creation of an underground army of over a thousand well-trained and armed saboteurs.

BVT, well aware of the political implications of such a plan, passed it on to the Dutch Government in exile, who turned out to be less than enthusiastic about the whole idea. There was a general feeling that the Netherlands, with a high density of population, were not a suitable place for what SOE had in mind, and much pressure had to be exerted by the British to get the Dutch to go along with the plan. Several levers were effectively used. The Dutch were not slow to recognize that, if they failed to co-operate, SOE would carry out the plan behind their backs anyway, creating the unwanted impression that the Dutch were unwilling to fight. In fact, Dutch co-operation would be severely limited by SOE anyway. All they were required for was to supply the agents and provide advice – and then only when asked. By this stage there was still no talk of equality.

On paper at least, SOE appeared to be doing quite well in the Netherlands. The files showed that there were eleven agents there, all doing good work (Lauwers, Taconis, Baatsen, Andringa, Ras, Klooss, Sebes, Dessing, De Haas, Jordaan and Molenaar). By the standards of most European countries this appeared no mean achievement, yet for the purposes of the Plan for Holland it was an almost insignificant number, and Dutch Section were urged by SOE to press on as quickly as possible with their 'good' work.

In reality, as has been seen, the situation was considerably worse than thought. Molenaar was dead, and all the other agents bar one were in German hands. Ironically the sole exception was Dessing, who was still being sheltered by Vorrink's organization, though he had no way of contacting his headquarters and in terms of operational value may be regarded as an unusable asset. De Bruyne was, in fact, unaware that Dessing had even been sent to the Netherlands.

The most important influence on the creation of the Plan for Holland was a report drawn up by the resistance leader Gerard Dogger, whose arrival in Britain had caused such friction between MI6 and CID. The report spoke of a large, well-organized Dutch underground movement known as the OD (Order Dienst), which was already known to the British. It was a large-scale organization spread throughout the Netherlands consisting mainly of former officials and army officers – consequently its political tone was also right of centre, which may have added to its appeal in British eyes. In all, it may be regarded as the single most important Dutch resistance organization of the war. According to Dogger, the OD could easily recruit the thousand men needed, leaving Dutch Section with the task of supplying instructors, weapons and explosives. As a way of achieving quick results, it seemed too good an opportunity to miss.

Clearly Dutch Section needed to send an agent to contact the OD and check the veracity of Dogger's claims. They found a suitable candidate in the bullish and eccentric figure of George Jambroes.

A teacher by profession, Jambroes had fought in the Dutch Army in 1940 and then had chosen to continue the struggle underground. He was a strongly opinionated man, which led him into taking risks which many felt were unjustified. One example of this was his habit of walking around after curfew armed with a gun, in defiance of the Germans. Fortunately for himself, as well as for the Germans, he never bumped into any patrols during these forays.

When the Germans introduced their race laws into the Dutch education system, Jambroes resigned from his teaching post, an act which promptly brought him to the attention of the SIPO. He was forced into hiding and decided to try to make his way to Britain. After an adventurous journey lasting six months which took him through Belgium, France, Switzerland, Vichy France and Spain, he managed to reach London in March 1942.

Once in London Jambroes was debriefed at the 'Patriotic School' (originally known as the Royal Patriotic Asylum. Later a school for the orphan daughters of soldiers and sailors killed in the Crimean War. Now used by MI5 as the interrogation centre where all refugees from Europe were screened), where he impressed his interrogators with his forceful personality. During his questioning SOE recognized in him a potential leader for the Plan for Holland and approached him. Though he had initially hoped to join the RAF, Jambroes did not need much persuading and accepted the offer, not least in order to get away from the Dutch community in London. In common with a lot of Dutchmen who had just escaped from occupied territory, he despised the comfortable life-style and general inactivity of the long-term expatriates – for someone keen to fight the Germans, there was something deeply annoying and disillusioning about them. But for SOE, Jambroes felt he might just as well have remained in the Netherlands.

Jambroes was extensively briefed by Dutch Section's

commanding officers, Blizzard and Seymour Bingham (see p.148). They explained to him the background situation to the mission, how an underground army, if mobilized at the right moment, could cut enemy communications, rail links and supply lines. His task was to set the plan in motion in the Netherlands, after which he would return to London to help direct operations.

His companion for the mission was to be thirty-three-year-old Sjef Bukkens, who had served in the Dutch Air Force in 1940, escaping to Britain via – of all places – Cherbourg. In September 1941, after a long conversation with Queen Wilhelmina's son-in-law, Prince Bernhard, he had volunteered for service with CID in the hope of seeing some action. However, the only action he had seen that winter was the unedifying sight of Dutch bureaucrats fighting among themselves as the ramifications of 'Contact Holland' were felt. Bukkens had initially been intended as Ernst De Jonge's radio operator but he had quarrelled with MI6, and De Jonge had left without him. After having been posted for his sins, he was recruited by SOE, who asked him to accompany Jambroes on his mission of 'the utmost importance'. Impressed by Jambroes' fiery character, Bukkens accepted the offer immediately.

As the date of his departure approached, Jambroes was given his final instructions. He was to travel to Amsterdam and try to contact the OD at one of five addresses he had been given. As a password he was to bring greetings from Gerard Dogger and announce himself with an old Boer motto, '*Alles sal rech kom*' – 'All will be well'. Should this not succeed, he could try the other four addresses, which included that of Koert Bolle, the doctor in Pijnacker who had secured a new set of identity papers for Klooss. This was the second time Dutch Section had sent someone to Bolle's address, and this after it had already been used by MI6.

On 23 June 1942 Jambroes and Bukkens were taken to a 'holding school', because of poor weather, and isolated from the world around them. Jambroes used the time to draw up a will in favour of his wife, in which he stated that if, after the war, the Netherlands were still occupied by

Germans, he would like his son to grow up in a country free from Nazi influence. The weather finally cleared and the two agents were dropped three days later, on 26 June 1942, along with four canisters of weapons and explosives. Dutch Section would rue the day they had put all their eggs in one basket.

After a safe landing, it was the old familiar tale of Poos, Slagter, the car and the handcuffs. Swearing profusely, Jambroes was led away, and within a few hours his resistance appears to have collapsed completely – perhaps through his feeling of betrayal, a personal fear of torture and death. Whatever the reason for Jambroes' capitulation, Schreieder knew the main points of the Plan for Holland that very evening. During the following weeks the details were filled in.

The significance of their night's work was not lost on either Giskes or Schreieder. The organization to be built up by SOE might well lead to important clues concerning the timing of an Allied invasion of Western Europe. Neither expected a message stating: 'The invasion will begin tomorrow night,' nor did they think it likely the Allies would attempt an invasion of the Netherlands – any commander who proposed that ought to have been court-martialled. However, an assault on northern France or Belgium might require the sabotage of supply routes through the Low Countries, and these orders would provide an excellent indication of an imminent invasion.

The implications of 'North Pole's' latest success quickly reached the higher echelons of Nazi Germany. Himmler himself was given a report on the matter and took a keen interest. The teacher who had escaped to Britain was back and might indirectly warn the Germans of an Allied invasion. Overnight the counter-espionage operations in the Netherlands drastically increased in importance.

At an operational level, Giskes had no problems playing back Bukkens' transmitter using the code captured on him. It is not known whether he obtained all the security checks (by this stage SOE were issuing two or three per agent) but it seems probable, as Dutch Section had no difficulty in accepting Bukkens' messages as genuine. Given their new-found importance, Giskes and Schreieder racked their brains to think of stumbling-blocks. One danger in particular stood out: was it possible that the OD had its own separate radio link with SOE? Their radio-detection units suggested not, but to be on the safe side Schreieder sent Van der Waals to some of the addresses given to Jambroes. Using information supplied by the SIPO, he posed as a messenger from Jambroes and managed to infiltrate the fringes of the organization. Van der Waals' early probings convinced Schreieder that the OD was unaware of the nature of Jambroes' mission.

Yet there remained the danger that, if Jambroes did not contact the OD, this would sooner or later be reported to London. It was at this stage that the MI6 agent Alblas sent a message to the effect that an important agent had as yet not contacted the OD. Alblas was subsequently arrested but Schreieder could only hope that London did not become too suspicious. The OD was in fact a widespread organization and whilst the SIPO had been able to keep tabs on much of its work, there was still a considerable amount they did not know.

Because of this, Schreieder simply could not risk allowing Jambroes to contact the organization. On the other hand, now that Dutch Section had learned of Jambroes' safe arrival, they would expect him to carry out his orders. To solve this problem, Giskes came up with a very neat solution: he informed SOE that in Jambroes' opinion the OD was a demoralized organization, riddled with traitors, and that for SOE to link themselves to it would be to run an unacceptably high risk of infiltration. There were enormous advantages for the Germans in this: by having to start from scratch, Dutch Section would be reconciled to the fact that it would take a long time to build up the required organization; in addition, the dreaded sabotage orders would be longer in coming. Dutch Section had no problem in reconciling themselves with Jambroes' judgement.

At the beginning of September 1942 'Jambroes' signalled he was ready to start receiving reinforcements. This message was passed on in paraphrased form to Colonel De Bruyne at MVT and only served to deepen the Dutch sense of injustice. Not allowed to see the original messages, De Bruyne had never even heard of a security check; nor was he allowed any access to the codes, security, transmitting, transport or choice of drop zones. These were a secret known only to SOE and the Germans. To add insult to injury De Bruyne was informed that only some time after the drop that his men had been sent. Ironically therefore Giskes and Schreieder knew of a drop long before the commander of the men who were being sent.

During the night of 4 September 1942 Dutch Section sent in four more agents as part of the Plan for Holland, to two different parts of the Netherlands. The one thing the drop zones had in common was that they were both swarming with excited Germans.

The first pair were the thirty-three-year-old engineer Karel Beukema and twenty-year-old student Kees Drooglever, a contemporary of Eric Hazelhoff Roelfzema, though not blessed with the latter's charmed existence. Drooglever refused to hand over his code, claiming he had not got one, and though he was disbelieved, the SIPO found nothing in his possessions which remotely resembled a code book. In desperation Schreieder had the DZ searched and a small pocket dictionary was unearthed which Drooglever had managed to throw away unnoticed. On being confronted with it again, he threw it against the cell wall in fury. His transmitter became the eighth 'North Pole' link.

The second pair of agents gave the Germans an even tougher time. These were twenty-three-year-old Arie Mooy and a thirty-nine-year-old naval commander, Roel Jongelie. Jongelie in particular stood out among his fellow agents – and not just on account of his age and balding head. Mentally he was a lot tougher than his younger colleagues and not so easily over-awed. Before the war he had undertaken several dangerous missions in the Dutch East Indies and early in the war had managed to escape with his ship through a Japanese blockade to reach Australia. His interrogations were hard-fought duels, and all he would tell the SIPO was that his safe arrival had to be announced by the phrase 'Erica left on time', adding that the message had to be sent within twenty-four hours or Dutch Section would be warned.

Suddenly the SIPO themselves were under time pressure. Schreieder knew from experience that no such request had ever occurred before, but on the other hand he noted that Jongelie appeared to have an unusual assignment. In the end Schreieder felt so pressurized that he woke Giskes out of his bed to see what he could make of the situation. However, interrogations were not Giskes' strong point and not surprisingly – in the eyes of the SIPO – he made no more progress than Schreieder. Jongelie continued to maintain that the message had to be sent. As he stood up to leave, Giskes tried one last trick. He announced that he had decided to send the message. As he reached the door, he quickly turned around, just in time to catch a fleeting glimpse of a smile on Jongelie's face. It lasted for only a fraction of a second but it was sufficient. Giskes informed Schreieder that he was certain the message should not be sent. As for what the correct message was, if any, Giskes had no idea. Nor did he expect to hear it from Jongelie.

The situation was too dangerous for the Germans. They decided that, for the purposes of 'North Pole', Jongelie would have to be 'killed'. The following day Dutch Section received a worrying message from the Netherlands: '*SORRY TO HAVE TO INFORM YOU THAT ARIE [Jongelie's cover-name] RECEIVED CONCUSSION ON LANDING. DOCTOR THINKS RECOVERY LIKELY ALTHOUGH CONDITION SERIOUS*'. London replied, urging that Jongelie receive the best medical attention possible, stating that money was no problem. They also sent him their best wishes. Things looked to be all right when another message came from the Netherlands: '*ARIES CONDITION IMPROVING. DOCTOR SAYS NO LONGER DANGEROUSLY ILL AND WILL RECOVER SOON IF ALL GOES WELL.*' But the optimism of the message appeared misplaced, for on 4 October 1942, Dutch Section received some sad news: '*CONDITION ARIE SUDDENLY DETERIORATED. DIED FRIDAY [2 October] ABOUT MIDDAY. BURIED YESTERDAY EVENING AT LARGE HEATH. HOPE THAT ONE DAY WE MAY REBURY HIM ELSEWHERE.*' The file on Arie was closed. At about the same time the real Jongelie was being transferred to the prison at Haaren.

During the summer of 1942 a new threat to 'North Pole' developed. Ever since April 1942 a new agent had been operating using the call sign OBX. The surveillance teams had been unable to pin-point him, and there was a danger that the agent might be in touch with the OD and warn London that Jambroes had never been seen in the Netherlands. OBX was in fact Willem Niermayer, one of the last MI6/CID men to be sent out.

Niermayer, a freelance journalist before the war, had been recruited by MI6 after the Army turned him down because of his asthma. After having been dropped 'blind', he had worked from several different addresses, taking care not to transmit from the same place more than a few times. However, his many train journeys had left him short of cash, and he was forced to ask MI6 for more. He was told he would be given the money by a certain 'Bram' who would be visiting him shortly. Amazingly enough, MI6, no doubt taken in by what appeared to be SOE's excellent contacts with the Netherlands, asked Dutch Section if one of the agents they would shortly be dropping could carry out the chore for them. SOE had no objections.

'Bram' arrived during the night of 1 October 1942. His coming had as usual been announced over a pre-existing radio link, and the Germans were waiting for him. Among 'Bram's possessions Schreieder found a special torch containing 5,000 guilders and a set of new identity papers complete with address and photograph. It did not take the SIPO long to surmise that this might be the agent OBX they had hunted so long for.

The job was made for Van der Waals. It took Schreieder several days to brief him, so complete had the Germans knowledge become, so high the stakes. What followed was a clinically efficient operation. After visiting the address on the papers, Van der Waals, posing as 'Bram', soon came into contact with the unsuspecting Niermayer, won his confidence and learnt a lot about his work. Niermayer was picked up by the SIPO shortly afterwards.

The Abwehr attempted to play back Niermayer's transmitter but again failed to hoodwink the professionals.

Niermayer succeeded in hiding at least one of his security checks, and this was instantly noticed by MI6, who immediately broke off contact. Nevertheless, the news of the elimination of OBX even reached Himmler, so pleased were the Germans to have removed another stumbling-block from their path. Now, it seemed, all they had to do was to avoid making any mistakes and Dutch Section would indirectly inform them of an impending invasion. Giskes sent a message to SOE saying that Jambroes was now in a position to receive more sabotage instructors. Blizzard was not slow to respond, and the month of October 1942 was to be the busiest yet.

During the night of 20/21 October three more agents were dropped. These were Pieter Kamphorst (aged forty-seven), Meindert Koolstra (twenty-five) and Michiel Pals (thirty), all of whom had been part of Queen Wilhelmina's escort to Britain in May 1940. Their transmitter would provide Giskes with his ninth link with SOE.

During 23/24 October two more agents arrived. Twenty-three-year-old Charles Hofstede and Charles Pouwels, aged nineteen, became the tenth link.

Elsewhere that night came the eleventh. The unlucky ones this time were Hendrik Steeksma (aged twenty-three) and Humphrey Max Macare (twenty-one). Four days later Dutch Section dispatched thirty-one-year-old Jan Dane and twenty-five-year-old Jacob Bakker, and link twelve was established.

During that night a total of eighteen tons of weapons and supplies were dropped in three different places, involving some sixty canisters. The logistical difficulties involved in transporting and hiding all this material did not appear to worry Dutch Section. Blizzard was by now completely blinded by the optimistic reports coming from the Netherlands.

On paper in London the Plan for Holland seemed to be getting under way nicely, and Blizzard decided it was time to recall Jambroes and debrief him on his splendid work. The order did not come as a surprise to the Germans, and they had prepared for this eventuality. So as not to arouse suspicion, Giskes deliberately continued to make the

arrangements for Jambroes' return and aimed to cause
the maximum inconvenience to the British. The best time
for a pick-up, he told Dutch Section, was during the week
of 15-22 November 1942. Despite its ill omen – the
operation was almost a carbon copy of Van Hamel's
pick-up arrangements some two years earlier – it was
arranged that a sea-plane should fly in low, collect
Jambroes between Hoorn and Edam and get out quickly.
Dutch Section provided detailed co-ordinates.

The day before the operation Dutch Section received a
message via the Bukkens line saying that Jambroes had
gone missing. The pick-up operation was postponed and a
week later SOE learnt the sad news that Jambroes had
been killed by the Germans in a gun fight. Nothing could
be done except send commiserations and appoint
Beukema Toe Water as new chief of the organization. The
file on Jambroes was closed – another victim of the war,
but Dutch Section was determined that the struggle in
which he had died would go on.

The fight continued during the night of 28/29
November 1942. Thirty-year-old Arie de Kruyff and
George Ruseler, aged twenty, who was setting foot on
Dutch soil for the first time, fell straight into German
hands. Giskes set up link thirteen.

There was to be no talk about unlucky numbers, for the
following night two more SOE men, twenty-four-year-old
Hermann Overes and twenty-one-year-old 'Ben' Ubbink,
met with the same fate. And 'Lauwers' ' radio link was still
transmitting without a security check!

By the beginning of December 1942 Operation 'North
Pole' – or 'Das Englandspiel' ('The Game with England') as
it was now christened by the SIPO/SD – had led to the
capture of forty-three SOE agents. For these men, who
filled the cells at Haaren, there were two main topics of
conversation, tapped in morse along the central heating
system: how had things gone so drastically wrong, and
how could they warn SOE?

12 'Misplaced Faith'

One of SOE's tasks during the spring of 1942 was to contact the Dutch Socialist leader Koos Vorrink, whose attempt to reach Britain in May 1940 had ended when he literally missed his boat. From that moment on, Vorrink had immersed himself in resistance work. In January 1942 he had set up the so-called 'National Committee' consisting of a large number of left-wing politicians whose aim was to form a post-war Dutch Government – a remote prospect in 1942.

Both SOE and MI6 recognized the importance of Vorrink's organization early on, and in February 1942 sent agents to contact him. SOE won the race when Dessing, as has already been seen, managed to penetrate Vorrink's tight security screen.

It had been far from easy. Dessing's mission had been prepared by a Dutch journalist in London, Meijer Sluyser, whose close involvement with SOE had led him to give up two addresses in Amsterdam which he knew would lead to Van Looi, a fellow journalist and Vorrink's right-hand man. For his introduction in Amsterdam, Dessing was given two copies of a photograph of Sluyser's younger daughter, clearly taken in Britain, which helped him to allay general suspicions about his accent and mannerisms. He was finally passed on to Van Looi, who in turn, and not before a further thorough screening, put him in touch with Vorrink.

At this stage Dessing found himself in trouble. His radio operator, Jan Molenaar, failed to turn up at any of the pre-arranged meetings, and Dessing was unable to contact Dutch Section. It would be many months before SOE learned that Vorrink had been contacted and that he steadfastly refused to go to Britain. Ironically Dutch Section were to remain ignorant for many months of their one true success in the Netherlands that spring. Realizing he was wasting his time, Dessing decided to try to get to Switzerland, and he managed to reach Britain in the autumn of 1943.

However, Dutch Section were nothing if not persistent and in the summer of 1942 they laid the groundwork for a fresh attempt to contact Vorrink. This time the agent was Van Hemert, who had also been armed with a photo of Sluyser's daughter. He was told that its meaning would be revealed only when the time came. The Germans too were confused by it, after having picked Van Hemert up at his DZ, and Schreieder decided to file it in case it should ever become important.

Van Hemert proved a difficult customer. It took a month before Giskes dared open contact with his transmitter, and then the first message which arrived in Britain was completely indecipherable. The following messages arrived without the correct security check. Inexplicably Dutch Section chose to disregard this uncomfortable evidence. For Blizzard and his colleagues, it seems, the only news was good news.

At the end of October 1942 Sluyser received a cryptic letter from Van Looi, sent via Switzerland:

I myself have been rather busy since my association with Loen [Dessing]. Nice work and a nice colleague. Only, circumstances have conspired against us ... A brother of Loen [Molenaar] was to have arrived but that remained mere talk. That was a great pity because he was in possession of the necessary technical knowledge [a radio transmitter] which our firm was lacking. We continued our work for a few months, as far as this was possible, but then had to close the firm down temporarily. Loen has now been to talk to ILG, the metalworker [code for Switzerland], with a view to returning to work for his old boss [SOE]. I am quietly continuing the firm's work in the hope that the necessary technical help will finally arrive.

In November 1942 Sluyser was asked to visit Queen

Wilhelmina, who told him that she wanted Vorrink working under her in Britain. This request was relayed to Dutch Section, who decided to activate Van Hemert. Before handing over his message Sluyser had specifically asked SOE whether they were certain that their agent was still safe. He was told there was no doubt; apparently Dutch Section had listened to recordings of Van Hemert's morse fingerprint and compared it favourably with that coming from the Netherlands. In their minds Van Hemert was safe. The missing security checks were not important. Consequently they sent Van Hemert a message telling him to go to a given address in Amsterdam and ask for the Wins family. They would then be able to put him in touch with 'Fia' (Van Looi). Schreieder realized that here was another job for his best V-man.

With almost perfect timing Van der Waals arrived at the Wins' home the day before he was to go into hiding. This time he introduced himself as 'Anton', a British agent who had just arrived in the Netherlands. Wins quickly put him in touch with Karel Van Staal, another of Vorrink's lieutenants, who was impressed by 'Anton's' credentials and had no hesitation in passing him as genuine. Van Looi, however, was considerably more suspicious, not least because the photo of Sluyser's daughter had already been used as proof of identity. Would the British Secret Service use the same trick twice? Nevertheless, 'Anton' was able to answer all the questions asked about his training and even showed off his SOE knife. This did impress Van Looi. Nine months earlier Dessing had also shown him such a knife.

'Anton' tempted Van Looi further by claiming to be in touch with a radio transmitter, the very thing Van Looi had been waiting for since 1940. Somehow Van Looi controlled his emotions and told 'Anton' that he would be convinced of his authenticity if he could arrange for Radio Orange in London to broadcast a message for him. It would have to contain a reference to his code-name, 'Fia', and that of Vorrink, 'Koert'. When the challenge was passed on by Van der Waals to his paymaster, Schreieder, after some discussion, Giskes sent Van Looi's request to SOE via Van Hemert's link. Dutch Section consulted

Sluyser on the matter and assured him that Van Hemert was still safe and well, doing good work. On the evening of 23 November 1942 Radio Orange broadcast the following: *'HERE IS A MESSAGE FOR KOERT AND FIA: HAVE FAITH'*. With this Van Looi's final doubts were swept away, and he took 'Anton' to meet Vorrink.

Schreieder was delighted. At last, after two years, the SIPO had managed to penetrate Vorrink's security screen, and Schreieder was determined to play the National Committee for all it was worth. The first step was to give orders to all German police and security forces in the Netherlands to stop following up leads against Vorrink's organization. There were to be no more arrests. With a bit of luck he could end up controlling a large section of the Dutch underground movement.

During the following weeks, Van der Waals played his role brilliantly, and both Vorrink and Van Looi came to trust him completely. At every meeting he brought them fresh evidence that he was in touch with Britain, such as presents of tea, chocolate, cigarettes and weapons. Shortly afterwards 'Anton' moved in to live with Van Looi in his house in Amsterdam, where he was not only at the nerve centre of National Committee work but also able to follow up his other major interest by making a strong impression on Van Looi's eighteen-year-old daughter Nellie.

In late December 1942 Vorrink handed 'Anton' a long report which he wanted transmitting to Queen Wilhelmina in London. In it he described German mistreatment of the Jews and proposed that, if this did not cease, the British should announce that several German cities would be heavily bombed. (Vorrink's view of the war was clearly quite limited. Bomber Command did not need any excuses by this stage.) Also mentioned were the names of Dutch collaborators involved in the rounding-up of Jews. Van der Waals duly presented the report to Schreieder, who re-wrote it, leaving out the part about the collaborators and generally modifying German behaviour. The resulting report was still such that it had to be divided into two sections so as to avoid a lengthy transmission, something which might make SOE suspicious.

The first part was sent on 12 January 1943, along with a

complaint about its length from 'Van Hemert'. Dutch
Section too were annoyed. Blizzard went to see De Bruyne
to tell him their agent should not be exposing himself in
order to send a political report which was of little interest
to them. In March 1943 Vorrink received a reply from
SOE which stated – after some considerable editing by
Schreieder – that his proposal of reprisals against German
cities was considered unacceptable because of the risk of
wide-scale retaliation against Dutch hostages. This, it was
pointed out, would hurt the Dutch more than the
Germans, a nicely worded ploy aimed to appeal to
Vorrink's sense of social responsibility. Ultimately,
whatever Vorrink might have thought of this, the whole
affair had only strengthened his faith in his trusty 'Anton'.

During this period Vorrink's main concern was to obtain
recognition from Queen Wilhelmina that the National
Committee be regarded as the official representative of
the Dutch Government in the Netherlands. With this in
mind, it had occurred to Vorrink that Dutch Section, for
political reasons, might not be passing on all his messages
to the Queen, and he therefore decided that his own
organization needed a transmitter. This request placed
Schreieder in a difficult position. There would be no
problem supplying Vorrink with a radio transmitter – the
Germans had captured enough of them in the past year.
The difficulty lay with the radio operator. Schreieder
recognized he could not afford to allow a genuine SOE
operator to come over, possessing, as he would, his own
code and security checks. Not only would he be impossible
to control but a quick check with headquarters would blow
'Anton's' cover and ruin the whole operation. There was
only one logical solution to the problem. He instructed
Van der Waals to inform Vorrink that he could have a
transmitter but that the British could not afford to send an
operator as well.

This seemed but a minor matter to Vorrink, as he
gratefully accepted the transmitter 'Anton' had acquired
for him. Only one message was ever sent, and this
amounted to an insider's joke. The Germans set up a
secret station in The Hague and transmitted a message to
Vorrink informing him that 'Anton' had been promoted

to the rank of captain whilst Van Looi was to be his lieutenant. After this the transmitter appeared to malfunction. In fact, it was never used again.

In early March 1943 Vorrink received a request from SOE via 'Anton' for the names of all those involved in the National Committee. The reason given was that the Dutch Government in London wished to know who exactly their official representatives might be. It seemed straightforward enough to Vorrink. He wasted no time in compiling the evidence, which he handed to 'Anton', saying he wanted the official recognition put down in writing and signed. To his disappointment he received a reply saying that the Government in exile could not recognize the National Committee since it simply did not have enough information about it. What was needed was a detailed account of the organization.

In order to help inform London, Vorrink decided that one of his best men, J. Van Tijen, should travel to Britain with a large amount of espionage material, including more reports on the persecution of Jews, a code used by German night fighters (obtained from a source within the Luftwaffe) and details of coastal defences, radar stations and troop positions. 'Anton' was asked to arrange for a seaplane to come and pick up Van Tijen, who also trusted 'Anton' implicitly. Van der Waals had taken him to witness a supply drop, laid on by Schreieder, and Van Tijen had no doubts that he could provide a seaplane.

It was at this point that Van der Waals almost threw the game away. The head of the rival OD, J. Six, learned of Van Tijen's imminent departure for Britain and asked him to take a message along. He was very disturbed to learn that the agent who had been organizing the matter had claimed to be a nephew of the Dutch Prime Minister, Gerbrandy. This was true. In order to bolster his importance, Van der Waals had been posing as the Prime Minister's nephew. However, Six had information suggesting that Gerbrandy's nephew was working for the Germans, and he took down a detailed description of 'Anton'. A few days later he telephoned Van Tijen to say that the descriptions did not match.

On being confronted with this news, Van der Waals

almost lost his nerve. After some quick thinking, he admitted he was not Gerbrandy's nephew but claimed that the Germans, unable to catch him, had been spreading rumours. He managed to convince Van Tijen and added that he too would be returning to Britain to draw up a report, which had the effect of further burying any doubts that might have developed.

The date for the pick-up was set, and Van Tijen left with his secret material, fully expecting to be in Britain before the day was out. In fact, he got no further than Zaandam station, which was where Schreieder chose to have him picked up.

By this time Schreieder had realized that things were becoming too complicated. Further arrests in other groups infiltrated by Van der Waals lead him to fear that 'Anton's' cover would not last much longer. In fact, there was increasing evidence that Van der Waals was now a known traitor to certain underground groups. Slowly but surely Schreieder saw his dream of being able to manipulate the centre of Dutch Resistance activities disappearing. If he held out longer, he might still be able to pull off some major coups, but failure might ensure he lost a sizeable number of the National Committee as well as severely endangering 'North Pole'. The risks, he finally concluded, were too great and he began to plan for the mass arrest of Vorrink's organization. To do this, Schreieder calculated he needed three weeks, and he offered Van der Waals 15,000 guilders if he could hang on for that long.

In order to bolster his V-man's credibility Schreieder hit upon two plans. First 'Anton' took Van Looi's young daughter out for an evening stroll during which they were 'ambushed' by the SIPO. Several shots were fired before they both managed to escape. The following day all the official Dutch newspapers ran notices offering 10,000 guilders for the arrest of a man whose description was unmistakably that of 'Anton'. Schreieder's second plan was to have a message broadcast over Radio Orange suggesting that Van Looi had arrived safely in Britain. This was arranged through 'North Pole'.

Schreieder knew that with Vorrink's arrest Dutch Section might ask questions about Van Hemert, who had been so closely linked with his work. In an attempt to avoid suspicion he decided to lay a false trail by making some arrests in OD circles and then informing SOE that Vorrink was in danger because of his 'links' with these people. The plans made for the destruction of Vorrink's networks were incredibly detailed and thorough. Long lists of suspects had been drawn up, with a staggering amount of detail about their personal lives and resistance activities. SIPO knew, for instance, where most would go if forced into hiding, where their favourite cafés and bars were and where they were most likely to be at any time of the day. Rarely in history has an underground organization been so thoroughly penetrated.

As far as Vorrink and Van Looi were concerned, 'Anton' lured them to the southern province of Brabant, where they were to meet local resistance leaders in order to discuss plans for co-operation. The Germans allowed the meeting to take place – Van der Waals was present – before arresting them at Eindhoven station. All three, 'Anton' still playing his part, put up heavy resistance before being overpowered and taken away in the back of a van.

As they were lying there, Vorrink suddenly heard a click as Van der Waals put the safety catch back on his pistol. To his horror Vorrink recalled 'Anton's' telling him before that he would never allow the Germans to take him alive. Yet nothing happened and during the next few days it began to prey on his mind that the Germans guarding them had not reacted to a threat they must clearly have heard.

As the day wore on, the plan was put into operation throughout the Netherlands. In all the SIPO arrested some 150 people that afternoon, including the entire leadership of the National Committee, its sabotage and espionage sections and anyone who had had the misfortune to come into contact with Van der Waals. There were inevitably some hiccups: one of those arrested resisted so violently that the Germans forgot to arrest 'Anton' as well, and Karel van Staal – one of Vorrink's lieutenants – had not been arrested at all.

Schreieder used Nellie van Looi to trap Van Staal, who

had meanwhile gone into hiding. She had earlier been arrested but was now 'liberated' by 'Anton', who 'overpowered' her guards before taking her to safety. Suspecting nothing, Nellie took a message to Van Staal, saying that 'Anton' too had escaped arrest and wanted to speak to him. Van Staal fell for it hook, line and sinker. Within a day he was lured to a secluded spot and arrested. That evening Dutch Section received a warning that Van Hemert was believed to have been arrested.

Later, Van der Waals became bored with Van Looi's daughter, and she was re-arrested by the SIPO, who sent her to work in Germany. Her cruel experiences weakened her heart, and she died in 1949.

Surprisingly the mass arrests of 1 April 1943 led to only one death sentence, that of the Luftwaffe source who had provided information on the night fighters. He was ruthlessly hunted down and shot. An unusual amount of leniency was shown by the Germans towards those arrested, perhaps motivated by the fact that they had taken mainly leading Dutchmen and politicians, and to execute them would have had a bad effect on the population as a whole. It seems clear that this decision was taken at the highest levels, and it has been suggested that Hitler saw the 'Nordic' type Vorrink as a future leader of the Netherlands. Whatever the reason, many of those arrested were free within a few months, and even the most important remained in the Netherlands until April 1944. After that the Germans became less concerned with the niceties of Dutch morale and had them sent to concentration camps. Van Staal and Van Looi both ended up in Buchenwald; Vorrink saw the war out in Sachenhausen.

'North Pole' had had terrible consequences for the Dutch Resistance, yet, despite all that had happened, SOE still remained ignorant of what was really going on in the Netherlands. Dutch Section's incompetence was reaching epic proportions.

13 'All Prisoners in Haaren – Stop – Dourlein'

In March 1943 the Seminarium prison at Haaren received its first woman agent. She was Beatrix ('Trix') Terwindt, a pre-war airline stewardess with plenty of initiative who had escaped to Britain via Switzerland in March 1942.

In London Terwindt had come into contact with Airey Neave who, having just escaped from occupied Europe himself, was working for MI9, the escape and evasion organization. Neave was very much interested in Terwindt. He was desperately keen to set up an escape line in the Netherlands which would link up with some of the Belgian and French lines already in existence. Terwindt for her part was eager to go. In London she had come into contact only with patronizing middle-aged Dutchmen who had laughed at her when she assured them she wanted to fight. She was frequently told she would be better off becoming a secretary, and this had grated. Now she could get her own back on them. Neave was the man who was going to provide her with a chance to fight.

MI9 had no facilities to train and dispatch agents, but Neave had heard that SOE Dutch Section had excellent contacts with the Netherlands. He approached Blizzard with the request that they train and dispatch Terwindt themselves. That presented no problems, and after her training she was dropped to a German reception committee which Dutch Section had unwittingly been kind enough to arrange for her.

Schreieder quickly realized from the material found on Terwindt that she had been sent by a different organization on a separate mission. After her interrogations, during which she successfully hid the fact that she had a code, Terwindt was transferred to Haaren. As a woman she was given her own cell, in which she suffered acutely from boredom and loneliness. In due course Schreieder offered her freedom if she would consent to make one visit to her contact, J. Smit, who was already well known to the Germans. She refused. Smit was arrested later and executed.

Haaren had been designed as a priests' seminary, not as a prison, and most of the small student rooms had been adapted with bars and special doors. A former prisoner has left a description of the excellent treatment received. The agents were provided with plenty of food, books, cigarettes and a weekly bath. The beds had sheets and blankets. Each day the prisoners were 'aired' for twenty minutes. Several cells were even provided with radios.

The prison was used as a clearing station for hundreds of suspects arrested by the SIPO/SD but none was ever allowed near the second floor. Rumour had it that the floor was being occupied by a group of agents, and Dr Steyns, the prison doctor, had once been able to sneak up here and whisper through a keyhole. Despite his claim to be a 'good' Dutchman, he was received with a stony silence by the inmates.

Several days after Terwindt had been dropped, three more agents arrived in German hands. twenty-nine-year-old Klaas Van der Bor, Kees van Hulstein, aged thirty-one, and Cornelius Braggaar, twenty-nine, provided Giskes with his fourteenth link with SOE. Van der Bor was already wanted by the SIPO for the murder of a German soldier earlier in the war. His face was on posters all over Dutch police stations, a fact which was well known to Dutch Section but which had not deterred them from sending him back to the Netherlands. Though Van der Bor refused to talk, Schreieder decided to treat him the same way as his colleagues and had him transferred to Haaren.

Things were moving again after a long winter break during which Giskes and Schreieder had worked overtime, trying to obtain information with which to keep their radio game going, and throughout there was in the back of their minds the fear that SOE might finally have realized what was going on and be playing them along.

During the night of 19/20 February 1943 another four agents arrived. Twenty-eight-year-old Gerard Van Os, Jan Kist, aged thirty, and their radio operators, Willem and Piet van der Wilden, aged thirty-two and twenty-eight respectively, took the number of agents past the fifty mark. To celebrate, the SIPO gave a large party in The Hague. It was exclusively a Nazi affair: the Abwehr were not invited, nor did they share in the generous cash awards which were presented.

And still the flood of SOE agents continued. 1/2 March saw thirty-year-old Pieter Boogaart, Piet Arendse, thirty-one, and Pieter Dourlein, twenty-five arrive on Dutch soil. Dourlein had been seen off personally by Major Seymour Bingham, the new head of Dutch Section. As he left, Bingham told his agent that he should be under no illusions that the war would be over quickly. In Bingham's opinion it would last well into the 1950s. This was hardly the sort of talk suitable for the occasion and served only to depress Dourlein. Captured, he was taken to Haaren along with his colleagues.

The news that new agents had arrived was spread along the piping system which ran through the cells, on which messages were tapped out in morse code. Some had even drilled little holes through to the next cell and were able to hold whispered conversations. Most of this talk concerned theories as to what had happened. Only Lauwers and Jordaan now still believed in a triple-cross. Most of the others were convinced there was a traitor in London. All Dutch Section's officers were scrutinized, and the finger of suspicion came to point at Major Seymour Bingham. Many recalled the strange way he had behaved and the enigmatic things he had said. The evidence was wild and unsubstantiated, but to the men in Haaren, bewildered and starved of news, it seemed the only possible explanation. They had been betrayed by Bingham, and somehow a message had to be got back to Britain.

In his cell, Johan ('Ben') Ubbink sat dejected. In the courtyard below he kept on seeing the faces of men he had met and known during his training, and this strengthened his resolve to escape. He had not spent half a year travelling around the globe to reach Britain merely to spend the rest of the war in a German prison cell. However, whenever he raised the subject of escape, he was told by his cellmates to forget about it. As far as they were concerned, it was simply not possible.

Next to Ubbink's cell was that of Pieter Dourlein. He too had been warned against escape by his cellmates, but Dourlein had never been one to be put off. He was hard as nails, and his war record was full of outstanding achievements. He had already escaped once before from the Germans, in 1941, after his attempt to cross the North Sea in a canoe had failed. Hunted by the SIPO, who had posters of him hanging all over the Netherlands, he had organized another attempt and successfully made it across to Britain in an open dinghy. In London he had been warned against joining SOE by a friend but had gone ahead anyway. His farewell letter to his wife suggests a certain fatalistic determination: 'You will never understand what drives and leads me. That is why I am going to do what I will. Never ask why. Life now is not worth much and I have seen so much suffering. I want to put an end to this. I am certain that the war will soon be over and that we will win it. This is why I am prepared to die.'

In fact, the first escape attempt had already taken place. Back in December 1942 Van der Giessen had managed to cut his way out of his cell window and had narrowly failed to bluff his way past the sentry on the front gate. As a result of this the cell window bars were regularly checked by the guards. This loophole was now closed and, despite racking his brains, Dourlein could spot no further weaknesses in the prison's defences. Meanwhile he had managed to contact the occupants of a cell on the floor below. They turned out to be from his part of the Netherlands, and on this basis he decided to trust them. They claimed to have contact with the outside world via a doctor who was completely trustworthy. Dourlein asked them to pass on the following message: '*WHOLE ORGANIZATION IN GERMAN HANDS. ALSO RADIO LINKS. ALL PRISONERS IN HAAREN. DOURLEIN AND BLEEKER*' (Boogaart's cover-name). He was assured the message would be passed on. Its importance was shortly re-emphasized by the arrival of three more agents, twenty-eight-year-old Klaas Wegener, Freek Rouwerd, aged thirty, and Ivo Van Uytvanck, twenty-five. They had been dropped during the night of 21/22 April 1943.

The prison doctor, M.J. Steyns, was popular with the Haaren prisoners and not only because his medicines included such things as sandwiches, eggs and alcohol. He was the prison's secret postman, smuggling messages in and out, from husbands to wives or boyfriends to girlfriends and vice versa, contrived when Steyns made his weekly visit to a nearby hospital for consultations about some of his patients. In this way he was able to pass on Dourlein's warning to a nephew who thought he could get in touch with a secret transmitter. In fact, this warning eventually arrived in the hands of Van der Waals – still playing the role of 'Anton', the British secret agent in Vorrink's organization. Needless to say, it was killed stone dead.

However, Steyns was not the only person who could smuggle out messages. The industrialist F. Philips, being held in Haaren as a hostage after a strike in his factories, was allowed visits from his private secretary, who made regular business trips to Switzerland. Before one of these trips Steyns cornered the man and asked him if he would take a special message to the British Embassy in Berne. The secretary agreed and at the beginning of May 1943, on his next trip, he handed over the warning to the British. He was politely assured that his message would be passed on. The news slowly filtered back to the agents in Haaren, who were delighted, believing that now the whole affair would be sorted out.

Meanwhile Dutch Section had been busy playing a number of escape lines into German hands. This occurred after they had had problems with the new head of the organization in the Netherlands, Beukema Toe Water, who refused to leave his post to go to Britain and draw up a report. All he would agree to was that his second-in-command, 'Nicolaas de Wilde', could go over to Britain via France. In order to do this, however, they would need several contact addresses of escape lines. SOE obliged and even dropped in a brand-new set of identity papers for 'De Wilde'. Van der Waals began to prepare for the biggest role of his double life.

A few weeks later Dutch Section received a message from their colleagues in F (French) Section informing them that 'De Wilde' had been arrested in Paris. This was done by the Germans over a captured French line – in this respect F Section made many of the same errors as their colleagues in Dutch Section. That the message had been safely delivered was demonstrated when Beukema Toe Water was warned by London to break off all contact with 'De Wilde'. All this masked a change of heart by Schreieder. He had finally decided not to risk Van der Waals in Britain but to hold him back for future work. From the German point of view it was just as well, for MI6 had received a reliable report from one of their agents in the Netherlands stating that a Dutchman called 'De Wilde' was known to be a traitor. This was duly passed on to Dutch Section, who found the news disturbing. Was it possible that there were two 'De Wildes' operating in the Netherlands?

Dutch intelligence officers in MVT were alarmed when they were shown the warning. To them there was no hard evidence that all was well in the Netherlands, despite repeated assurances by their British colleagues. Jambroes had left almost a year earlier, and as yet no one had returned to confirm anything. Neither did the flow of worrying messages stop. MI6 received the following warning in June 1943: '*IT HAS BEEN KNOWN WITH COMPLETE CERTAINTY FOR A LONG TIME THAT TWO MEN BOTH CODE-NAMED DE WILDE ARE WORKING FOR THE ENEMY*'.

It was clear to anyone involved in Dutch Section's work that, if either of these 'De Wildes' was Beukema's second-in-command, the consequences for the entire Dutch organization would be appalling.

Two days later MI6 received from Switzerland the warning sent by Dourlein and passed on by Philips' secretary. Unfortunately it had changed somewhat from its original form, to: '*EIGHT PARACHUTISTS AMONG WHOM DOULIN AND DRAKE ARRESTED WEEKS AGO, CODE FRIEND MARIUS KNOWN*'. Nevertheless, it gave Dutch Section food for thought.

In the meantime, SOE had managed to 'persuade'

Beukema Toe Water to return to Britain. He had decided to try his luck crossing the North Sea instead of on the long journey through France and Spain. He informed Dutch Section that he would be leaving during the night of 15 July 1943 in a small boat and asked the British to have MTBs standing by. However, a week passed without any sign of the commander of SOE's secret Dutch army, and finally the search was called off.

It had been clear to Giskes and Schreieder that another shooting accident would look too suspicious, and they decided that the best way forward would be to allow Beukema simply to disappear in the North Sea. As far as the Germans were concerned, their *Englandspiel* still held good, for in late May another three agents had been dropped. These were twenty-one-year-old Oscar de Brey, Anton Mink and Laurens Punt, both twenty-four years old. Giskes had his eighteenth link with SOE. In Haaren the overcrowding was such that the Germans were forced to house the men three to a cell.

By this time it had become clear to Dourlein that, despite his warning having reached Britain, Dutch Section had still continued dropping agents. He became more determined than ever to escape and began to study every angle of the prison and its routine. It remained a discouraging survey, for the walls were thick and high, the windows all barred, the perimeter was covered in barbed wire and sentry posts, along with machine-guns, patrols and searchlights. Outside all this lay a moat surrounding the prison.

Dourlein's first schemes were wild ideas. He intended to knock out the guard who came into the cell to take them for occasional questioning and then to escape in the ensuing confusion. His cellmates refused point-blank to have anything to do with the idea arguing that he would be shot dead before he had even reached the first floor. Unperturbed, Dourlein continued to time patrols and searchlights from his window. He discovered, by measuring the distance and practising on the floor, that it was theoretically possible for him to squeeze through the bars above the cell door. His comrades still wanted nothing to do with his ideas, so he turned to his neighbours. Ben

Ubbink was immediately enthusiastic. The two drilled a hole through into each other's cell and were able to discuss things more easily. Both turned their blankets into ropes and managed to remove the nails of the boards which covered the bars above their doors.

The plan they developed was simple. At weekends the guards who walked up and down the corridor were reduced from three to one. At 5.30 p.m. the guard would go off and collect the food trolley and take it round all the cells. This was a lengthy affair and also a noisy one, due to the rattling trolley. It was at this time that they intended to squeeze through the bars above their cell doors and run to a small store-room which they knew was just around the corner. Whilst the guard was returning the empty food trolley, they would creep to the toilets, where they would await darkness. They had estimated the drop from the toilet window to the ground below as some nine metres, but after that they would be on unknown territory.

The escape was planned for Saturday 30 August 1943, and when the day arrived, tensions rose in the agents' cells. Dourlein's comrades begged him not to go through with the plan – it would be suicide, they said. But Dourlein remained unmovable. But that night as they listened for the footsteps of the guard, they heard the unmistakable sound of a second German and after a hasty consultation decided to postpone the attempt for twenty-four hours.

The following evening things were back to normal, and there was only one guard pushing the food trolley. The moment he disappeared round the corner, Dourlein removed the wooden panel above his cell door and started to squeeze through the bars, whilst his comrades stood by to hand him his clothes and rope. After a fierce struggle during which he could see Ubbink doing likewise, he dropped down to the corridor outside. Out of sight round the corner they could hear the sound of the trolley returning, and they quickly made their way to the store-room. To their relief it was open; another question had been answered in their favour. Once inside, they dressed quickly and waited for the guard to return the trolley. On hearing him go past, they crept quietly to the toilets, where they hid in one of the three cubicles. Only

then did they have time to sit down and take stock of what
had happened. Indeed, this was the first time either man
had seen the other, and after introducing themselves
formally they settled down to wait for midnight.

From time to time a guard would come in and try their
door. As calmly as possible they would take it in turn to
mumble '*besetzt*', their faces covered in sweat. At 8 p.m.
they heard the guard opening the cell doors so that the
clothes of the agents could be put outside. This was a rule
introduced to prevent escapes but Dourlein had reckoned
that, with three sets of clothes in each cell, it would be
possible to avoid detection. This indeed proved to be the
case.

Finally, after what seemed like an eternity, darkness fell
and with it came a thunderstorm. The two agents could
hardly believe their luck as a strong wind got up and the
rain started to beat down heavily.

They waited until midnight before leaving the toilet and
creeping towards the window. They knew that if anyone
came into the room in the next five minutes all would be
lost, and in case of this eventuality Dourlein had armed
himself with a piece of lead piping. Quickly they lowered
themselves down the knotted sheets and found themselves
within fifteen metres of a sentry box. Fortunately the
weather had blotted out any sound and they were not
spotted. Conscious of the fact that they were probably
being watched from all the cell windows above, they
crossed a grassy field to the cover of the chapel. Here they
slid along the wall until they reached a small incline where
they would be safe from the searchlights.

Relaxing momentarily, they studied the route ahead.
What faced them was a massive wall of barbed wire,
interspersed with sentry boxes. It appeared that all the
sentries were sheltering inside from the rain, and they
decided to take their chance. Slowly they crept towards the
barbed wire. Ubbink went first but Dourlein, too impatient
to wait, followed him quickly, tearing his clothes in the
process. Once through the wire, they reached the last
obstacle, the moat, which they waded through: the water
only reached their navels. Climbing the high bank on the
other side, they found themselves in a farmer's field, free

men. They had dared and won and in doing so had achieved the near impossible. It was now imperative that they reach shelter before the next morning, when the Germans would undoubtedly launch a massive search.

Oscar de Brey, one of the last SOE agents to be dispatched during the *Englandspiel* in May 1943. He was murdered in Mauthausen on 7 September 1944

Beatrix Terwindt was dispatched to Holland on 13 February 1943 on a mission for

Haaren. The prison where the captured SOE were held

Pieter Dourlein, he and Ubbink became the first SOE agents to escape from Haaren

Belooning F. 500.-.

Onderstaande Personen:

Johan Bernard UBBINK
geb. 22.5.21 in DOESBURG,
laatst gewoond hebbende:
           te ARNHEM,
stuurman

         en

Peter DOURLEIN,
geb. 2.2.18 in VEERE,
laatst gewoondhebbende:
          te AMSTERDAM,
metselaar

worden door de recherchecentrale gezocht
terzake straatroof.
Ieder, die inlichtingen kan verschaffen, wenden
zich tot de plaatselijke politie.

A Gestapo poster produced after the escape of Dourlein and
Ubbink from Haaren, naming them for the crime of street
robbery. Their escape ended the *Englandspiel*

HET CONTRA SIGNAAL

SOL JUSTITIAE, ILLUSTRA NOS!

TER VERANTWOORDING!

De vele arrestaties in de meest uiteenlopende kringen van allerlei personen, die hetzij direct, hetzij indirect bij het „illegale werk" betrokken zijn en de ondervinding in eigen milieu hebben bewezen, dat de Duitse Sicherheitsdienst zich bedient van talrijke ongure elementen, die er hun beroep van maken via connecties, waarmede zij vaak reeds jaren lang omgang hebben en die voor hun een legitimatie zijn van hun „goed Nederlanderschap", illegale groepen op te sporen en uit te roeien.

In de verschillende „illegale bladen" troffen wij regelmatig waarschuwingen tegen dergelijke personen aan. Bij ons is nu de vraag gerezen, of dit wel de meest geschikte plaats is voor publicering, aangezien wij ~~moeten aannemen, dat deze bladen~~ geregeld vanwege hun grote oplage en onvoorzichtige verspreiding in gestapo-handen komen.

Vele van deze waarschuwingen bevatten zeer gebrekkige signalementen en vage beschuldigingen, die opsporing uiterst moeilijk maken.

Wij stellen ons daarom ten doel systematisch zo nauwkeurig mogelijk signalementen, foto's en andere gegevens te verzamelen, die tot uitschakeling en terechtstelling van deze verraders aanleiding kunnen geven.

Dit blad beoogt geen massale verspreiding, maar dient *absoluut alleen* te worden verstrekt, aan die groepen en personen welke direct of indirect medewerken aan het onschadelijk maken van deze misdadigers. *Men houde dit blad dus voor zichzelf en geve het nooit door.* Wij hopen met de uitgave van dit opsporingsorgaan tegemoet te komen aan herhaaldelijk van bevoegde zijde gehoorde wensen.

Voor eventueele noodzakelijke aanvullingen en verbeteringen, welke zo juist mogelijk moeten worden verstrekt, houden wij ons ten zeerste aanbevolen.

Geeft deze gegevens door aan de U bekende ingewijden, wij zorgen voor de rest.

1. ALDEWERELD, J., geboren 12-8-1904 te Amsterdam. Engeland waarschuwde tegen deze persoon, die zich valselijk uitgeeft als werker van G.S.3. Zie foto en Rennes en J. M. de Droog.

2. BEEKHUYSEN, D., chauffeur. Signalement: slank, hoog in de schouders, mager, slecht gebit. Zie 13 Mendel.

3. BILSEN, FRANCISCUS K. J. VAN, Geboren 5-1-'11 te Ginneken. Signalement: lang en fors, 1.85 m., grijzend blond kortgeknipt haar, blauwe diepliggende ogen, breed in de schouders. Voorheen inspecteur van politie aldaar en hoofdagent te Vlaardingen. Thans ambtenaar van de C.C.D. wonende te Tilburg, Ringbaan Oost 14F. Deze werd met steun van de Duitse autoriteiten hoofdagent te Vlaardingen en doet het thans voorkomen alsof hij buitengewoon vaderlandslievend is en tengevolge daarvan zijn ontslag bij de politie te Vlaardingen gekregen zou hebben. Hij treedt thans op als verspreider van het illegale blad de stem van Vrij Nederland. Men neme zich voor hem in acht. Zie foto van Bilsen no.

4. BURG, CORNELIS VAN DEN, Geboren te Den Haag 22 Juli 1911, alias van Ederveen, woont bij zijn ouders, Pletterijkade 48, Den Haag. Signalement: Lang, slank, 1.80 m. bruine gelaatskleur, dunne neus, magere ingevallen wangen, spreekt nasaal. Is Gestapo-agent en zegt voor de Engelse dienst te werken. Als introductie biedt hij Amerikaanse revolvers aan. Hij zegt van Engeland uit opdracht te hebben actiegroepen te verenigen en van wapens te voorzien. In Nijmegen bewerkstelligde hij talrijke arrestaties. Hij werd daarbij gewond, doch is thans uit het ziekenhuis ontslagen. Ongetwijfeld zet hij zijn duister bedrijf voort. Zie foto van den Burg no. 4.

5. DAM, VAN, zie 13 Mendel.

6. DIGGELEN, CORNELIS MATTHIJS VAN, geboren 9-3-1906 te Rotterdam. Laatst bekende adres: Bezuidenhoutscheweg 353. Zie foto no. 10 Kampers.

7. DE DROOG, JOHNY M., Gestapo-agent, zoekt kwasi adressen voor onderduikers en parachutisten en tracht zich illegale organisatie's in te dringen. Hij bezigt daarbij als introductie zijn foto uit het politieblad. Zijn arbeidsveld was eerst Nijmegen en is nu Limburg. Zie foto J. M. de Droog.

8. PHILIPSEN, zie no 15.

9. GERBRANDY, zie foto en no. 19 Rennes.

10. KAMPERS, ADRIANUS, geboren 30 Juli 1902 te Warmenhuizen, laatst bekende adres Runstraat 13 3 hg. Amsterdam. Hij is een misdadiger en was voorheen revolversmokkelaar tezamen met v. Diggelen. Kampers verricht spionnagewerk voor de Gestapo en was onlangs als zodanig werkzaam te Brussel. Zie de foto Kampers en van Diggelen no. 6.

11. KRAMER WILLY, adres Berkenlaan 31. Zeist, alias Leo Lens. Leo Gerritsen. Is verloofd met juffrouw de Graaf, onderwijzeres te Utrecht. Werkte laatst als Gestapo-agent in Brabant. waar hij vele slachtoffers heeft gemaakt. Zie foto.

12. LIGTEN, JOHANNES BERNARDUS VAN, geboren 1 Maart 1910 te Amsterdam. Signalement: lang 1.84 m., slank, haar en wenkbrauwen donkerbruin, chic type. Woonadres: Kijfhoeklaan 78, Den Haag? Is Gestapo-agent, zie foto.

13. MENDEL, JACOB LION. 33 jaar oud, alias Breukeler. Laatst bekende adres v. Lennepkade 29 te Amsterdam. Bezocht aldaar dikwijls de Poort van Kleef, Paleiscafé en de Rode Leeuw. Signalement: lang 1.75 m., bruin achterovergekamd golvend haar, hooguitgeschoren hals. Draagt bij voorkeur een laag wit boordje en zwart vilten gleufhoed. Zogenaamd in Maart 1943 als jood gedeporteerd naar Westerbork, werkt nu nog voor de Gestapo. Had bijna slachtoffers gemaakt bij de O.D. Werkt samen met Dirk Beekhuysen, van Dam uit Monster en Nieuwerbrug. Zie foto Mendel no. 13.

14. NIEUWERBRUG, zie Mendel no. 13.

15. NOPPEN en PHILIPSEN, rechercheurs, twee hoogst intieme medewerkers van Kommissar Horack van de Bijzondere Afdeling van de S.D. Geven zich uit voor Oranjegezind en leden van Vrij Nederland. Hebben in sommige kringen ook inderdaad de naam „goed" te zijn. Noppen gaat zeer vertrouwelijk om met Gestapo-agent Pijpers en naar men zegt heeft hij zelfs zijn promotie aan dit sujet te danken.

16. POOS, L. A., adres Amalia van Solmsstraat, Den Haag, 41 jaar, werkt samen met Slagter. Beide werken voor de Gestapo en hebben reeds vele slachtoffers gemaakt. Zie foto.

17. PRONK, CORNELIS ALBERTUS DOMINICUS, geboren te Amsterdam 29-6-'99, beroep journalist. woonplaats Miletstraat 46 hs. Amsterdam. Signalement: lang 1.71 m., flink postuur, haar en wenkbrauwen donkerblond, gelaatsvorm ovaal, gezonde gelaatskleur, hoog voorhoofd, blauwe ogen, grote neus, lidteken in de hals. Pronk is in Juli 1935 reeds in aanraking geweest met de politie te Amsterdam wegens een zedenschandaal. Thans is Pronk, naast functionaris der W.A., ook een agent-provocateur. Zou o.a. vele leden der z.g. Orde Dienst aangebracht hebben. Zie foto Pronk.

18. PIJPERS JOSINI, 55 jaar oud, Huijgensstraat 12, Den Haag. Is Gestapo-agent. spionneerde reeds vorige oorlog voor de Duitsers. Voor de oorlog bij de politie gesignaleerd wegens vele misdrijven. Bevriend met Noppen.

19. RENNES, Londen waarschuwt tegen een zoon van Dominee Rennes uit Heeg. Geboren 12-9-1908 te Amsterdam. Rennes werkt samen met een persoon zich noemende Gerbrandy. neef van onzen minister-president. Vide Aldewereld en foto Gerbrandy

20. SCHOTEN, VAN, oud 32 jaar, adres Hoofdweg 185 te Amsterdam. Werkt voor de Gestapo in jodenzaken.

21. SLAGTER. rechercheur te Den Haag. Zie foto en no. 15 Poos.

22. STIENSTRA, oud ongeveer 35 jaar. Broer van den inspecteur van de Prijsbeheersing Stienstra te Den Haag. Noemt zich ook Willy den Hartog, Anton Damen. Laatst bekend adres Amstelkade 150 te Amsterdam. Signalement: lang 1.85 m., ovaal gelaat, tanige gelaatskleur, haar donker, enigszins grijzend, gang slungelachtig, hoog in de rug, zwaait met scheiding. Heeft een tijd lang meegewerkt aan een organisatie in het Zuiden en daarna verraad gepleegd.

23. VASTHOUT waarschijnlijk valse naam. Signalement: lang en slank, smal gelaat, blauwe ogen, blond dik haar met scheiding. Draagt wit zijden das. Is S.S.man. Heeft zich een tijd lang bezig gehouden met Engelse vliegers zogenaamd om ze naar Engeland terug te voeren, in werkelijkheid werden ze, nadat ze bij wijze van test om hun juiste identiteit te bewijzen inlichtingen verschaft hadden, doorgezonden naar het krijgsgevangenkamp. Werkt samen met no. 26 v. Wezemaal.

24. VOS, HENDRIK DE, geeft inlichtingen aan de Gestapo. Werkte in Limburg. Zie foto.

25. WAALS, ANTHONIUS VAN DER, geboren 11-10-1902 te Rotterdam. Alias: Anton de Wilde, Ton van Dissel, Casimir. Bart van der Velde. Signalement: 1.80 m., slank postuur, bleke gelaatskleur, donker enigszins grijzend haar, scheiding links, enigszins spleetogen, spitse neus tussenschot duidelijk zichtbaar, dunne lippen en gouden boventand, kin horizontale gleuf. Onder de naam Bart v. d. Velde drong hij zich in een vaderlandse organisatie en leverde vele van haar leden aan de Gestapo over. Hij deed dit o.a. te Bergen op Zoom en Utrecht. Hij zegt te werken voor de Engelse inlichtingendienst en Majoor Somers. Hij wist, of kon bewerken, welke zinnen er door Radio-Oranje zou komen. En wel herhaaldelijk, zij het dan dat de opgegeven zinnen voor- of achtervoegsels kregen. Volgens de S.D. werd in Juli 1943 te Rotterdam in de Zestienhovenstraat vermoord, welk bericht vals is. Hij is ongetwijfeld nog actief werkzaam. Executie dringend noodzakelijk. Zie foto.

26. WEZEMAAL, VAN, Deurne, oud 35 jaar, Brederostraat 91 te Amsterdam, alias Josef Versenaer. Beroep leraar M.O. Duits. Signalement: lang 1.85–1.90 m., zwaar gezette man, haar donkerblond, kroezig, rond gelaat, ogen grijs-groen, opmerkelijk kleine nagels, vriendelijk voorkomen, merkwaardige uitspraak van de s. verder licht Amsterdams dialect Is S.S.man Hielp Engelse vliegers z.g. naar hun land terug. Deze vliegers werden echter, nadat zij hen voldoende inlichtingen over basis. vliegtuigen enz. verschaft hadden, naar een krijgsgevangenkamp gebracht. Als bewijs van aankomst in Engeland liet hij spreuken over Radio-Oranje doorkomen. Ook Hollanders zijn het slachtoffer geworden van deze „weg". Van Wezemaal is onlangs in Limburg aangeschoten en ligt zwaar gewond in het ziekenhuis. Hij werkte samen met Vasthout no. 23.

27. WIJK, VAN, 23 jaar, oud. Adres Bieschboschstraat 48, Amsterdam. Werkt voor de Gestapo in Joodse aangelegenheden.

Bewaart dit blad, maakt er gebruik van, maar geeft het nooit door. Laat het nooit in 's vijands handen komen.

Volgende no.'s zullen zo mogelijk ontbrekende foto's en verdere aanvullingen geven.

A Dutch Underground pamphlet warning against known Dutch
traitors. No. 3 on the list is Van Bilsen

Anton Van der Waals at his post-war trial

14   The Writing on the Wall

On Monday morning 31 August 1943 Giskes received the news he had dreaded for so long. A nervous SIPO officer told him that two agents had apparently escaped the previous night. Giskes was furious – unless the men could be recaptured during the next few hours, the implications for 'North Pole' were obvious. If they came into contact with anyone even remotely involved in underground work, their news would spread like wildfire.

At Haaren, everything had been turned upside down. At exercise time one man was found missing from cell 45, and after a hasty search cell 46 also turned out to be one short. Worse still, there was no immediate explanation as to how and where the escape had taken place, and initially the Germans concentrated their investigation on the Dutch SS guards. Outside, roadblocks were set up and posters issued bearing Dourlein and Ubbink's photographs. Ubbink's family were all arrested and their house was watched, although Dourlein's bed-ridden father was not disturbed.

For Schreieder the escape could not have come at a worse moment. His old boss had just been transferred to Italy and now, instead of impressing his new one, he had a disaster on his hands.

After quick deliberation Giskes and Schreieder decided upon the only course of action which might conceivably save 'North Pole'. A message was sent to SOE: '*DAVIDS [Code-name for Dourlein] AND ULDENHOUT [Ubbink] CAPTURED WHILE AGO BY GESTAPO. TURNED ROUND AND NOW WORKING FOR THE GERMANS. HAVE BEEN SENT TO ENGLAND UNDER COVER STORY OF HAVING ESCAPED FROM HAAREN. BE*

CAREFUL. GERMANS TRYING TO SPREAD CONFU-SION.' There was considerable subtlety in this message. Giskes was banking on SOE's tendency to believe in their whole organization rather than two individals. It seemed unlikely that this would be accepted by the British for long, especially if the two men reached London, but, as Giskes argued, Dutch Section had proved so gullible before that it was worth a try. In any case there was now nothing to lose.

Unaware of this slur on their characters, Dourlein and Ubbink had quickly reached the outskirts of Tilburg. Here, in desperation, they decided to try a Catholic church, reasoning that the local priest might be able to help them. They were taken to a small room in the back of the church, where they explained their predicament. The priest told them to wait whilst he went to get someone who knew more about these things than he did himself. An hour later he returned with a large, powerful-looking man who introduced himself as Frans Van Bilsen. He questioned them separately and told them he would find them a place to hide while he checked their story.

That evening Van Bilsen took the two agents to a farm near Moergestel, only some five kilometres from Haaren. Their story had soon been verified. Van Bilsen's brother, a Dutch policeman in Den Bosch, had seen the German telexes there. According to his brother, everything was in uproar and the whole area was being turned upside down. Whole estates in Tilburg and Den Bosch were being cordoned off and searched.

By an amazing piece of luck, Dourlein and Ubbink had managed to stumble on the most active resistance worker in the area. Van Bilsen, like his brother, had been a policeman before the war. Early in the war he had been sacked twice from his job, and on the first occasion had complained to the Germans, who had reinstated him as chief inspector at Vlaardingen. Subsequently he had deeply regretted this and had begun to get involved in underground work, which included spying within the police force, carrying out small acts of sabotage and setting up of his own underground newspaper called *De Stem van Vrij Nederland* (*The Voice of Free Holland*). He was both publisher and editor, and it had a growing circulation. Soon after his reinstatement by the Germans he fell foul of a Dutch Nazi who suspected Van Bilsen of illegal activities. Although there was no evidence, he was sacked a second time, after which he took a job as a porter in a Tilburg factory, which gave him plenty of time to pursue his underground activities.

The German search for the two missing prisoners continued for several weeks. Posters, put up on most street corners, offered 500 guilders for information leading to the recapture of men supposedly wanted for armed robbery. Van Bilsen acquired one of these posters and took it to the farm where Dourlein and Ubbink were hiding. Dourlein was incensed to see the Germans were offering only a miserly 500 guilders for them, and he wrote an abusive letter to the head of the SIPO, complaining. Van Bilsen went along with the joke and arranged to have the letter sent from the North of Holland.

Despite the difficult circumstances the Germans set about their work with their customary competence. Whilst Schreieder busied himself with the details of the search, Giskes sought to counteract the damage done to 'North Pole'. To do this he used his old V-man George Ridderhof, who had been operating in Belgium since 1942. In early 1943 SOE Belgian Section had passed on information concerning a resistance group which operated jointly from Belgium and the Netherlands, the latter's network being known as Dienst Wim. When the Dutch Section agent Kist arrived in the Netherlands with orders to contact the organization, Van der Waals had been sent to infiltrate it. This he did with his usual ruthless efficiency, and soon after the entire Dutch end was rolled up. After this Ridderhof was ordered to contact the Belgian side of the organization. Posing as 'George Van Vliet', he managed to win the trust of those in command. In so doing, Ridderhof contacted a certain Knoppers, whom the Germans knew had been in contact with Dienst Wim, and persuaded him to go to Britain to report on the Dutch situation. According to 'Van Vliet', things were going very well there. The unsuspecting Knoppers was passed down a

German-controlled escape line to Spain and from there to Britain. When Knoppers informed Dutch Section of what he had heard, though he was only partially believed, SOE's trust in 'George Van Vliet' strengthened – so much so that in October 1943 two agents, Van Schelle and Grun, were sent by Dutch Section to contact Van Vliet in Brussels. *En route* their plane was shot down but both agents survived the crash and made their way separately to Ridderhof's address. After allowing Van Schelle to work for some six weeks, Giskes decided that it was time he returned to London to report – again the hearsay – that all was fine in the Netherlands. The unsuspecting Van Schelle was returned the same way as Knoppers had been. Again he praised Van Vliet as a loyal underground worker, thus strengthening his credibility with SOE. In fact, if there was one thing that Major Seymour Bingham was certain of in the autumn of 1943, it was that 'George Van Vliet' was completely reliable.

It should also be noted here that during the Dienst Wim affair, Dutch Section supplied Giskes with several addresses in Paris which gave the Abwehr further leads into French Section's 'Prosper' network, which was completely destroyed by the Germans in late June 1943.

A further mention should also be given to the bizarre story of Knoops, who was dropped 'blind' by Dutch Section over northern France in September 1943 (the RAF had by then banned flights to the Netherlands). He had been dropped as a control agent – the first – and made his way to Amsterdam. Once there he failed to contact those he was looking for, namely some of the longer established radio lines, and decided to return to Britain. He was back in London within forty days of having been dropped, a not inconsiderable feat, but could provide Dutch Section with little information.

As part of his deception campaign Giskes also arranged for a cargo ship to be blown up in Amsterdam harbour in broad daylight, and the destruction – attributed to sabotage – was given wide coverage in the press. The facts of the matter were kept so secret that only a handful of Germans knew what had happened.

Whilst Giskes was busy toying with Dutch Section,

Schreieder had had no luck in his search for Dourlein and Ubbink. After a few weeks he had been forced to tone down the scale of the search, and his gloom deepened. As the intensity of the German searches began to diminish, Van Bilsen decided the time had come to move the two men to a safer address. It turned out to be an eventful car journey the highlight being their crashing a German road block. Somehow they escaped again and reached their new destination safely. Here they decided to wait until SOE could come and collect them.

On the very first day, Dourlein had asked Van Bilsen if he could get a message through to Britain. Van Bilsen had promised to do his best but, as the days turned into weeks, there was no news. The strain began to tell. The two agents often quarrelled about trivial matters, and they even had a fight on one occasion. In their quieter, more optimistic moments they arranged with Van Bilsen that, once back in Britain they would set up a raid to free their comrades in Haaren. The code-word would be announced over the BBC.

Finally Van Bilsen's contacts managed to get Dourlein's message through via Switzerland. In due course a reply was received from SOE telling them to make their own way to neutral territory. The news came as a great blow to Dourlein and Ubbink, who recalled that Dutch Section had always promised to collect them if anything went wrong. After all they had been through, this disillusionment was hard to bear. Both realized they would have to take the initiative again, and Van Bilsen calmly got on with the job of providing them with false papers and money for their forthcoming journey. The main problem was a lack of French money. Try as he did, Van Bilsen simply could not get hold of any, and the problem was solved only when Ubbink's brother, himself wanted by the Germans, claimed to know a way of depositing money in a bank account in Paris.

At last, on 11 November 1943, some 2½ months after their escape from Haaren, they were ready to set out on their journey. Crossing into Belgium, they took a bus to Antwerp, where they said farewell to Van Bilsen, who had accompanied them on the first part of their journey. It was an emotional parting. Both men were only too aware of the debt they owed Van Bilsen, without whose help they would have got nowhere.

They arrived safely in Paris, having travelled via Brussels without incident, but once in the French capital they found themselves stuck. The contact address they had been given turned out to be empty, and no one could tell them where the landlord had gone. In fact, he had already been arrested by the SIPO. To make matters worse, the bank in which Ubbink's brother was supposed to have deposited the money claimed to have received no such authorization. For four days they waited without food. The situation became so desperate that Dourlein suggested they knock down a German officer and take his money. After all, he argued, they were wanted for armed robbery anyway. Fortunately for some anonymous German, their money came through just in time.

Soon after, they were on their way to the Swiss frontier. They got off the train at the small town of Belfort, where only some quick thinking by Dourlein saved them. As they were leaving the station, Ubbink noticed the Germans carefully checking everyone's papers. They returned to the platform but there were no other trains due, and after a while the Germans started to look at them suspiciously. Realizing they had to do something quickly, Dourlein picked up a baggage trolley and strode off towards the goods department. Ubbink, quick on the uptake, lifted a heavy box onto the trolley and followed. The goods department had a back exit, and the French railway workers inside stood back as the two agents slipped through into the street outside. It was an excellent example of the value of clear decisive thinking in moments of crisis.

Their next contacts were the Birnie family, who lived in a small mountain village not far from the Swiss border. After a hot meal and rest they were guided across the mountains by some of the local Maquis who used the route to trade with the Swiss for guns and ammunition. Both found the climb desperately difficult after so many months of inactivity but they finally staggered into a Swiss refugee camp. Here they were fortunate enough to come

into contact with a Dutch businessman who gave them
money for their rail tickets to Berne. They were
particularly careful to avoid any contact with the Swiss
authorities because of the inevitable delays which would
then occur. In the back of their minds was also the
unpleasant thought that, as wanted men, they might be
handed back to the Germans.

Once in Berne, they wasted no time before going to the
British Consulate, where they asked to see the intelligence
officer. The date was 22 November 1943. They told their
story, were complimented on a fine escape and were told
that London would be immediately informed. After their
initial debriefing they were taken by taxi to an hotel. The
following day they repeated their tale to Dutch officials.
Again they were very well treated.

In fact, 22 November 1943 was a crucial day for all
concerned with 'North Pole'. MI6 received a message from
Switzerland reporting:

*LIEUTENANT JOHAN BERNHARD UBBINK, COVER-
NAME UDEMA AND CODE LETTERS CEN, PARA-
CHUTED INTO HOLLAND DURING THE NIGHT OF 1
DECEMBER 1942, AND SERGEANT PIETER DOURLEIN,
COVER-NAME DIEPENBROEK, CODE LETTERS ACO,
DROPPED DURING THE NIGHT OF 10 MARCH 1943,
HAVE BOTH ARRIVED HERE. BOTH REPORT THAT
THEY WERE MET BY A RECEPTION COMMITTEE WHO
KNEW THEIR COVER-NAMES, YET TURNED OUT TO
CONSIST OF DUTCH NAZIS AND GERMAN SD, WHO
IMMEDIATELY ARRESTED THEM. DURING THEIR
INTERROGATIONS IT BECAME CLEAR THAT THE
GERMANS WERE COMPLETELY AWARE OF THE
WHOLE ORGANIZATION WITH ITS CODES AND
PASSWORDS. FOR A LONG TIME THE GERMANS HAVE
BEEN TRANSMITTING TO ENGLAND PRETENDING TO
BE AGENTS. THEY GUESS THAT AT LEAST 130 MEN
HAVE BEEN ARRESTED IN THIS WAY SO THAT THE
WHOLE ORGANIZATION IS IN GERMAN HANDS.
DURING THE NIGHT OF 30 AUGUST 1943 THEY
ESCAPED FROM PRISON. THEY SUSPECT MAJOR
BINGHAM OF TREACHERY WITHOUT DARING TO
ACCUSE HIM OUTRIGHT AND PRESS FOR THE
UTMOST CAUTION WITH THIS MESSAGE.*

This message was passed on to both Dutch Section and MVT. It must have been particularly galling for SOE to receive such disastrous confirmation from their rivals.

Meanwhile MI6 sent its own agents in the Netherlands the following warning:

'SISTER SERVICE TOTALLY INFILTRATED BY GERMANS. WE THEREFORE URGE YOU TO BREAK OFF ALL CONTACT WITH THEIR AGENTS AND KEEP CLEAR OF THEM. PLEASE WARN OD AND OTHER ORGANIZATIONS.'

Bad news also reached Giskes and Schreieder on 22 November 1943. Until then it had still been possible to believe in the double-cross, despite the disappearance of Dourlein and Ubbink. Though Dutch Section had not sent any agents since May, the radio traffic and supply drops had continued as normal, and SOE appeared to have accepted the 'turning' of Dourlein and Ubbink. It was still possible that the British might indirectly inform them of an imminent invasion. However, that day saw the last of these lingering hopes crushed. Schreieder received a phone call from Haaren to say that another three agents had escaped. Giskes was informed soon afterwards.

The three escapers turned out to be Van der Giessen, Van Rietschoten and Wegener. They had shared the same cell, and their absence had been noticed within a few hours. Ever since the Dourlein and Ubbink break-out the guards had been under orders to check the prisoners every few hours. That evening the guard had entered their cell at 10.30 and found it empty. The alarm was immediately raised.

In fact, Van Rietschoten had managed to keep hold of a small saw supplied by SOE, which had been sewn into the lining of his jacket. With this he had been able to cut through the ceiling of the cell into a loft directly above. Each night the hole had been camouflaged and after four weeks it was large enough to squeeze through. Once in the loft they discovered to their amazement that there was an unbarred window. Having witnessed what had happened to Dourlein and Ubbink, they sensibly decided to sit back and wait for a rainy night. The storm arrived in the evening of Monday 22 November 1943, when they agreed that the attempt was on. Unfortunately their rope (made from a blanket) proved too short, and Wegener twisted his ankle rather badly on landing. Despite this he managed to follow the other two through the wire to the farmland outside. Once there, they decided to split up. The time was 8 p.m.

After several hours of agonized limping, Wegener collapsed in a ditch. In the distance he could hear the sounds of tracker dogs, and it seemed only a matter of time before they caught up with him. But, as he sat back to await the inevitable, by a minor miracle the pursuing Germans and their dogs failed to find him – the rain had washed out his tracks. The following day he managed to crawl to the address in Heeze he had been given before his escape. Here he was taken in and looked after. Within a week he had recovered enough to start thinking about warning SOE.

Van Rietschoten and Van der Giessen also managed to get clean away from their pursuers. They were hidden at a local farm where they were to remain for some time. More about them later (p.162).

Ironically Klaas Wegener's attempts to warn SOE fell foul of the very warnings which MI6 and the new Dutch Secret Service BI (Bureau Inlichtingen) had been sending to all their agents from the summer of 1943 onwards. Wegener had met his wife, who attempted to contact an MI6/BI agent called Pierre d'Aulnis whom Wegener had known in London and who he assumed might by now be working in the Netherlands. The gamble paid off in the sense that d'Aulnis, who had been dropped by MI6/BI in June 1943, soon heard from his contacts in The Hague that Wegener was looking for him. He was instantly suspicious. MI6 had warned him to break off all contact with agents from Wegener's service, and it seemed only too probable that the Germans had allowed Wegener to escape in order to follow him. He decided to avoid his former colleague at all costs. It is an indication of how jumpy the OD had become that one local leader even decided to shoot Wegener the minute he turned up.

It did not take Wegener long to realize he was mistrusted and, like Dourlein and Ubbink before him, he decided his only option was to return to Britain via France and Switzerland. Sadly his luck ran out, and he fell victim to a penetrated escape line just after having crossed the frontier into Belgium. By this time, however, he hardly cared. He had walked in midwinter for several hundred kilometres and had suffered terribly in the open. His return to Haaren came almost as a relief.

By late 1943 the RSHA high command decided that the time had come to relieve Giskes and Schreieder of control over their agents. Schreieder did manage to persuade his superiors to leave behind the five most important, whom he argued were vital to the continuation of 'North Pole'. These were Lauwers, Jordaan, Van der Reyden, Terwindt and Ter Laak. The others were transferred to the high-security prison at Assen, close to the German border. When Trix Terwindt demanded that she be taken along with her colleagues, she was told somewhat ominously by Schreieder that she really was better off staying where she was and that he would do his best to keep her there as long as possible. How long this would be was very uncertain, for in the topsy-turvy world of the Third Reich Schreieder himself, having been held responsible for the escapes, was now facing the prospect of a court martial and a concentration camp,

On 1 December 1943, unbeknown to their comrades in Haaren and Assen, Dourlein and Ubbink crossed the frontier from France into Spain. They had been in Switzerland for only three days before being passed along an MI6 escape line, via Grenoble to Toulouse and from there to the foot of the Pyrenees, where they set out to cross the mountains with two guides and fourteen fellow escapers. For four days they struggled in terrible weather conditions, with very little food, and finally staggered into Spain more dead than alive, their shoes literally stuck to their feet with blood. Then Spanish bureaucracy delayed matters for two weeks, during which time they recovered from their ordeal and wrote long detailed reports about everything that had happened to them. These included their suspicions against Seymour Bingham, still head of Dutch Section, and praise for Frans Van Bilsen. Dourlein wrote: 'What this man did for us is undescribable. Nothing was too much for him, and he gave himself over totally to the cause. This man must not be forgotten after the war. His organization is well constructed, but he needs supplies from England and with this help will be able to do big things.'

By yet another irony of fate, the name of Frans Van Bilsen was already known to SOE. The Dutch underground had printed a list of the names of known Dutch traitors, along with their photographs. A copy had arrived in Britain and included such notables as Van der Waals, Poos and Slagter. But underneath them was the name of Frans Van Bilsen and the allegations that he had been made Chief Constable of Vlaardingen by the Germans and that he was now posing as a resistance worker, having been 'sacked' from his job.

The existence of the list was known to Van Bilsen himself, and he was naturally concerned about it. He had just finished editing the Christmas 1943 edition of his newspaper, including an article Dourlein had written about the situation in Britain. His friends warned him to go into hiding whilst they cleared his name and counteracted the effects of this miscarriage of justice. Van Bilsen agreed to do so after one last job. He was to collect some ration cards for people in hiding in Venlo, a simple task which would take less than a day. His wife begged him not to go but he remained adamant. But the list had already reached Venlo and he was recognized collecting the cards. On his return he was ambushed by the local resistance group and left for dead. Somehow he managed to stagger to a hospital. However, his reputation had preceded him, and none of the doctors seemed much interested in saving his life. He died a day later from loss of blood. One more cruel irony.

For Major Seymour Bingham, head of SOE Dutch Section, the writing was also on the wall. Just before Christmas 1943 he received Dourlein and Ubbink's reports from Spain, which confirmed his worst fears. It was not merely a *few* of the radio links which were in German hands, as had been hoped, but all of them. He had helped preside over one of the worst intelligence disasters in history. An official commission of inquiry was set up to discover what had gone wrong.

Yet, only shortly before, things had appeared to be going so well. When Bingham had succeeded Blizzard as head of Dutch Section in February 1943, relations between SOE and MVT improved noticeably. The Dutch were allowed more access to the operations going on in the Netherlands and were on friendlier terms with their British counterparts. Now all this counted for nothing. Bingham was relieved of his command in early 1944 and posted to SOE's mission in Australia. He was succeeded by Major R.I. Dobson.

It took more than six weeks to arrange for Dourlein and Ubbink's passage to Britain from Spain. The delay was undoubtedly in order to give SOE time to prepare for their reception, as will become clear. When they finally arrived back on 1 February 1944, Dourlein had been away for eleven months, Ubbink fourteen. As far as they were concerned, they had returned to blow the whistle on Bingham's treachery and to organize a raid on Haaren to free their comrades. They were immediately disillusioned. There were no representatives from Dutch Section there to meet them, nor had the Dutch MVT bothered to send anyone. Instead they were taken by a sergeant to a holding station outside London and placed under house arrest. They were given strict instructions not to discuss their case with anyone and were closely followed wherever they went. Each was allowed to send one letter, which they did, to Colonel De Bruyne, complaining of their treatment.

Things soon got worse. Three days later their debriefing began and quickly assumed the guise of an interrogation. Dobson examined their reports and questioned them closely on their escape and journey to Switzerland. The strain was too much for Ubbink. His memory began to deceive him, and he started to contradict himself, thus increasing his anxiety. Nor was his command of English good, and he had a lot of trouble expressing himself. Dobson's attitude began to turn hostile.

Meanwhile Dourlein received a letter from De Bruyne. (For Ubbink there was no letter. He had upset the officious De Bruyne by admitting that he had not originally held the rank of sergeant before his mission.)

I have just received the letter you wrote me on 2.1.44. Firstly I would like to express my joy that you at least have managed to return. You will understand my feelings of misery when I discovered that men sent by us with such care and effort should immediately, on arrival, fall into enemy hands. Your return is, therefore, of such value, that we can now be fully informed about how all this could happen and also to discuss what can be done to help our comrades who are still prisoners over there and to see how we can continue with our original work. I understand that you find it annoying to be held by British Security for a few days in order that they can debrief you, but nothing can be done about this. It is a cast iron law that anyone entering this country after having been in contact with the enemy should be subjected to a very thorough investigation. A cast iron law, Diepenbroek [Dourlein's cover-name], but one which is entirely understandable. There are already hundreds of examples of why this investigation is necessary ...

These were prophetic words. Giskes' message about both men having been turned had succeeded beyond his imagination in creating an atmosphere of suspicion. Added to this, their praise for the alleged traitor Van Bilsen, and Ubbink's contradictions, had made SOE highly suspicious. As the tone of the questioning got progressively nastier, Dobson confronted both with the list naming Van Bilsen a traitor. Neither could believe it. Ubbink in particular angrily denied the allegations. He told Dobson that he had lived with Van Bilsen for several weeks and had witnessed his resistance work at first hand. There was no way he could have been a traitor. The man had risked his life to save them, and Ubbink was determined to remove this slur. Nevertheless, Dobson refused to believe him.

Ubbink became ill and visited a doctor without permission. He was immediately ordered into hospital. On his release the interrogations continued as before.

SOE appeared less than happy with the fact that Dourlein had written in his report that they had been well treated in Haaren. But Dourlein was adamant. For some reason he had been well treated by the Germans, and he was not going to lie about it. Dobson then openly accused

Dourlein of working for the Germans. Dourlein reacted furiously, throwing himself at Dobson, hitting him hard before being dragged off. Dobson had the nerve to repeat the exercise with Ubbink a few hours later. Ubbink, being milder-mannered than Dourlein, was too shocked to reply.

After six weeks of questioning, Dourlein received another letter from De Bruyne, who claimed not to understand why the British were so suspicious of their story. He could only warn Dourlein not to be difficult and to accept the delay as a necessity. By now, however, the damage had already been done. Both had become totally disillusioned with the British. It was not that they wished to dwell on what they had achieved – this was only their duty as they saw it – but they were deeply injured by the lack of respect shown them. Little things made all the difference: for example, they were allowed no interpreter, which would have made things a lot easier. In the event accusation followed accusation.

Nor could they rely on much help from De Bruyne, their commanding officer. He had resigned his command of MVT on 4 February 1944 and therefore had little further influence on SOE affairs. He did raise the matter with some Dutch Ministers, but they in turn ran into a brick wall. To the Dutch it seemed clear that the recently reorganized Dutch Section saw these ghosts from its tarnished past as an embarrassment, best hidden from sight.

By May 1944 the case was still dragging on. Another letter to Dourlein from De Bruyne said that he could visit them only after a decision had been taken on their future. This was of little comfort to either man. It did not seem improbable to them that they would be executed. After all, the penalty for treason was death.

On 27 May they learned their fate. It was felt that, with the invasion of Europe coming up, they were too great a security risk. Both were to be imprisoned in Brixton indefinitely. Neither Dourlein nor Ubbink was really aware of what was going on as they were led to their cell. They soon learned that, compared with Brixton, Haaren had been luxury. They had been imprisoned without trial in one of Britain's dirtiest prisons, along with thieves and murderers. Dourlein collapsed on one of the filthy bunks in deep despair. Ubbink managed to get hold of a pen and paper and wrote a desperate letter to De Bruyne:

> For the last time I wish to draw your attention to the case of Dourlein and myself. We have been arrested and imprisoned in Brixton without any form of trial. I include the order to imprison us which was given to us on our arrest. It is clear that we are not trusted. I want to make it clear that if those who decided this based it on information received from occupied territory, this originated from the Gestapo. We have done nothing that was not our duty and those people who think the Germans helped us to return to England are wrong. I swear by almighty God in whom I believe, that I am not guilty. This, Colonel, you may consider an oath. I request that you contact the Queen [Wilhelmina] and the highest officers in the intelligence service. If this does not help, I request that you complain to the House of Lords. I would very much like to talk to you and if this is not possible I would ask you to put us in touch with an intelligence officer. If this is not possible, I would ask you to bring our case in front of a court where I can defend myself. If the people who arrested us are of the opinion that it is better if we are separated from the outside world, then there are plenty of places where this could happen outside a prison in which I find myself between walls and bars. I consider it damaging to my feelings of self-respect to be sitting in the same prison as deserters and criminals. I humbly ask you, Colonel, with the utmost strength, to do everything possible to help us in view of the fact that Dourlein and myself are unable to do anything ourselves. I do not think that I can live for much longer under these conditions and fear that I will lose my sanity.

On finishing his plea, Ubbink showed it to Dourlein. He merely shook his head, convinced it was a waste of time. SOE had succeeded where the SIPO, for all its ruthlessness and cunning, had failed. Dourlein had given up all hope.

15   The Staircase of Death

During the first few weeks of December 1943, it became abundantly clear to Giskes that 'North Pole' was on its last legs. No agents had been sent since May and, though the supply drops had continued until October, they too ceased after that date. All that remained were the radio links, and Dutch Section's orders became more and more difficult. For instance, Taconis was told to liquidate twelve high-ranking Dutch Nazis, whilst Andringa was asked to organize a large and ambitious raid. Giskes forced to have Andringa 'killed off' on paper to avoid embarrassment, was under no illusions that Dourlein and Ubbink must have reached their destination.

Further proof was obtained on 5 February 1944 when the SIPO tracked down the MI6/BI agent Borissum Buisman. Among his possessions they found the message from MI6 warning that SOE's Dutch Section had been completely infiltrated and should be given a wide berth.

The remaining radio game lingered on for a month until finally, in March 1944, Giskes suggested to his superiors that he put an end to it. Berlin agreed and told Giskes to write the last message himself, although the final draft was to be telexed to Berlin for approval. It had occurred to Giskes that with a bit of luck he could be ready to transmit the message on April Fool's Day 1944. Permission was forthcoming, and on Saturday 1 April SOE received Giskes' message, in clear language, on all ten of the radio links it still maintained with the Netherlands:

TO MESSRS BLUNT [Blizzard], *BINGHAM & CO, SUCCESSORS LTD, LONDON. WE UNDERSTAND THAT YOU HAVE BEEN ENDEAVOURING FOR SOME TIME*

*TO DO BUSINESS IN HOLLAND WITHOUT OUR
ASSISTANCE. WE REGRET THIS THE MORE SINCE WE
HAVE ACTED FOR SO LONG AS YOUR SOLE
REPRESENTATIVES IN THIS COUNTRY TO OUR
MUTUAL SATISFACTION. NEVERTHELESS WE CAN
ASSURE YOU THAT, SHOULD YOU BE THINKING OF
PAYING US A VISIT ON THE CONTINENT ON ANY
EXTENSIVE SCALE, WE SHALL GIVE YOUR EMISSA-
RIES THE SAME ATTENTION AS WE HAVE HITHERTO,
AND A SIMILARLY WARM WELCOME. HOPING TO SEE
YOU.*

But neither Giskes or Schreieder had much cause for
amusement. The collapse of 'North Pole' had resulted in
bitter recriminations between the Abwehr and the state
organizations. High hopes and expectations had been
raised in Berlin – too high. It did not matter that some
sixty British agents had been captured and that a secret
army had been prevented from rising in their rear, nor
that an enormous amount of supplies had been captured,
including 15,200 kilos of explosives, 3,000 sten guns, 5,000
pistols, 300 Bren guns, 2,000 hand grenades, seventy-five
radio transmitters, 300,000 rounds of ammunition, 200
bicycle tyres, ten raincoats, twenty pairs of boots, ten pairs
of shoes and 450,000 guilders (£40,000 taking the contemporary rate of exchange) for the men in charge of Nazi
Germany, the failure to learn details of the forthcoming
Allied invasion of France far outweighed all this.

The SIPO tried hard to place the blame for the failure
on Giskes, who, they claimed, had insisted that the agents
be treated humanely. It was this that had allowed them to
escape. Giskes defended himself strongly, pointing out
that both Himmler and Heydrich had agreed to take a soft
line with the agents concerned. It was at this time,
however, that Giskes lost the supporting cover of Canaris,
who had been removed as head of the Abwehr. He was
only too well aware that the Nazi Party clique in the
Netherlands were just waiting for an excuse to destroy
him.

Schreieder had been through an even more worrying
time. He had been held formally responsible for the

escape of five agents from Haaren. Rauter, head of the
SIPO/SD in the Netherlands, had tried to have him indicted
for treason by negligence. The affair had reached Berlin,
and even Hitler was consulted. For several months Schreieder faced the prospect of a concentration camp, and it
was only after much discussion that the decision was taken
not to try him. He was, however, denied all the privileges he
had enjoyed during 'North Pole', including extra personnel, and was no longer allowed access to the captured
agents. They would subsequently be dealt with by the SS.

In April 1944 the SOE men were transported from Assen
to Poland. They included Ter Laak, originally left behind
in Haaren but caught trying to smuggle a message out in a
laundry basket.

By this time Giskes had set to work in Belgium. He had
acquired a new V-man who was providing him with some
fine successes. The new traitor was the infamous Chris
Lindemans, alias 'King Kong', who had started to work for
the Germans after several years of genuine resistance. He
had already presented Giskes with one escape line running
from Belgium to the Spanish border. Now he reported
being in touch with two men who were on their way to
Britain. Giskes, wishing to strengthen 'King Kong's' standing with the British, authorized him to give the two men sets
of identity papers as long as they themselves could provide
the photographs. These were duly obtained and Giskes was
surprised to recognize Van Rietschoten and Van der
Giessen, who had escaped from Haaren five months
before. With 'North Pole' now over, he decided there was
no point in arresting the two. His reward would lie in the
trust SOE would place in Lindemans.

A couple of days before Van Rietschoten and Van der
Giessen were due to leave for Britain, 'King Kong' reported
them both carrying suitcases full of spying materials,
including micro-films. This changed matters. Giskes was
clearly unable to allow this information to fall into British
hands and reluctantly he called in the SIPO to have the two
men arrested. They were returned to Haaren and,
although their interrogations produced almost nothing,
the Germans found enough leads in the suitcases to arrest a
large number of people.

As part of the tougher policies now being pursued by the Nazi hierarchy, orders came through from Berlin that Van Rietschoten and Van der Giessen should be executed forthwith. Officially they would be shot whilst trying to escape. Schreieder tried hard to get the order cancelled, and even the local SIPO did not wish to carry out the executions. But it was all in vain. On 10 June 1944 Ernst May, one of Schreieder's officers, visited both men in their cell and told them frankly what was going to happen. They took the decision calmly, saying that they had expected it and were prepared. All May could do was to leave them a handful of cigarettes. They were shot that evening.

The news of D-Day slowly seeped through to Dourlein and Ubbink in their Brixton cell. Since their imprisonment, Colonel de Bruyne, convinced of their innocence, had been trying his best to get them released. He had contacted the Dutch Government and had even extracted a pledge from Prince Bernhard to put up bail for them. SOE had also finally given him permission to visit the two men in Brixton.

It was a depressing meeting. De Bruyne was unable to tell them anything about how long they might be imprisoned for. Furthermore his plan to rescue the agents from Haaren had been rejected by Gubbins as being too risky. Yet again it seemed to the Dutch that SOE were not really concerned about the men they had sent to the Netherlands.

A week after De Bruyne's visit, his patience was at last rewarded. Dourlein and Ubbink were informed that they would be released the next day. It seemed too good to be true, and they could hardly believe it when they were taken to see Gubbins himself, who offered his sincere apologies for what had happened to them. Both were offered commissions with SOE. Not surprisingly they turned them down, and after this things cooled again.

Dourlein and Ubbink were destined for more humiliation at the hands of officialdom. After a week's leave, Dourlein was informed by the Dutch Naval Minister that the Navy had decided to accept him back, at the rank of corporal. The letter went on to explain that he had been promoted to sergeant only because of his SOE activities and that this now no longer applied. Dourlein could hardly believe it. After all he had been through, he was being demoted at a time when promotions were being handed out left, right and centre, to people who had done nothing.

Ubbink too faced demotion. He was forced to resign his commission and in protest decided to leave the Dutch Navy. Again it was deemed that his rank as lieutenant was due only to his SOE work. Ubbink decided to join the merchant navy. The mission he had volunteered for with such enthusiasm had ended in complete disillusionment and degradation.   Despite their escape, Giskes had managed to have the last laugh. Another less than savoury chapter in SOE's history was over.

During the months of August and September 1944 the Allied armies fought their way from Normandy to the Dutch border. This news reached Lauwers and Jordaan in their cell at Haaren, and it seemed to them, as to the Dutch people as a whole, that their liberation was at hand. On 4 September Radio Orange announced that the British had reached the outskirts of the southern city of Breda. This was not true, but nevertheless it resulted in a mass exodus of Germans and Dutch Nazis from the southern Netherlands, known ever afterwards to the Dutch as *Dolle Dinsdag*, Mad Tuesday. Its effects were noticeable even to Lauwers in his cell as he heard German demolition teams blowing up bridges.

Unfortunately for Lauwers and Jordaan, the Germans had not forgotten them. Later that day they were transferred to Vucht concentration camp and officially handed over to the SS. Lauwers began to fear the worst. Fate seemed to be plucking him from his liberators at the last possible moment. After spending one night in Vucht, the remaining three agents, Lauwers, Jordaan and Van der Reyden, were put on a transport to Germany.

The prisoners were packed eighty at a time into wagons meant for forty and were not given anything to eat or drink. The journey lasted three days, during which the SS shot two people after an escape attempt. Their final destination was Sachsenhausen near Berlin, where they were shaved, de-loused and given concentration camp clothing. The following day they were marched to a nearby labour camp, where their real suffering began.

Jordaan's condition began to deteriorate rapidly and when he disappeared, listed as sick, Lauwers did not expect to see him again. He was wrong. In February 1945 Jordaan returned to the camp, reduced to a walking skeleton but still fighting for his life.

By this stage the Russians had launched their final offensive across Poland and were threatening Berlin. Hitler himself ordered that thousands of political prisoners be transported to areas in southern Germany and Austria.

Jordaan was put on a transport for Mauthausen, where a new kind of Nazi cruelty awaited him and his fellow prisoners. The journey took almost a week. On arrival the SS lined up 400 of the sickest people and made them stand out in the open all night. The temperature was −10°C and the SS guards delighted in spraying their prisoners with cold water. Three SS men amused themselves by axing people to death. Very few survived the night.

Despite his wretched condition, Jordaan had not been included in the 400.

He did not know that Trix Terwindt was also a prisoner in the camp. Despite Schreieder's efforts to have her kept in the Netherlands, she had been sent to Ravensbrück. In a last gesture Schreieder told her guards to treat her well, and he arranged that she should be taken to the camp by taxi. On arrival at their destination the taxi could not be found and she had to walk to Ravensbrück. In a macabre irony the commandant subsequently berated the guards for not having obeyed orders and waited for the taxi. Terwindt was left to wonder whether Schreieder was really as ignorant of what was going on in German concentration camps as he had seemed. After spending some time in Ravensbrück she was transferred to Mauthausen, where her health started to fail her. She could only hope that the Americans would reach the camp before her strength gave out.

The story of the remaining 'North Pole' prisoners is a sad one. They were transported halfway across Europe in cattle-trucks to the Polish town of Rawitcz. They had been classified under the *Nacht und Nebel* decree, and towards the end of August 1944 a strong detachment of SS men arrived to guard them. Forty-seven prisoners were put on a transport for Mauthausen, including forty SOE and MI6 agents, and seven British commandos captured during the raid on St-Nazaire.

Of the eleven agents unaccounted for, no trace has ever been found, and they are still officially listed as missing. These were the MI6 men De Jonge and Orrt and Dutch Section's Bakker, Kist, Macare, Mooy, Overes, Parlevliet, Pouwels, Rouwerd and Van Steen. Attempts made thirty years later by a Dutch Television team to trace these men met with no success. It is, however, known that a number of French Section's agents who were being held at Rawitcz during this period were murdered in Gros Rosen concentration camp, and it is possible that the missing men likewise died there.

Before the war Mauthausen had been a quiet Austrian village, surrounded by very beautiful countryside. Its only distinguishing feature was its granite quarry, which had provided stone for some of the finest buildings in Vienna. After the Anschluss in 1938 this quarry had been taken over by the SS, who decided to build a concentration camp on the site. During the next few years Mauthausen was to become synonymous with death. In 1941 Heydrich designated the camp for those prisoners not worth 're-educating'. Its commandant, Frank Ziereis, was a bloodthirsty sadist. One example of his attitudes will suffice. In 1942 he presented his young son with a pistol as a birthday present, complete with ammunition and forty prisoners as target practice. To his delight his son finally managed to shoot dead all forty. This was the man who would now decide the fate of Dutch Section's agents.

Before Ziereis could have his fun, he had to go through certain formally laid down procedures. The new prisoners were lined up outside the administration block and registered. After this they were given striped camp clothing to wear, including a red triangle indicating them political prisoners. This was merely a formality, for the SS had no intention of allowing them to mix with other prisoners. Ominously they had their registration numbers written on their chests and were then marched off towards the quarry. Its high, steep rock face had been christened 'the wall of parachutists', referring to the hundreds of prisoners who had either been pushed over or jumped over the edge. In 1941 a group of Dutch Jews had been forced over and, much to the amusement of the watching SS men, the last few had jumped holding hands.

The new prisoners were put to work in the quarry and forced to carry heavy granite blocks up a staircase known as 'the staircase of death'. As they struggled up it, they were mercilessly flogged by the guards, who made sure they were on the inside of the path, since it had been known for a prisoner to throw himself into the void, dragging an SS man with him.

Four agents who decided they had had enough and threw down their blocks were quickly driven to the top of the quarry and shot to pieces by a heavy machine-gun. With this the other prisoners' last hopes disappeared and, once it became clear that they were going to be killed anyway, the number of refusals started to rise. More and more were taken up to be shot. After two journeys up the staircase, the SS decided to halt for the day. Nineteen prisoners had been killed and were for the most part completely unidentifiable, the heavy machine-gun bullets having torn their bodies apart. The survivors were left in their cells facing an unpleasant night. All they could hope for was as dignified an end as possible.

The following day the survivors were taken back to the quarry. This time a whole gallery of SS men and their wives had come to watch the forthcoming spectacle. They were to be disappointed. As soon as they reached the quarry, most of the men made it clear that they would not do any work. Together they walked up the staircase towards the machine-guns. A few struggled on, unwilling to give up, but their numbers dwindled quickly and by 8 a.m. on 7 September 1944 all the remaining prisoners were dead.

Their deaths had not gone unnoticed within the camp. Indeed, they left a lasting impression on the longer-term prisoners who had witnessed the massacre. As they watched the bodies being cremated, a Russian prisoner, Iwan Mostowoj, and two Yugoslavs, Velibor Maric and Uros Malinic, decided at great personal risk to remove the ashes of the agents and bury them inside the camp. One day they hoped to be able to tell the world what had happened, in order that these brave men should be properly honoured.

16   Aftermath

When the Americans liberated Mauthausen during the last few days of the war, the scene that met their eyes was truly appalling. Several hundred 'walking skeletons' came out to greet them. Others crawled out of the hospital to witness the moment for which they had waited so long. For a good many it was too late. Between 7 and 10 May 1945 another 2,000 ex-prisoners died as a result of exhaustion or starvation. A week after the Americans had arrived, the death rate was still running at 450 a day. Among all these bodies was that of Han Jordaan who had just failed to live to see the day of liberation. He was twenty-six years old.

Ironically Trix Terwindt was not there to greet the US soldiers. A week before, she had been sent, along with all Mauthausen's female prisoners, to a neutral country, as part of a deal made by Himmler with the Red Cross. She had crossed the Swiss frontier more dead than alive, and for a time her life hung in the balance. She pulled through but her experiences in Ravensbrück and Mauthausen were to scar her for life. At Mauthausen she had been hit in the neck by a grenade fragment, which caused her neck to become deformed, and not until 1976 did surgeons dare to operate. They appear to have been successful. After the war she resumed her work as a stewardess for the Royal Dutch Airlines.

Both Wim Van der Reyden and Huub Lauwers survived their concentration camp experiences. Van der Reyden, who weighed one hundred kg. at the time of his arrest, had been reduced to a mere forty-five when the Russians arrived. On his return to Britain he found that no one seemed to know who he was. Rabagliatti and Van't Sant, the men who had sent him via 'Contact Holland', had long

169

since vanished, as had the possessions he had left behind in Britain. Apparently unwanted, he returned to the Netherlands without even having been debriefed. In late 1945 he married a British girl and joined the merchant navy as a radio operator. In 1947 he accepted a shore job and a year later settled in Norwich to work as an electrician.

After the war Van der Reyden suffered at the hands of a Dutch press keen to unravel the mysteries of the *Englandspiel*. He was accused – by men who had never faced a torture chamber – of having said too much to the Germans, and of handing over his code too quickly. It was conveniently forgotten that he had kept his full security check from the Germans and that because of this their attempt to double-cross MI6 had failed. In 1977 Van der Reyden was still living in Norwich as a school inspector.

Lauwers too was liberated by the advancing Russians, on 26 April 1945. He made his own way back across the Elbe and for a while was suspected of having tuberculosis. This turned out to be a false alarm and in early May 1945 he was flown back to Britain. At this stage he was still convinced that SOE had played a triple-cross. Hundreds of hours of reflection in his many prison cells had entrenched this belief. Nevertheless, such knowledge had not embittered him. He recognized the fact that he had probably been sacrificed to save more lives elsewhere. Such things happened in war-time. However, his initial enthusiasm for a debriefing soon began to evaporate when no one seemed particularly interested in his case. After a while his patience snapped and he left the house where he was being held in order to visit a local pub. On his return he discovered that all hell had been let loose. He was threatened with a court martial and stunned his MI5 interrogator by saying that he would welcome one. He argued that he had spent enough time behind bars and now wanted some freedom of movement. Only now was he told that his case had been subject to an official inquiry in 1944 and that those responsible had been removed from their commands. He was not told what the inquiry's conclusions were but for the first time it became clear to him that Dutch Section had made some serious mistakes.

In August 1945 Lauwers was ordered to report to the Dutch Secret Service, BBO (Bureau Bijzondere Opdrachten), in Utrecht. Before he left he asked the British to hand over the details of his case to the BBO but they neglected to do this. He therefore arrived back in the Netherlands to find himself viewed as the traitor responsible for the death of fifty agents. In fact, Kas De Graaf, the Dutch officer responsible for his case, was convinced he was meeting a man destined for execution. When, at Lauwer's request, De Graaf flew to Britain to collect information about his case, he was told by Major Dobson, still head of Dutch Section, that Lauwers was not a traitor. Dobson confirmed that after his arrest none of Lauwer's messages had contained a security check, adding that this fact had also been noticed by Dutch Section. De Graaf was astonished and asked how this could have happened. Dobson could not tell him.

De Graaf effectively cleared Lauwer's name and offered him a job with the BBO in the Dutch East Indies. This offer was subsequently cancelled when the British decided they wanted to debrief Lauwers again. After this he worked with the BBO in Utrecht until it was disbanded in October 1946. After the war Lauwers became a dentist and maintained close connections with the University of Utrecht. In 1947 he married Wout Teller's widow, whom five years earlier he had managed to save from the Germans.

In later life Lauwers suffered from the effects of his terrible experiences. The accusations that he had been a traitor hit him hard, but despite this he is not a bitter man. Even the rejection of an application for a medal, the Militaire Willemsorder, has not bothered him. He does not consider himself a hero.

Pieter Dourlein was also badly treated after the war. After his petty demotion from sergeant to corporal, he was given the choice of going to America for marine training or taking a flying course as a wireless operator/air gunner. He chose to fly and after completing his training applied for the sergeant's stripes which he had been promised. His request was turned down and he was told he would have to fly for a year before he could be promoted. With the war still raging, his chances of this seemed somewhat small but, a born survivor, he did just that, serving out the war with 320 Squadron. Finally, on 1 January 1946, he was promoted back to his former rank.

After the war Dourlein became very disillusioned with life. He tried to get a job with Dutch Naval Intelligence but was turned down, and gained the impression that he was still not completely trusted. He later admitted that, had he not married a British girl in 1946, his life would have taken a turn for the worse. In 1947, still serving in the Navy, he was posted to the Dutch East Indies. When his commanding officer decided that he had done enough in the war to warrant a medal and told him to apply for one, Dourlein refused, saying he was not going to humiliate himself by asking for one. The matter then became an order. In October 1950 he was awarded the Militaire Willemsorder, fourth class, by Queen Juliana, representing the official rehabilitation he had been waiting for since 1944. In the 1950s he recorded his experiences in a book, *Inside North Pole*, which translated well into English. He continued to serve in the Dutch Navy until 1969, when he was pensioned off and his death in 1976 robbed the Netherlands of one of its greatest war-time heroes.

Ben Ubbink also continued to be haunted by his past. In 1944 he had resigned from the Dutch Navy in order to avoid the humiliation of being demoted, which he was convinced was due to the failure of the Plan for Holland. He served out the rest of the war in the merchant navy. In 1950, after Dourlein had been awarded the Militaire Willemsorder, Ubbink received a letter saying he had been awarded the Bronzen Leeuw, a lesser decoration. Ubbink felt bitter and cheated. The Dutch authorities made it clear that Dourlein's award included his service as an airgunner in the latter stages of the war. Ubbink, who had served on convoys during the same period, was unable to reconcile himself with this and refused to accept the award. It took three years and much diplomatic activity before he was finally persuaded to accept. In common with his surviving comrades, Ubbink suffered in later life from the effects of his war-time experiences. He retired early for health reasons and today cannot get by without a psychiatrist. The nightmares still remain.

These are the only survivors of 'Operation North Pole'. The fifty-four agents who did not live have only one memorial. It is at the bottom of 'the staircase of death' at Mauthausen. It contains the names of the forty Dutchmen and seven Britons who were murdered there. The Russian and two Yugoslavs were traced after the war, and they told where the ashes had been buried. This spot is now marked by a gravestone from the Dutch War Graves Institute. A translation reads simply:

> ON 6 AND 7 SEPTEMBER 1944 IN THIS CAMP
> 40 DUTCH AND 7 BRITISH PARACHUTISTS
> WHO HAD BEEN DROPPED INTO GERMAN OCCUPIED
> TERRITORY WITH A SPECIAL ASSIGNMENT
> WERE PUT TO DEATH BY THE NAZIS.
> THEIR BODIES WERE CREMATED
> IN THE CAMP CREMATORIUM.
> AT THIS SPOT UNDER
> EXTREMELY DANGEROUS CIRCUMSTANCES
> SEVERAL YUGOSLAVIAN
> AND RUSSIAN PRISONERS
> BURIED THE ASHES OF THESE PARACHUTISTS.

The memorial was set up on 7 September 1965 at a ceremony attended by some forty-five relatives of the dead men.

Of the Germans, the SS men responsible for the massacre are mostly dead. The camp commandant, Ziereis, was hunted down after the war by some of his ex-prisoners. He was shot whilst trying to escape and died a few days later from his wounds. Most of his henchmen were tried and hanged after the war, with one notable exception. The former SS man in command of the guards at Mauthausen, Hans Gogl, continued to live quietly in Mauthausen after the war as a clockmaker. In 1964 he was tracked down by Simon Wiesenthal – himself a former inmate of Mauthausen – and brought to trial on a charge of war crimes. Gogl was acquitted by an all-Austrian jury but Wiesenthal, undeterred, continued his research and discovered Gogl's part in the murder of the 'North Pole' agents. In 1978 a second trial took place, during which Gogl claimed not to be able to remember the forty-seven prisoners. He was acquitted a second time, leading Wiesenthal to describe what had happened as not so much a miscarriage of justice as an Austrian phenomenon.

Lieutenant-Colonel Giskes was captured in Belgium in April 1945, flown to Britain and interrogated at some length. When the British had finished with him, he was handed over to the Dutch authorities. Eventually he was declared 'clean' by the Dutch and allowed to return to Germany. His memoirs of the war years are recorded in a book called *London Calling North Pole* which caused quite a stir in Britain when it first appeared. Giskes spent his last years in an old people's home near Munich, where he died in 1977, aged eighty-one, just a few weeks before a Dutch Television team were due to interview him.

Joseph Schreieder was also arrested and interrogated after the war. The Dutch used him as a witness in several post-war trials, although he himself was never prosecuted. On his return to Germany he too wasted no time in recording his experiences. He paid tribute to the courage of the agents who had paid for their capture by him with their lives. The publication of his book enraged Amsterdam. In a symbolic act, eight Dutch journalists obtained a copy, tore it in half and threw both halves through the windows of the publisher who had printed it. Attached was a note saying, 'On behalf of the dead of the *Englandspiel*.' Having done this, the journalists walked down to the local police station, reported what they had done and paid a fine.

After this Schreieder joined the Bavarian Security Police. Ironically his new job led him to work closely for a number of years with his war-time opponent Eric Hazelhoff Roelfzema when the latter was a director of Radio Free Europe which operated from Munich.

Schreieder's former boss, Dr Harster, was less fortunate. In 1947 a Dutch court sentenced him to twelve years imprisonment. In common with most Nazi war criminals he was parolled long before his time was up, in 1953, having served only half his sentence.

For the Dutch traitors who had offered their services to

the Germans it was an entirely different story. George Ridderhof, Giskes' V-man who had infiltrated Lauwers and Taconis' network in early 1942, had continued his life of betrayal in Belgium, providing the Abwehr with a number of useful leads. He was arrested after the war and sentenced to death by a Dutch court. All appeals were turned down and he was executed on 1 March 1947. By this time Chris Lindemanns, alias 'King Kong', had already committed suicide in his cell in Scheveningen. Leo Poos and Martin Slagter, the Dutch policemen who had met the agents at the drop zone for initial debriefing, were both given life imprisonment. Each served eighteen years before being released in 1963.

Anton Van der Waals had a busy time after the war. In 1944 he had murdered two domestic servants so as to take their identities for himself and his newly married wife. Together they lived quietly under these names until April 1945, when Van der Waals was recognized by the British as a traitor and arrested. He was taken to Utrecht, where MI6 decided they could make use of his skills. At the time it was feared that a long-term underground movement would rise in Germany made up of fanatical ex-Nazis. As Van der Waals was well known to the Germans it was felt by the British that he could be used to infiltrate these groups. He was packed off to Berlin with the assurance that, if he co-operated well, the British would see to it that the Dutch courts judged him lightly. Once in Berlin, however, there was little for him to do. The expected Nazi resistance did not materialize and Van der Waals soon got bored and decided to defect across Berlin to see what the Russians could offer him. He soon found that life in the East was even less appealing and returned to the West claiming to know all kinds of information about the Russians. The British were furious and immediately arrested him.

In the meantime the Dutch authorities had been searching high and low for their most wanted traitor. Several enquiries could make no headway and finally the British were asked to help. Having no more use for Van der Waals, the British admitted to holding him and discreetly handed him over to the Dutch. His trial was an extensive affair, lasting a year and a half. Almost inevitably he was found guilty and sentenced to death. He was hanged in January 1950.

After the war the Dutch set up a Parliamentary Commission of Inquiry to investigate the behaviour of the Government in exile and the effectiveness of the various Dutch war-time Secret Services. Dutch newspapers outdid each other in speculation at the results which an investigation of the *Englandspiel* might bring. Some suggested that SOE had deliberately sacrificed its agents in order to feed the Germans false information. Further speculation concerned the possibility of there having been a traitor in London. The name of Seymour Bingham was mentioned, despite the fact that he had joined Dutch Section after Lauwers had been dispatched. These reports were quite unjustified and personally damaging for Bingham, who at one stage was forced to threaten a Dutch intelligence officer with legal action.

Meanwhile, behind closed doors, the Parliamentary Commission was patiently interviewing all the Dutch and German survivors who could shed any light on the matter. In all several hundred people testified. The British refused to allow their officers to be questioned in this way but did let the Commission have 'informal chats' with the men concerned. These were strictly off the record, and no full account of them has ever appeared.

In the end the Commission's findings were an anticlimax. It stated that no evidence had been found to suggest there had been treachery in London or that SOE had deliberately sacrificed some of its agents. Instead the whole affair was due to 'errors of judgement'. Today this is still the official explanation of 'North Pole', otherwise known as *Englandspiel*.

There were and still are, however, many people who feel that the 'errors in judgement' were made by the Commission of Enquiry. Their claims deserve attention. Was the *Englandspiel* part of a British deception plan designed to make the Germans believe there would be an invasion of the Netherlands in 1942 or 1943?

These theories, and the Commission's findings, will be examined in the following chapters.

Part II

17   SOE's Technical Flaws

'Operation North Pole', *Englandspiel* was in essence a radio game, played by both sides to the sounds of morse code. The official view that the whole affair was an unmitigated disaster for SOE due to 'errors of judgement' is strongly supported by analysis of SOE's training, radio, security and coding procedures. As such it offers insight into many of the cardinal sins of intelligence work.

The recruitment and training of Dutch Section's agents were in many ways inadequate. It was undoubtedly difficult to find high-quality agents in the small community of Dutch refugees in Britain, yet by using people who were not suitable to resistance work, SOE was creating weak links which could and did have fatal consequences for the entire organizatioin.

Ernst May, one of Schreieder's interrogators and code specialists, was in a position to observe at least forty of the captured agents under psychological pressure. He maintained later that not all of them had been chosen carefully enough by SOE. Some had been away from the Netherlands for many years and had no current contacts, whilst a few had never even been in the country before. Some wished only to return home, and a good few were opportunists. According to May, there were only a handful of die-hard idealists.

One weakness in the training was that the various courses which the agents completed did not follow on from one another. In the ensuing overlap, the agents were allowed leave in London, where they became a security risk. Accounts abound of how talkative agents could be amongst themselves about the course they had just completed. This lack of security was a major reason why

Dutch Section lost most of its first training group in the rebellion which brought down Laming.

Initially SOE had to rely on MI6 for its communications with its agents but in May 1942 it established its own independent communications network. In so doing it merely duplicated MI6 procedures, so that the early criticisms made of MI6 also apply to SOE.

The training of the all-important radio operators was too short. This was undoubtedly caused by the lack of time available, but again, by sending in half-trained operators, Dutch Section was creating weak links within its networks. Some, such as Lauwers, knew something about the subject but most had to be trained from scratch. They were taught morse code and how to operate their radio sets but remained dangerously slow in tapping out their messages. Time and time again Dutch people would remark at the clumsiness of the early operators who provided the German surveillance units with an easy target. Nor did the agents know anything about the technical side of the equipment they were using. Even a small faulty connection could and did put them out of business.

The radio sets themselves were inadequate. Each radio operator was given a compact radio set which could run off either mains or batteries, although none of the latter was supplied. Each set worked on a crystal which allowed the operator to work on two different wavelengths only. Each operator was subsequently given two crystals, which doubled the number of frequencies available. This was clearly not enough for security, and made things a lot easier for the German surveillance units. Either SOE should have given its agents more crystals or they should have used radio sets which did not operate using crystals. Such sets did exist at the time.

A major weakness of the transmitters used was their inability to reach Britain without the help of a large outside aerial. This inevitably meant a greatly increased risk for the agents in the field faced with this sudden and unexpected problem. It is also worth noting that none of the agents was allowed to test his transmitter in Britain before he left on his missions. Had this been done, it would have been possible, for example, for SOE to rectify the manufacturing fault in Lauwers' set, which lost them two valuable months.

Agents were also constantly told that the Germans did not have the technology to pin-point their transmitters. This was simply not true, and by 1942 there was ample evidence to demonstrate this. Had agents been made aware of this danger, they could have operated far more safely by constantly changing address and moving from area to area. As it was, time and time again German detector-vans were able to close in on the unsuspecting agents and pin-point their exact whereabouts.

In terms of radio procedure, SOE appears even more culpable. Each agent was given a fixed time at which to transmit back to his home station. When one considers that the agent was also limited to only four frequencies, it becomes clear how easy things are made for the Germans. Security demanded that an agent be able to contact SOE at any time, in spite of the added inconvenience. Instead the home station worked on the same frequency with up to thirty different agents. Whenever a new agent came on this frequency, SOE merely changed its call sign, which was pointless since the Germans were well aware that all these call signs were coming from one location somewhere north of London. Yet the agents, who could have benefited from having several different call signs, were given only one.

The time allowed for each transmission was set at no more than ten minutes, but this was far too long. It simply gave the German surveillance teams too much working time, as is evident from events in the early part of the war. Those ten minutes were also badly divided. During that time an agent was expected to transmit his own messages and receive any in return from SOE. If need be – and it frequently *was* necessary – one or both sides would have to repeat part of their messages, thus adding to the time spent on the air, which in practice often exceeded ten minutes.

Finally both agent and home station would have to indicate that they had received their messages. There should have been a set time when the SOE transmitted all its messages to a particular country, so that all the agent had to do was to tune in and take down his own message. To be sure that the messages would reach those they were intended for, they could be repeated at different set times. By adding a serial number to the messages, it would be possible for the agent involved to find out if he had missed a message. Had this system been employed in the first half of the war, it would have effectively more than halved the amount of time the agent had to spend on the air. This system was applied very effectively by the Dutch in the Dutch East Indies, where agents were limited to three or four minutes and forty words. There is no reason why it could not have been applied equally successfully in Western Europe. Moreover, the home station in Britain did not need an outside serial in order to reach its agents.

SOE constantly referred agents to previous messages, which necessitated their keeping a file, a dangerous security risk. There are numerous examples of agents being captured along with their previous messages, which allowed the Germans an important insight into the work that the agent had been doing and could provide them with many leads. Although the nature of the work was such that it was difficult to avoid referring back, this should never have become general practice.

Yet another mistake was that many agents had only one way of communicating with Britain, namely via radio. The more reliable alternative of a code in 'innocent' letters sent to addresses in Switzerland was not given to the agents, although this would have greatly increased the security of the Dutch networks and would almost certainly have made 'North Pole' impossible.

On the security front SOE displayed far more than just a lack of efficiency. There were at least six main ways in which SOE could check on the true identity of the person operating the transmitter at the other end. The first was the posing of test questions where the correct reply for the agent to some 'innocent' question would be a nonsensical answer which had been pre-arranged before the agent left. Secondly, security could be maintained by the inclusion in the messages of certain security and identity checks. Again these had to be pre-arranged. Thirdly, the home station could be reassured by recognition of an agent's morse code 'fingerprint' (a trained operator's style is as distinct as someone's handwriting), and fourthly by recognition of the sound of the radio transmitter itself. The fifth possible check as by using the 'innocent' letter technique of sending a harmless message every few weeks to Switzerland. Finally there was always the option of dropping a 'control' agent unannounced.

It is important to stress that none of these methods was foolproof; each had its own drawbacks. But taken together these methods, if applied properly, would have made 'North Pole' a non-starter.

The test question would probably have been the quickest way to discover whether an agent was in enemy hands or not. A seemingly innocent question such as, 'How are you coping with the pressures of work?' would not rouse much suspicion with a German operator, who would have no way of knowing that the correct answer was 'Red tulips are beautiful.' Most importantly the agent, if captured, need not be under any pressure to hand over the correct reply, and even if he did tell them something, the Germans would have had no way of knowing whether it was correct or not. Of course, if the agent cracked completely, he might well tell all, so that a correct reply could not be taken to mean that everything was still all right, but an incorrect reply would be a strong indication that something was amiss. For some inexplicable reason, SOE made little or no use of the test question until after the *Englandspiel*.

The security option which SOE did rely on heavily was that of the identity check and the security check. The identity check would be uncovered by the Germans the minute they had the agent's code, for it consisted merely of three letters at the start of each transmission. If the Germans had been monitoring the coded messages, it would be a simple matter to discover the agent's identity check.

The early security checks were also far from adequate. Lauwers, for instance, had only to make one spelling mistake in the sixteenth letter, or multiple thereof. In view of the fact that his transmitter was very weak and that atmospheric pressures would cause messages to arrive incomplete and otherwise mutilated, one spelling mistake was clearly not much of a guarantee of an agent's safety. More importantly, it should have been clear that, if the agent's code was captured or forced out of him – and SOE specifically allowed its agents to do this – the security check would be blatantly exposed in the previous messages monitored by the Germans. If an agent had continuously been making a spelling mistake in the twelfth, twenty-fourth or thirty-sixth letter of each message, this would show up clearly under analysis. It was only a bad lapse by Giskes, who failed to check Lauwers' messages properly, which allowed Lauwers to conceal his true check. This simplistic system would have worked properly only had the Germans not been aware of the existence of the security check. Unfortunately they were, not least because Dutch Section had told them in the spring of 1942 to, 'INSTRUCT NEW OPERATOR IN USE OF SECURITY CHECK.'

Security checks were developed during the war as their weaknesses were realized. By 1943 agents were being sent to the Netherlands with two or three different checks but by then the damage had already been done.

The problems regarding security check were compounded by the discrepancy between what the agents were taught about security checks during their training courses and the interpretation made of them by senior officers at Dutch Section. The agents were constantly told that omission of their security check meant that SOE would automatically assume they had been captured. Yet in practice this was simply not the case. When Lauwers omitted his security check, this was instantly noticed by SOE but after some discussion ignored; the same happened when Jordaan omitted his check. When Van Hemert's first message was entirely indecipherable and the following four messages did not contain his security check, Dutch Section not only failed to investigate the matter but used Van Hemert's link to drop another seven agents. It is also known that Dourlein gave the Germans a security check he had stopped using after his training. Again no suspicion was aroused.

The inescapable conclusion is that senior officers at Dutch Section did not consider the security check vital in determining whether their agent was still safe. It was this failure of communication which above all else led to 'North Pole', and a large part of the responsibility for it must be laid fairly at Dutch Section's door.

Analysis of an agent's morse code 'fingerprint' offered SOE a further security measure. Every experienced radio operator develops a distinct way of transmitting, in the same way as people develop their own handwriting. For example, an operator tapping out the letter C (dash,dot, dash,dot) might make the first dash slightly longer than the second. To the expert ear these characteristics stand out a mile. The 'fingerprint' might show itself not in the way the operator taps out his letters but also in the manner in which he adjusts his set before transmitting or warms up for transmission. To make use of this 'fingerprint', a recording of the agent's style should have been made before he left for occupied Europe, to compare it with his messages when they came in. Unfortunately SOE did not bother making any such recordings until 1943, although the technical capacity certainly existed before then. It is true that a well-trained professional operator could fake an agent's 'fingerprint' but it seems unlikely that the five or six German operators who transmitted over the eighteen captured radio lines could fake perfectly and consistently the styles of agents whom they had never even heard transmit because they had been captured immediately on landing.

Recognition of a transmitter's tone was a security measure already much used in the First World War, at sea. Usually a transmitter has its own distinct tone: it can be either high or low pitched, clear or rough sounding. Of course, during 'North Pole' the Germans had the good sense to use the transmitters captured alongside the agents Nevertheless, a check might have revealed something.

There are several examples of letter codes being used by SOE. Lauwers, for instance, was told to send a postcard to Switzerland indicating his safe arrival in the Netherlands. However, this appears to have been the only time he was required to do this. In October the technique was also effectively used by Van Looi about Dessing's attempt to return to Britain via Switzerland. But it does not appear to have been used very often by SOE, and no mention is made by Giskes or Schreieder of newly arrived agents being obliged to confirm their arrival by post to Switzerland. It appears that Dutch Section was satisfied with a radio message from the reception committee.

The advantages of this method of communication seem to have been overlooked. The postal service to Switzerland was reasonably good during the war and interception of 'innocent' letters unlikely. Plausible addresses and characters could have been found, and the agent might have sent a fortnightly postcard. The continuing reception of these cards or letters would provide another strong indication of whether or not the agent was still operating in freedom. The disadvantages, as always, were that, if the Germans discovered the trick, it could be used to mislead in the same way as radio transmitters were. In addition there would be an inevitable time factor involved, which would mean that SOE could never be certain of their agent at any moment. Letters might also get lost or go to the wrong address, so that non-delivery need not mean the agent had been captured. Nevertheless, safeguards could have been built into the system to prevent the Germans misusing it, and it represented a cheap alternative method of checking up on an agent. That Dutch Section never appears to have considered the regular use of letter codes may be regarded as an oversight. Had they been in operation in 1942-3, 'North Pole' would have been inconceivable.

Perhaps the most obvious method available to Dutch Section of checking on its organization in the Netherlands was the deployment of a 'control' agent, someone dropped 'blind' and unannounced who could then check that the agents in the field were still going about their work. Certainly this was the Germans' greatest fear during the entire *Englandspiel*, the one thing they could do little about. Incredibly the first 'control' agent was not dropped by Dutch Section until September 1943, which once more suggests a lack of imagination in those in charge of Dutch Section. Again, the arrival of a 'control' agent every six months would almost certainly have blown 'North Pole'.

Additional checks to maximize security include analysis of an agent's personal characteristics, or his use of language in the messages sent, and this option *was* used by Dutch Section. For example, the decision to continue accepting Lauwers' messages as genuine was made after an analysis of his character which suggested that he was absolutely reliable and would under no circumstances work for the Germans. The weaknesses inherent in this are self-evident, and it should never have been used as more than an additional indicator.

One more point remains inexplicable. Why was no attempt made to check on the co-ordinates of the transmitters in the Netherlands? Had this been done, it would have been obvious that all the messages from the Netherlands were coming from a handful of different places. For instance, agents who were supposed to have been operating in the south were transmitting from the north. This could and should have been noticed.

A further weakness in security was Dutch Section's inexplicable reliance on the reception committee. (None of the agents dropped blind by SOE was captured on landing whereas all those dropped to reception committees before March 1944 were arrested immediately.) A reception committee by its very nature was an enormous security risk: a large number of people had to be informed, thus increasing the chances of infiltration, and all involved had to be out after curfew and be home by morning without being noticed. Nor is it clear what the benefits were supposed to be of being met by a large group of underground workers. A well-briefed agent would have no problem making his way to a contact address, and the fewer people who knew of his presence the better.

As we have seen, in terms of security Dutch Section fell well short of what could reasonably have been done. The gross errors of the *Englandspiel* can be directly traced to these weaknesses in security, and it is indeed hard to understand what Dutch Section did exactly rely on when they assessed the safety of their agents. In fact, the term 'errors of judgement' seems inadequate to describe Dutch Section's security during the *Englandspiel*: a complete lack of understanding, imagination and technical expertise is apparent in the whole affair. Nor does it seem surprising that many Dutchmen have been unable to accept such crass incompetence as being the whole story.

A crucial part of the agent's training concerned coding. From the German point of view, it was essential to obtain an agent's code as soon as possible after his capture. This was best done on the drop zone, when the agent would be carrying his code on him; if the agent had been working for some time, the chances of finding his code were far more problematical. Usually, in this case, the Germans would strike a deal with the agent, promising immunity in return for the whereabouts of the code book. Most agents soon agreed to this, especially as during their training they had been told they could hand over their code if under pressure.

The early codes were based on the 'play fair' and 'double transposition' systems. 'Play fair', which came first, was found to be too easily broken and was phased out by 1942. Its successor was slightly more complicated. The agent chose a particular book in any language based on the Western alphabet. SOE headquarters would have a copy of the book identical down to the same publishing date. The agent would then be given a key set of figures which he would apply to a given page of his book. The system could also work with a poem, such as was used by Lauwers and Alblas. This had the advantage that it could be memorized, and was consequently safer than a book. Its major drawback was that it gave the agent fewer possibilities for his code. Despite being an improvement on the 'play fair' system, 'double transposition' could be broken, as it involved the moving of only two letters. It was later replaced by the so-called 'one-time' pad, a pad which could be destroyed after use. (More details of these code systems can be found in M.R.D. Foot's book *SOE – The Special Operations Executive 1940-46*.) Each Dutch Section agent was sent out with slight variations on these codes which the Germans were soon able to master.

Estimates of the numbers of messages sent by all Dutch Section's 'agents' during 'North Pole' vary between 900 and 4,000. Giskes' estimate of some 1,700 – and he had no reason to lie about this – corresponds closely to that of Brook (head of SOE in Western Europe), who put the number at between 1,000 and 2,000.

These messages could be divided up into four main groups. First there were questions of a personal nature in which the agent asked for certain items, such as boots or money, or if Dutch Section enquired after his health. Second, some messages concerned the success or failure – usually the latter in Dutch Section's case – of assignments or acts of sabotage. The third group was concerned with the planning of operations, such as the notification of the arrival of more agents or weapon drops. Finally there were the messages which related to the intelligence gathered – which was, after all, the agent's main priority.

According to Schreieder, it was noticeable that most messages continued to be sent by Dutch Section via the older-established radio links which had been 'turned' by the Germans in the spring of 1942. Fortunately, from the German point of view, they did not receive too many messages concerning sabotage. The aim of Jambroes's organization was to train an underground army to be activated only when the Allies were close to the Netherlands. A large-scale campaign of sabotage would only hinder this objective. Those orders that the Germans did receive were usually allowed to fail to the extent that fake stories about them would appear in the Dutch press. These continual failures were yet another indication that things were not going well in the Netherlands. Dutch Section failed to take the hint. The military information which Giskes fed to SOE was brought to him by Section IIID of the Abwehr, officially responsible for finding such 'chickenfeed'. This included troop-movements, strengths of local garrisons and coastal defences. Occasionally Giskes would arrange with the commander of the Wehrmacht in the Netherlands that more important information be passed on, and these titbits would be presented to Dutch Section as big *coups*.

However, the Germans' main hope – that they would learn the date of the Allied invasion – was not fulfilled. Clearly they were not expecting to be told the exact time and location of the invasion, but messages to the effect that the Dutch organization should be on standby would provide good indications. In retrospect this does seem to have been a forlorn hope. Not only was 'North Pole' over long before D-Day but an Allied invasion of northern France was unlikely to involve a Dutch underground army, a point which seems to have been lost on the Nazi hierarchy.

None of the messages sent by SOE contained information concerning Allied military intentions, and in this sense the *Englandspiel* proved a failure for the Germans. Dutch Section's incompetence allowed the Germans to penetrate numerous resistance groups, arrest hundreds of suspects and collect tons of weapons and explosives but this had very little effect on the war as a whole.

Of the messages themselves, none survives – officially – on the British side; a few may be hidden away in Foreign Office files. After the war SOE burned all its war-time messages, leaving no evidence of their contents or composition. On the German side, all the messages were likewise destroyed. Those messages in Schreieder's hands were burned on orders from Berlin in September 1944. This was done in Haaren, by May, Schreieder's code specialist, who kept a select few which were subsequently disposed of in April 1945. It was left to the Dutch themselves to provide the handful of surviving messages which are known about and which appear in this book.

All in all, SOE's technical failings provide powerful ammunition for those who are convinced that German successes in the *Englandspiel* were due entirely to 'errors of judgement'. Nevertheless, several other conclusions have been reached by Dutch observers since the war, all with disturbing implications. It is to these allegations that we must now turn.

18   Warnings

The last 'North Pole' agents were dropped in May 1943, and officially several reasons have been given as to why Dutch Section halted its operations after that date.

First, the Dourlein message which had been smuggled out of Haaren arrived in Britain no later than the end of May 1943. It came via two messengers: the secretary of the Dutch industrialist F. Philips, who handed it over to the British Consulate in Switzerland, and an MI6/BI agent, who warned London in late June.

The second reason for the halting of operations was given as the failure of any agent to return from the Netherlands to confirm, in person, what exactly had been achieved. Originally Jambroes was to have returned to Britain after a few months, handing over command to Beukema Toe Water. But, as has been seen, Jambroes did not return, having allegedly been killed in a gun fight with the Germans in November 1942. By the new year Dutch Section were requesting Beukema Toe Water to return to Britain. Toe Water – that is, the Germans using his radio link – flatly refused, claiming he was too important to the organization to be withdrawn. Giskes offered a compromise, asking Dutch Section if they would accept the organization's second-in-command, 'Nicolaas De Wilde' – none other than Van der Waals. It was decided that 'De Wilde' would travel through France on papers which were dropped specially for him. SOE subsequently learned via one of its 'turned' French Section lines of 'De Wilde's' arrest in Paris.

Finally, in June 1943, Beukema Toe Water 'agreed' to return to Britain and proposed to cross the North Sea in a small boat. Dutch Section were kept in suspense for several days, and a massive sea search was launched. When this turned up nothing, Dutch intelligence officers in London were overcome with a sense of frustration. One by one Dutch Section's attempts to have someone return from the Netherlands had been thwarted. The Dutch had long lost any confidence they might have had in Dutch Section. By the summer of 1943 there was absolutely no hard evidence that everything was fine in the Netherlands.

During the late spring of 1943 several worrying messages arrived in Britain. The arrest of the Dutch Socialist leader Koos Vorrink, along with his National Committee, became widely known and led to the suspicion that Van Hemert, who had 'worked' closely with Vorrink, had been betrayed. More details were emerging all the time, and most spoke of a major traitor operating within many Dutch resistance groups.

Two warnings are known to have fallen into the hands of Van der Waals at the last minute. In February 1943 two members of Schreieder's reception committee were drinking in a restaurant with a number of Dutchmen after a successful operation. After consuming a lot of alcohol, the Germans began to boast to their Dutch colleagues about the achievements of their section in capturing dozens of agents along with tons of weapons and explosives. They were overheard by an underground worker who passed the information on to the OD, where it filtered through to Van der Waals. Schreieder was subsequently unable to determine which of his staff had been so careless. The second warning was smuggled out of Haaren in April 1943 and came from the agent J. Kist. This too was intercepted by Van der Waals.

The RAF also played a part in the autumn of 1943 by halting its flights to the Netherlands. The Special Operations Squadron's losses over the Netherlands were five times as high as those in other countries. In fact, the Germans had determined to attack one in three planes, and by September 1943 twelve RAF bombers with eighty-three crewmen had gone missing. Surviving crews reported attacks out of the blue where no night fighters were to be expected, whilst navigators were telling of drop zones suspiciously well lit-up.

These factors all played a role in the halting of SOE operations in the Netherlands during the summer of 1943. More interesting and far more damning are the warnings which Dutch Section received *before* May 1943 and which it either ignored or failed to notice.

The first warning Dutch Section received concerning German penetration of their organization came in March 1942, when Huub Lauwers omitted his security check for the first time. He never used his check again, although his line continued to transmit to SOE right up to March 1944. Why did Dutch Section not react?

Lauwers' missing check *was* instantly noted and brought to the attention of Blizzard and his colleagues. They discussed the matter and decided there was sufficient evidence to suppose that Lauwers was still operating in freedom. What this evidence was is unclear. Lauwers was told by a Dutch Section officer after the war that it was generally recognized that an agent in the field, under enormous psychological pressures, could sometimes do strange things, including forgetting his security check. In fact, in gathering their evidence Dutch Section questioned the Dutch authorities about Lauwers. They were content to hear that here was a young man who would never work for the Germans. This appears to have been the sum of Blizzard's evidence. He could not check Lauwers' 'fingerprint' as no recording of it had been made. Neither could Lauwers be asked any test questions, as he had not been given any. Nor could an 'innocent' letter shed any light on the matter.

Yet Lauwers had always been reliable and very conscientious in the use of his security check, and his very last act before leaving for the Netherlands had been to assure Dutch Section that if he ever omitted his check he would have been arrested. Then suddenly he was off the air for a week, missing three contact times. After an initial transmission in which three messages arrived with his security check, he stopped using his check for good. Even if one instance was not enough for Blizzard, the following *two years'* omission should not have been explained away by the Dutch authorities' assertion that Lauwers would never work for the Germans.

Further evidence of the lack of communication between the training school and Dutch Section's staff officers lies in the fact that during their training all agents were told they could, if need be, transmit for the Germans *as long as they omitted their security check*.

At the very least Lauwers should have been 'quarantined', awaiting further investigation. Instead Dutch Section continued sending him important messages and announcing the dropping of further agents via his line. This decision demonstrates all too clearly the lack of imagination shown by Blizzard throughout this period. It was a mistake MI6 would not have made.

Lauwers' attempts to warn Dutch Section by hiding the warning 'caught' in several messages – including on one occasion in clear language three times in succession – have never been mentioned by SOE. (On the German side Giskes was told that Lauwers had been messing about, and he had him replaced by a German operator.) In view of the statement by SOE's coding expert Leo Marks that all the messages which arrived were recorded in their entirety, this seems strange at first glance.

Relevant here is the testimony of Anthony Cory James and his wife, both of whom worked in SOE's signal section during the war. Cory James stated to a Dutch magazine after the war that he had constantly warned his superiors that all was not well in the Netherlands, until he was told that if he mentioned the matter again he would be drafted into the Army for front-line service.

If Dutch Section's ineptitude was evident in the case of Lauwers, it was even more clearly demonstrated in the second warning it received. In May 1942 Han Jordaan was arrested by the SIPO after a short acquaintance with Van der Waals. Jordaan, like Lauwers, had always conscientiously used his security check until he suddenly went off the air for a short time. When he reappeared, to announce that a new operator had taken over from him, the message did not contain a security check – the first time the check had ever been omitted. At the very least this should have made Dutch Section suspicious. Instead, as has been seen, they sent the damning reply: '*INSTRUCT NEW OPERATOR IN THE USE OF SECURITY CHECK.*'

Major Charles Blizzard and Captain Seymour Bingham had blundered even more badly than in the case of Lauwers. Not only had they ignored the omission of the security check but they had also compromised their only true security link with Jordaan. The best they could have achieved was to remind Jordaan of something he was already well aware of and had been applying regularly and consistently. In the worse scenario they were handing the Germans a radio line and making a mockery of the meaning of security. In addition they also informed the Germans – if they didn't already know (and they had accepted that Jordaan had no security check) – of the system of security checks.

Dutch Section had now ignored two very clear warnings, and both Lauwers and Jordaan continued to be used to send in supplies and agents, with disastrous results.

No less disastrous was Dutch Section's oversight of the third warning it received from the Netherlands. In July 1942 the arrival of a new agent was announced over the Lauwers' link. Gerard Jan Van Hemert was duly dropped and arrested during the night of 23/24 July. He refused to hand over his security check, and his first message did not reach Dutch Section until a month later. On arrival it was found to be completely indecipherable, suggesting that Van Hemert had also succeeded in misleading the Germans concerning his code. His following messages contained no identity check, a fact which was also noted by the signals section and passed on to Dutch Section.

It seems almost as if Blizzard, by this stage, had become allergic to bad news about his Dutch agents. In any event, he chose to ignore this uncomfortable information. Not only was no enquiry set up but a further seven agents were subsequently dispatched to drop zones which had been organized by 'Van Hemert' or his 'contacts'. In addition, 'Van Hemert' was allowed to contact Koos Vorrink, which led to a large part of the Dutch Socialist resistance being destroyed. It is perhaps not surprising that many Dutchmen have been unable to accept this as merely coincidental, yet it is entirely in character with Dutch Section's appalling record of mismanagement.

Between July 1942 and May 1943 Dutch Section appear

to have received up to seven more major warnings that
there was something seriously amiss in the Netherlands.

The first is based on the testimony of Schreieder, who
stated that by July 1942 the Germans were in a position to
decipher the coded messages of the MI6 agent Aart
Alblas. At that time Alblas was still at large, and in one of
his last messages he warned MI6 that Jambroes, dropped
into the Netherlands during the night of 27/28 June, had
failed to contact the OD. It was this warning which led
Schreieder to spare no efforts in having Alblas picked up.
After the war SOE denied ever having received such a
warning from MI6, who in turn denied having received it
from Alblas. There are three main possibilities: that Alblas
did not send the warning; that it did reach MI6, who for
reasons unknown failed to pass it on to SOE, and that SOE
did receive the message and chose to ignore it. The latter
might explain Dutch Section's apparent hesitation for
three months before they sent in the next four agents
destined for the 'Plan for Holland'. The truth must remain
a question of conjecture.

A second possible warning may have reached Dutch
Section in August 1942, for the Dutch resistance worker
J.de Geus in a declaration after the war, claimed to have
sent a warning that a number of radio lines had been
'turned' by the Germans. This warning was supposedly
sent via an OD transmitter, but though De Geus was quite
certain that it had been received in Britain, there is no
independent confirmation of this.

A third possible warning also came in August 1942,
when Mrs Brave-Maks, private secretary to Prince
Bernhard of the Netherlands, handed over a report from
the Dutch to Colonel Brooke Booth of MI5 which stated
that the Dutch did not believe all was well. After the war
this report could not be found, and Mrs Brave-Maks' own
copy also mysteriously disappeared.

A fourth possible warning is reported as having come
from Commander D.W. Child, who returned to Britain in
late 1942 after having been hunted by the Gestapo. He
told MI6 that a number of SOE radio lines had been
'turned' in the Netherlands, although where he obtained
this information is unclear.

The fifth warning emanated from George Dessing, the fifth SOE agent to be sent to the Netherlands and ironically the only early agent apart from Homburg to return safely to Britain. After the war, in a report to the new Dutch Secret Service, BNV, Dessing told how at Christmas 1942 he had sent a warning from Brussels to SOE via Belgian Section concerning his 'meeting' with Andringa in Amsterdam. After he had arrived back in Britain in September 1943, Dessing was told by Bingham that his message the previous Christmas had not been passed on by Belgian Section for six months. This seems very odd in view of the statements made after the war by Maurice Brillouet, a Belgian resistance worker who in late 1942 gave Dessing shelter in his house. Brillouet confirmed that Dessing did send a warning in his own code via a radio link in Brussels. He also stated that his organization, understandably wished to confirm with SOE that Dessing was who he claimed to be. To this end they continually asked for information concerning him at an estimated frequency of twice a week for some two months but never received a reply to any of their queries, although all their other questions were answered, leading to the conclusion that Belgian Section must have received the questions about Dessing.

Given these circumstances, it hardly seems credible that Belgian Section would not have enquired of Dutch Section who this Dessing might be, especially as the possibility existed that he might be a German agent endangering their whole Brussels network. Was this another disquieting piece of information which Dutch Section chose to ignore?

Dessing knew from his brief meeting with Andringa in the café in Amsterdam that something had gone wrong in the Netherlands. Even with only this piece of information it should have proved possible for Dutch Section to work backwards to the conclusion that the entire network was in German hands.

There is more than just circumstantial evidence to suggest that by the beginning of 1943 SOE was warned of what was going on. The sixth possible warning is based on the testimony of Leo Marks, SOE's code specialist. Having become alarmed by the number of messages coming from the Netherlands which did not contain a security check, Marks decided to instigate his own unofficial enquiry. By his own admission he contrived a trick in the coding of messages which the Germans were unaware of. Though reticent about the precise details, Marks concluded that, at the very minimum, a large number of the radio links with the Netherlands were in German hands. He put his findings in a report in which he boldly claimed that in his view all the Dutch links were controlled by the enemy. Marks knew that to get his report to the highest levels he would have to say what he thought very forcefully. Signals section brought the report to the notice of Colin Gubbins, head of SOE, who had a meeting with Marks. According to Marks, Gubbins read the report carefully and 'took it very seriously'. Subsequently he asked Marks not to mention the report to anyone and to go straight back to him if there were any further developments. Marks went on to say that Gubbins did 'everything he humanly possibly could as a result of the report' but declined to say more, giving as his reason the Official Secrets Act. Despite the fact that he had already clearly broken it by speaking about his report and Gubbins' reaction to it.

This may well tally with Major Bingham's statement to the Dutch Parliamentary Inquiry in 1950 that in the spring of 1943 Dutch Section's operations were thoroughly investigated by MI5, who apparently cleared Bingham and his section.

Two important things happened after Marks' meeting with Gubbins. First Blizzard was removed from Dutch Section, to take over as head of Italian Section, and was succeeded by the unfortunate Bingham. Secondly and more disturbingly, Dutch Section sent in another nine agents between March and May 1943. Why? Perhaps MI5's clearance of Dutch Section had led to a false sense of security. It is possible that these agents were sent by radio lines which were still regarded as completely reliable, as Marks by his own admission had no evidence that all the lines were in German hands.

Is it possible that Dutch Section deliberately sacrificed these agents as part of the Double-Cross Committee's campaign, as has been argued by so many Dutchmen?

There is no evidence for this beyond an incredulity concerning the decision not to drop these men 'blind'. But, as has been seen many times before, this ineptitude was characteristic of Dutch Section. The matter will be further discussed in the following chapter.

A seventh possible warning Dutch Section may have received came from Haaren. On about 20 April 1943 Dourlein managed to tap out his warning to the prisoners in the cell below him. This message was, as has been seen, smuggled to Switzerland and handed to the British Consul who in turn passed it on to Britain. This happened on 14 May 1943, as confirmed by Mr Philips' secretary, who had taken the message to Switzerland. After the war he recalled having been told by the British: 'Your message has been received in London and the case is being investigated.' Yet a week later, on 21 May, Dutch Section sent another three agents to drop zones which were at the very least suspect and supposedly under investigation, and which were in fact German-controlled.

In addition to these clear-cut warnings Dutch Section ignored many less specific indications that of problems with its networks in the Netherlands. Why was it that the failure of all sabotage orders was so readily accepted? How was it that, of all the tons of weapons dropped into the Netherlands, none was ever used against the Germans? Why did all Dutch Section's strategic plans in the Netherlands run into such grave difficulties? Why was the fact not questioned that all the drop zones were north of the Rhine and Maas, whereas a good deal of the supplies dropped were destined for the south, thus making it necessary for those who collected them to cross closely guarded bridges to deliver them? Why was no attempt made by SOE to trace the location of Dutch transmitters? Why were all those questions not officially asked? At important moments agents died or went missing, and the list of setbacks continued to dwarf the handful of 'successes'.

It should be stressed that at no time would SOE have been able to learn anything from the Enigma intercepts. All traffic to Berlin went via the more secure SD telex system which the British were never able to crack.

Officially the first sign of a warning came in June 1943 when the OD passed on Dourlein's warning via an MI6/BI link. Dutch Section continued to receive warnings throughout the summer of 1943. In July Trix Terwindt managed to persuade a Dutch guard to smuggle a warning out of Haaren for her, and this message did reach Britain. The first detailed report Dutch Section received about the catastrophe in the Netherlands came in November 1943, when Dourlein and Ubbink arrived in Switzerland and were interviewed by both British and Dutch intelligence officers. By this time Dutch Section had already halted the dropping of weapons and supplies to the Netherlands and were maintaining only a nominal radio contact.

An even more detailed report by Dourlein and Ubbink was received in December 1943, when the two agents arrived in Spain. By then there could be no doubt about what had happened. SOE commissioned its own inquiry into the whole affair, which concluded that 'North Pole' was due entirely to 'errors of judgement'. Not surprisingly this internal report – which of necessity must have been incomplete – has never been made public.

The warnings which Dutch Section are known to have received or were claimed to have received are only those which have come to light after the war, from interviews with survivors and from statements from ex-staff officers involved in the *Englandspiel*. There may well have been many others from those who did not survive the war. It does not seem likely, for instance, that all the captured agents handed over all their security checks. According to Schreieder, they all handed him something but he had no way of knowing whether this was the whole story or not. However, those agents about whom something is known – Lauwers, Jordaan, Van Hemert, Jongelie, Dourlein, Terwindt – all misled the Germans. Only Ubbink was bluffed into handing over his check. In all thirty-four of the agents dispatched possessed codes and security checks. The Germans were naturally forced to conclude that they had all co-operated, as Dutch Section seemed to have no qualms about responding to the transmissions. Given Dutch Section's record, this could well be far from the truth.

In conclusion, it is abundantly clear that there were many warning signs that something had gone horribly wrong in the Netherlands. It does not require a leap of the imagination to suggest that something more sinister was going on behind the scenes. Was Dutch Section part of the Double-Cross Committee, as has been suggested? This possibility will be considered in the following chapter.

19 *Englandspiel* or Germany-Game

'The *Englandspiel* was not a result of "errors of judgement" as the official explanation would have us believe but a deliberate triple-cross played by the British to mislead the Germans.' This is a view widely held by a generation of Dutch journalists and writers since the war. In spite of the fact that the Dutch Parliamentary Inquiry found no evidence to support this allegation, there are still many Dutchmen who are convinced that there was more to the *Englandspiel* than has been officially admitted. To support these theories many wild leaps of imagination have been made, using evidence that is at best circumstantial, at worst patently absurd. By plotting a careful path through this hysteria, it becomes clear that Dutch Section were no more capable of running a successful triple-cross than they were of running ordinary operations in the Netherlands.

The first theory to be looked at is the suggestion that Dutch Section dropped Lauwers and Taconis into the Netherlands to be arrested in order to start a triple-cross. Sitting in his prison cell at Haaren, Lauwers certainly – for a time – suspected this might be the case. But on what evidence?

The agents had their drop zone marked by leaflets, but these were dropped as the official cover for their bomber and it does not seem unreasonable that SOE should wish to drop leaflets on their drop zone in order to mislead anyone who might have glimpsed something.

Secondly, that the men were dropped wearing identical clothing seems to have been a common mistake – all the early radio transmitters, for instance, were hidden in identical suitcases, so this is not in itself evidence of anything suspicious.

The use of silver coins no longer valid currency also appears to have been a genuine mistake by Dutch Section; MI6 is known to have experienced the same problem in late 1941, when several of their agents found similar problems.

The contacts Lauwers and Taconis were given were thought to be unreliable, and at least one turned out to be a Dutch Nazi. However, if SOE had wanted both men picked up by the Germans, why would they have bothered to warn them against this address?

Lauwers' radio set was discovered in the Netherlands to have a faulty connection. This could have been a simple manufacturing problem or could have happened on landing, as radios were frequently damaged. There is no evidence to suggest Dutch Section had deliberately tampered with the set beforehand.

The poor quality of the false papers both men were given was attested to time and time again by the experience of both SOE and MI6 agents in the Netherlands. In the early part of the war all the forging was done by MI6, and it appears that they had genuine problems forging Dutch papers. So again there is no hint of foul play.

The claim that Dutch Section sent Lauwers and Taconis an arms shipment before they were ready for it seems to be a matter of judgement. In the event the agents proved quite capable of arranging the drop zone and the storing of the weapons.

It is clear from all this that there is absolutely no evidence that Lauwers and Taconis were deliberately sacrificed.

A second theory runs along the lines that Dutch Section realized Lauwers had been 'turned' because of the omission of his security check and decided to use him for the purposes of a triple-cross. In support of this is their apparently ignoring the warnings which Lauwers transmitted by radio in the first few months after his capture. This theory, however, has been effectively demolished by probably the most distinguished opponent of the 'conspiracists', the Dutch historian Louis De Jong. Though not doubting that Lauwers *sent* his warnings, De Jong concluded there was no reason to suppose Dutch Section *received* the warnings. Until June 1942 all radio traffic from Western Europe was received by one station, controlled by MI6; after that date SOE set up its own reception station, which essentially duplicated the procedures used by MI6. The messages were recorded mainly by young women whose job it was to write them down in series of five letters – no doubt monotonous work. It is important to understand that they did not read words into these letter sequences, which would explain how, when they saw the letters 'caught', they did not equate them with the word 'caught'. Nor is it surprising that the letters 'ght'and 'cau' at the start and end of the letter sequences were not joined together. Once the MI6 staff had noted down the rows of letters, all attention was focused on the decoding of the message itself and on determining whether the security check was present or not. After this was done, there was no need to look at the original recording again, and indeed only the message itself, with mention of security check, was sent to Dutch Section.

The third warning sent by Lauwers – 'WORKED BY ... JERRY SINCE' was concealed inside the so-called 'jumbled letters' – letters unconnected with the actual message but which preceded it, intended to make things more difficult for the German decipherers. Again the jumbled letter sequences were of no interest to MI6 staff and were likely to be ignored. For instance, 'gwork ... edbym' is not at all an obvious warning; nor is 'pkjer ... rysin ... cewdq'. Nor were these jumbled letter sequences recorded on the reports of the messages sent to Dutch Section, so that neither Blizzard nor Bingham had an opportunity to assess them.

Several further points are made by De Jong. First, though SOE training undoubtedly stressed the importance of the security check, this seems in many cases to have been lost on the staff of the country sections. There are many precedents, especially in French Section, of SOE's assuming agents were still operating in freedom despite the omission of their security checks, often with disastrous results. As has been pointed out before, the omission of Lauwers' security check was noted by Dutch Section and was discussed at several meetings before a decision was taken on the basis that other factors suggested Lauwers was still safe. This was indeed a grave error but SOE made many such mistakes during the war. It is the inability to accept this fact – so inherent within the way SOE operated – that has led many astray into fanciful theorizing.

A good example of this is the 'Grand Deception Theory', which purports to show why SOE needed to play a triple-cross.

The theory runs as follows. The British knew very well how a double-cross should be played. During the first half of the war no fewer than twenty-nine German agents were 'turned' by MI5 in order to feed the Germans with false information. This was done so efficiently that several of the agents received medals from both the Germans and the British.

After Dunkirk, the theory continues, the British had to look to other means of fighting and delaying the Germans until they could build up their armies to take on the Germans in conventional warfare. The waging of an intelligence war was one of the few options open to the British between 1940 and 1942. To this end, all British agents were dropped as potential double-cross candidates. This is not to suppose that any agents were deliberately sacrificed but that, once it had been noticed that an agent was in German hands, he or she could be used to mislead the Germans. Thus when SOE noticed that Lauwers had been captured, this information was passed to the 'Double-Cross Committee' who decided to use Lauwers as a triple-cross candidate. The *Englandspiel* was allowed to develop from there. Accordingly, the Netherlands were seen as a good place for such a triple-cross. The terrain was totally unsuited to a guerrilla campaign, and the country was of only minor importance in the overall scheme of European resistance. Indeed, it was a country where SOE could afford to sacrifice its operations in the interests of a larger deception plan.

As to what this larger deception was, it has been suggested that it was an attempt to keep as many German troops off the Russian Front as possible. At this stage it was considered of vital importance to keep the Russians in the war. One intelligence source has suggested that the deception plan kept an extra 400,000 German troops away from the Eastern Front, whilst Leopold Trepper, a leader of the Communist underground group 'Rote Kapelle' in Germany, estimated this figure at 1·2 million. The author Dennis Wheatley, himself involved in misleading the Germans during the war, is reported to have told Dr Hans Hers (captured along with Lodo Van Hamel in 1940) that the deception plan as such did keep a large number of Germans in the West, guarding beaches in anticipation of an invasion which never came, and that Hers' suggestion that the *Englandspiel* was part of this was 'acceptable, even true'. Hers is also said to have been told by Admiral Bertram Ramsay that a deception plan was played during the years 1942-4 and that the *Englandspiel* was part of it.

In common with the other 'conspiracy' theories about the *Englandspiel*, the Grand Deception theory suffers from one major drawback: there is absolutely no hard evidence for it.

That the British were engaged in a large-scale deception of the Germans is not in doubt, but in an attempt to link the *Englandspiel* with this deception Dutch observers seem to have lost sight of the known facts, which argue strongly for the opposite. For instance, if the *Englandspiel* was part of a deception plan aimed at misleading the Germans, why were so many things done which were not strictly necessary? For example, why were agents told to contact Dutch underground organizations, thus giving away hundreds of loyal resistance workers? Why was it necessary to compromise an MI6 agent, Niermayer, by sending him a message through a Dutch Section network? Why was it necessary to blow so many escape lines, thus losing valuable aircrew?

Even more damning for the conspiracists is the way the *Englandspiel* is known to have developed. By dropping their entire, and vital, second network 'blind', Dutch Section was in no position to control a triple-cross. There would have been too many imponderables, too many potential trip-wires, to sacrifice fifty agents and hope that no official warning would come out of the Netherlands. Furthermore, given Dutch Section's known incompetence, it is inconceivable they *could* have carried out such a triple-cross requiring as it would have extraordinary skill and foresight. Nor, incidentally, did Giskes and Schreieder think much of this proposition when it was put to them during their post-war questioning by the Dutch. Both had naturally considered the possibility many times during the *Englandspiel* but had rejected it after analysis of the way their double-cross had developed.

In 1984 the waters of the *Englandspiel* were further muddied by the former SOE code specialist Leo Marks' statement (already studied on p.197) that in January 1943 his report outlining reasons for believing that a large number of, if not all, SOE's radio links with the Netherlands were in German hands, had been accepted by Sir Colin Gubbins. The question remains as to why, if Gubbins had done 'everything humanly possible' to have the report taken seriously, another nine Dutch Section agents (Arendse, Boogaart, Dourlein Van Uytvanck, Wegener, Rouwerd, De Brey, Mink and Punt) were sent to the Netherlands via these dubious reception committees. Marks' failure to elucidate further has provided the conspiracy theorists with a field day. Did Gubbins authorize the sacrifice of the last nine agents in order to turn the *Englandspiel* around on its axis? Was he prevented by a higher authority from stopping Dutch Section's operations, for some shadowy deception?

There is no evidence in any of the surviving messages in Dutch hands of possible triple-cross material. Nor was Marks' report, by his own admission, conclusive. He had stated that in his view *all* the radio links with the Netherlands were in German hands, but this was an unfounded exaggeration in order to get his report sent to the highest possible level. Gubbins need not have seen it as conclusive.

The solution to this confusion caused by Marks is nothing so dramatic. Gubbins in fact followed standard SOE procedure when doubts arose over certain operations. When he brought in MI5 to analyse the suspect messages, they too could find nothing which pointed to infiltration, as was testified by none other than Major Bingham to the Dutch Parliamentary Inquiry in an informal discussion in 1950. Furthermore it explains why Marks did not go on to explain what exactly Gubbins had done about his report; there was simply no story.

Nevertheless, these facts have not prevented some extraordinary feats of imagination, as people have striven to show why it was necessary for the British to 'sacrifice' fifty agents.

Van der Waals, fighting for his life at his war-crimes trial, suggested that Schreieder had been a British agent, something denied by all sides and not least by an indignant Schreieder himself – 'I would be ashamed to say I had worked for the British.'

Van der Waals' lawyer, Van Starp, put forward an even more fantastic idea, namely that the *Englandspiel* had been intended to destroy the Dutch Resistance, so that Britain could play a dominating role in post-war Europe, claiming that the political Left had been a special target, as witnessed by the destruction of Koos Vorrink's 'National Committee'. Apart from there being absolutely no evidence for this, it should be remembered that the *Englandspiel* took place in the early to middle part of the war, when Britain was still struggling for survival and not in any position to go about betraying resistance movements. The time for large-scale betrayals, according to this theory, would have been the last few months of the war, but by then SOE's aid to the Dutch Resistance was more than ever before.

It has also been suggested that SOE offered up its organization in order to allow MI6 a smoother run. But apart from the lack of evidence, this would have been incredibly counter-productive given the numbers of resistance workers who were inevitably caught up in the net.

These allegations infuriated both former MI6 and SOE officers when they first heard them after the war. Colonel Cordeaux, one-time head of MI6 Dutch Section, expressed a widely felt indignation to the Dutch Parliamentary Inquiry, who promptly published his letter:

Dr Donker [Head of the Enquiry] has been enquiring into one allegation of which I had heard nothing until last Tuesday. It is that both the SOE service and also my own service, the SIS(MI6), were both aware that the SOE service had been penetrated and was controlled by the Germans. It is alleged that we therefore decided in collaboration to continue running the SOE service under those conditions in order that we might form a cloak for the more successful running of the SIS. In other words it is alleged that we agreed jointly to recruit large numbers of the bravest Dutchmen and deliberately sent them out month after month to what we believed was certain torture and death at the hands of the Germans. It is difficult to imagine a more horrible allegation.

Dr Donker said at the beginning of this inquiry that he understood there might be occasions when a secret service was justified in betraying one of its agents to the other side. If this were ever true, it could only be so in a case where the agent was working entirely for financial gain and was quite prepared to betray his employers if it paid him to do so. Such an idea could have no bearing whatsoever on the present case. In addition to the stigma which this allegation casts on the service to which I belonged, I look upon it as a very personal matter in view of the close relations which I had with the Dutch Service during the war. I should like to say therefore in the presence of Dr Donker and Mr Mason that I should like to be informed after the Netherlands Government have studied Dr Donker's report whether or not they completely reject this allegation and also the allegation that the SIS had evidence that the SOE service was controlled by the Germans but for some reason kept that evidence to themselves.

As we now know, in 1950 the Dutch Government did reject this allegation, along with all the other charges put forward by the conspiracy theorists.

No evidence has been produced since the war to change the official British explanation of 'errors of judgement'. Careful analysis of the known facts bears this out. Mistrust of the *Englandspiel* derives merely from the inability of certain people to accept that a British Secret Service could make such elementary blunders. Today we are more aware of the unfortunate fallibility of SOE.

20   A Traitor?

There is one further theory concerning the *Englandspiel* which deserves attention. This is the possibility – much debated in the Netherlands after the war – that there was a traitor in London informing the Abwehr of Dutch Section's operations. In fact, this was a possibility which the Dutch Parliamentary Commission of Inquiry took far more seriously than the proposition that the *Englandspiel* had been part of a triple-cross by the British. It is also a theory which many of Dutch Section's agents in Haaren took to heart. To them, sitting for long periods in their cells with plenty of time to reflect, this was a constant topic of conversation. To a major in Dutch Intelligence after the war, the treachery theory was more than just speculation: Kas De Graaf was convinced there had been a traitor in London. Most of these theories focused on the activities and character of one man, Major Seymour Bingham, one-time head of Dutch Section and a man who played a leading part in operations during the *Englandspiel*.

Seymour Bingham came from an unusual background. The Bingham family had moved to the Netherlands early in the century, though maintaining their British nationality, and he had been called up during the 1914-18 war but too late to see any fighting. After the war he had gone to the United States of America, where he remained until 1933, when he returned to the Netherlands. During the 1930s he had worked as a director for the well-known Dutch firm Brynzeel and only left at the outbreak of the Second World War, when he was called up for a second time. He was transferred to the British Consulate in Amsterdam, where he worked until the German invasion in May 1940, remaining in the Netherlands until the day before the Dutch surrender. During this period he appears to have been working for MI5, for on his return he was employed at the 'Patriotic School', the camp where all refugees arriving from the Continent were screened by the security services.

People who worked with Bingham during this period thought him an odd character but no one ever doubted where his true loyalties lay. Then, towards the middle of 1941, Bingham developed a drinking problem which led to his dismissal from MI5. At this point he was recruited by Laming, Dutch Section's first chief. Bingham overcame his alcoholism and threw himself whole-heartedly into his new job. He worked hard and gave the impression of being completely trustworthy. There was only one drawback: during the next two years he was unable to avoid incurring the dislike of many Dutch officers.

By February 1942 Bingham had been promoted to become second-in-command of Dutch Section under the enigmatic Major Charles Blizzard. A year later, after Blizzard's transfer to Italian Section, he took over command. After the *Englandspiel* had been sorted out – in British eyes – by the official inquiry in early 1944, Bingham was quietly posted to SOE's Far Eastern Section in Australia, where, according to reports, he was equally unsuccessful in his work. Nevertheless, he was never formally blamed for any of the mistakes made during the *Englandspiel*.

The evidence offered against Bingham after the war by various Dutch sources was entirely circumstantial and would never have held up in open court. First it was noted, from the testimony of those agents who survived (Lauwers, Dourlein and Ubbink), that during their interrogations they were asked by the Germans for information regarding all Dutch Section's officers with the sole exception of Bingham. Then the Dutch intelligence officer Kas De Graaf, who seems to have waged a vendetta against Bingham, discovered that SIPO had employed a man called Bingham during the war years. Efforts by the Dutch authorities to track down this particular Bingham met with no success, but led to wild speculation.

These allegations can be conclusively refuted, as indeed

can the suggestion that there was *any* traitor in Dutch Section. Both Giskes and Schreieder went to great lengths after the war to deny they had been assisted by a source in London – something which would have detracted greatly from their own achievements. Schreieder declared that the name of Seymour Bingham was known only to him as an officer who worked for Dutch Section and that it would have been impossible for him to have worked for the Germans without his knowledge. Furthermore, Giskes' final telegram to Dutch Section in March 1944 was addressed to Blizzard, suggesting the Germans were unaware that Bingham had been promoted head a year before. In this respect the reports from surviving agents that they were asked little or nothing about Bingham may be due to loss of memory or mere coincidence; after all, there were more important things to talk about during an interrogation than one of the many officers who had been involved in the dispatch of the agent.

There is absolutely no evidence to suggest that the 'Bingham' who was employed by SIPO in the Netherlands during the war, was Major Seymour Bingham. The Dutch authorities were able to trace quite a number of families called Bingham living in the Netherlands during the war. Nor does it seem likely that Bingham who, if he had been a German agent, must have been in touch with a German courier, would have gone the whole war undetected by MI5, whose known record against German agents in Britain was one hundred per cent.

Had there been a traitor in London, as Schreieder rightly pointed out in 1948, the entire history of the *Englandspiel* would have been different. For example, the evidence is clear and substantiated that at the beginning it was a slow and difficult process for the Germans to track down Dutch Section's agents. This would not have been so had the Germans had a man inside SOE informing them of Dutch Section's operations. Neither Sporre, who was never caught, nor Homburg, who fell foul of a Dutch traitor, seems to have been 'blown' from London, and both Lauwers and Taconis were able to operate in freedom for some five months (November 1941 to March 1942) before falling prey to Dutch traitors. During that time Lauwers was able to transmit many important messages, and Taconis was able to set up the nucleus of a sabotage group, both damaging to the German war effort. And there are further questions which do not fit the known facts. Why were the Germans not aware that Lauwers had not given up his security check and that Van Hemert had likewise failed to hand over his? Perhaps the greatest single blow to the treachery thesis was dealt by the Dutch Parliamentary Inquiry in 1950, which unequivocally cleared Bingham of all the allegations against him.

The charges against Seymour Bingham are totally unfounded and represent a smear on the reputation of a loyal, hard-working British officer. Indeed, it is hard to understand why Bingham should have become such a target, as it was Blizzard who was responsible for most of the *Englandspiel*. Yet, despite his official exoneration, Bingham continued to be hounded by Dutch observers. When Kas De Graaf wrote decisively that there had been a traitor in SOE and that his name began with a B, Bingham threatened him with legal action, after which De Graaf let it be known that he had meant Guy Burgess, the Soviet agent whose own short employment by SOE had been terminated by Gubbins himself.

There remains one further matter to be cleared up. The name of François Van't Sant was often mentioned by German interrogators in order to explain how they knew so much about Dutch Section. Accordingly this strengthened suspicions against Van't Sant, both during and after the war. A lifetime of intrigue had left Queen Wilhelmina's private secretary with a large number of political enemies, and suspicions were not confined to the Dutch. The first head of Dutch Section, Laming, is known to have conducted a 'hate campaign' against Van't Sant, asking any Dutchman who came his way if he had any evidence that Van't Sant was less than trustworthy. Laming did not trust Van't Sant because he was said to have worked for money in World War I and been paid a handsome sum after the war by the British. Eventually Laming became so obsessed with the matter that it led to his downfall.

Nothing was ever found against Van't Sant, and he too

was completely exonerated by the Dutch Parliamentary Inquiry as well as by that great Dutch authority Louis De Jong. That MI6 trusted him there is no doubt, and it was with their blessing that he became head of the first war-time Dutch Intelligence Service. Nor is there the remotest evidence that the early MI6 missions in which he was involved (those of Van Hamel, Zomer, Schrage and Alblas) were betrayed from London.

The search for a traitor to explain why Dutch Section performed so miserably has been emotional and some-times almost hysterical. If such a traitor were to be found, it would offer a simple solution to the *Englandspiel*, but the truth is just as simple. The Germans undoubtedly knew a great deal about Dutch Section, its methods and its operations. They knew because they heard it from the mouths of the agents themselves.

21 Secret Anglo-Dutch Relations

Relations between the various British and Dutch Secret Services during the war followed a very tempestuous course indeed. Essentially they revolved around a series of shadowy personalities.

When the Dutch Government fled to Britain in May 1940, it officially disbanded its pre-war Intelligence Service GS III. In the eyes of most Dutch politicians GS III had fallen badly from grace. It had failed not only to warn of the German invasion but to organize a network of agents who would remain in the Netherlands should the Germans overrun the country. The result was that the Dutch Government in London had no links whatsoever with the Netherlands, and in the heat of the moment it was decided not to employ ex-GS III officers in the new Dutch Intelligence Service, CID.

Ironically, things started well. The relationship between Van't Sant, the first head of CID, and his counterpart, Colonel Euan Rabagliatti, head of MI6 Dutch Section from 1940 to 1942, was excellent. This was not simply due to the desperate war situation leading to minds being concentrated, but because the two men established a good personal rapport. Each respected the other, and their trust was implicit. We are left with Eric Hazelhoff Roelfzema's observation as to how Rabagliatti saw Van't Sant: 'Take Van't Sant. Now when Van't Sant takes you to lunch, do you know what he would really like? He'd really like to sit at separate tables, back to back, and talk through a tube under the carpet.' This was high praise indeed. In short, the men liked each other, a rare occurrence, it seems, for chiefs of intelligence sections.

Van't Sant recognized that CID, which was dependent

on MI6 for virtually everything, would have to take a back seat. CID received copies of messages sent from the Netherlands only in paraphrased form and were not officially informed about security checks. Nevertheless, it was also a subtle ploy by Van't Sant. By accepting second place, he was rewarded by Rabagliatti with far more personal involvement in operations than his successors had had. The fruits of this co-operation were also borne out in the operations conducted during this period. Van Hamel's mission, despite his capture, may be regarded as a great success, and both Zomer and Schrage did good work. Alblas, dropped in July 1941, proved to be the most effective agent of all, working for over a year. And later on, Hazelhoff Roelfzema's 'Contact Holland' was to produce some of the most spectacular undercover operations of the war.

The honeymoon period between MI6 and CID came to an end on 14 August 1941, when Van't Sant was forced to resign his position as head of CID.

In stark contrast to this happy co-existence, relations between SOE Dutch Section and CID were awful. Although Laming and Van't Sant had no official working relationship, there existed between them an enmity which became worse as time went on. Laming mistrusted Van't Sant and spread the story that MI6 had paid the Dutchman a large sum of money for his services in World War I. That this did not endear Van't Sant to his colleagues in the Dutch Government needs no comment, nor incidentally did it improve Laming's standing with MI6. Laming further antagonized the CID by refusing to inform the Dutch of his section's operations in the Netherlands in 1941 and he continued his attempts to discredit Van't Sant. Finally the feud reached such a state that the Dutch Prime Minister, Gerbrandy, was forced to ask Churchill to move Laming for the sake of relations between the two countries. Laming was transferred to the Middle East in February 1942 and succeeded by Blizzard. However, if the Dutch were hoping for more involvement with SOE, they were to be disappointed: Blizzard would prove even less forthcoming than Laming.

Van't Sant's successor at CID was a Dutch marine

captain, Derksema. He immediately annoyed MI6 by presenting them with a list of demands for a more equal status for the CID. The Dutch wanted to be informed of all the agents being sent to the Netherlands and more of a say in actual operations. MI6 did not share Derksema's vision of a new working arrangement and quietly ridiculed the Dutch for appointing a captain to command their Secret Intelligence Service. Rabagliatti in particular found it difficult to work with Derksema, and the earlier rapport completely disappeared. A major stumbling-block was MI6's refusal to send an agent to the Netherlands to undertake political work for the Dutch Government. The British claimed they were interested only in military intelligence and were not prepared to waste a valuable agent on something they regarded as almost irrelevant. It was an attitude which infuriated the Dutch Government, who needed political information to help form their policies.

Further difficulties arose over the Van der Reyden affair. As has been seen, Wim Van der Reyden had been recruited by MI6 in early 1942 with the consent of the Dutch Prime Minister. Somewhat pointedly, Derksema was informed only at the last moment. It then appeared that CID had records showing that Van der Reyden had been a member of the Dutch Nazi Party in the 1930s. Derksema informed MI6, who in effect told him to mind his own business. When Derksema again enquired about Van der Reyden, he was told that he had already been sent to the Netherlands. Acrimonious letters were exchanged and relations hit a new low. It was clear to the Dutch Government that something would have to be done, and in February 1942 Derksema was relieved of his command of CID, to be replaced by Colonel De Bruyne. He left an embittered man. Nor did relations improve with De Bruyne's appointment, for with the 'Contact Holland' affair on the horizon, things were about to go from bad to worse.

'Contact Holland' had been the initiative of Bob van der Stok (later to escape through the tunnel 'Harry' from Stalag Luft III in March 1944, one of only three out of fifty who made it back to Britain). Van der Stok, a pre-war fighter pilot, arrived in Britain in July 1941 along with Eric Hazelhoff Roelfzema and Pieter Tazelaar. Together they had contacted MI6 and laid out their plans. These involved the creation of a sea route to the Netherlands via parts of the coast which they knew well. At this stage Van der Stok, disillusioned by the bureaucratic wranglings necessary to get the operation set up, opted out and decided to join the RAF. Hazelhoff Roelfzema persisted and in effect became the operational commander. The first operations of 'Contact Holland' were carried out in October 1941 and, after some initial difficulties, seven agents were eventually put ashore. The operations were carried out at night from MTBs, and Hazelhoff Roelfzema personally took the agents ashore. (A full account of these feats can be found in his book *Soldier of Orange*.)

Behind the scenes, the strings of 'Contact Holland' were pulled by MI6 and Van't Sant, whose interest was unofficial as he no longer had any formal connection with the intelligence services. The relationship between the latter and Hazelhoff Roelfzema was excellent. This happy state of affairs was now undone by the intervention of De Bruyne.

The new head of CID considered that, as Hazelhoff Roelfzema was technically a CID officer (he was appointed liaison between MI6 and CID), 'Contact Holland' should come under his direct control. In addition De Bruyne harboured a number of strongly held resentments against MI6. It annoyed him that Colonel Rabagliatti continued to maintain contacts with Van't Sant behind CID's back; this was, of course, very bad manners. He was also dissatisfied with the secondary role the Dutch were being given by MI6 and, on a personal level, despised Rabagliatti, whom he saw as dishonest and devious. Soon De Bruyne became convinced that MI6 were deliberately delaying the arrival of messages on his desk from the Netherlands.

On 12 April 1942 the MI6 agent Pieter Tazelaar returned to Britain after the failure of his 'Contact Holland' mission – when he had been left without a radio transmitter. He was accompanied by the twenty-one-year-old Dutch resistance leader Gerard Dogger, whose arrival had been eagerly awaited by the Dutch Government in

London. Both men had a lot to say about the situation in the Netherlands, and De Bruyne had given Hazelhoff Roelfzema strict instructions that the two of them should be brought to him before anyone else for debriefing. MI6, however, were keen to speak to the two men first and persuaded Hazelhoff Roelfzema, who was in an impossible position, to take the men to see Queen Wilhelmina. It was only two days later that both were finally taken to see De Bruyne, who furiously sacked Hazelhoff Roelfzema for his pains and threatened him with a court martial.

The battle between De Bruyne and Rabagliatti was continued by both from behind their typewriters. Each sent a series of letters to the other and to their superiors. De Bruyne requested that MI6 should not use Hazelhoff Roelfzema for further operations. Rabagliatti not only refused but wrote to De Bruyne in early May 1942 saying that in his view Hazelhoff Roelfzema was the officer best suited to lead future operations in 'Contact Holland'. To this end he had received official permission from the Dutch Prime Minister, Gerbrandy, to employ Roelfzema. This calculated snub was the final straw for De Bruyne, and the same day he handed in his resignation as head of CID.

About this time 'Contact Holland' also came to an end. One of the men put ashore by Hazelhoff Roelfzema was captured and told the Germans enough to enable them to ambush the following operation. Hazelhoff Roelfzema's MTB found itself surrounded by German motor boats and – while Roelfzema characteristically went to sleep below decks – had the greatest difficulties in extracting itself.

CID slumbered on until it was officially disbanded in November 1942. De Bruyne had been succeeded by Warners but neither MI6 nor SOE approved of him and the Dutch Government were discreetly informed. Around this time it also dawned on MI6 that Rabagliatti, having driven two heads of CID to resign, might not be the most suitable choice to deal with the Dutch. He was quietly transferred.

The Dutch answer to SOE was set up in December 1941 and called Bureau Voorbereiding Terugkeer (Bureau for the Preparation of the Return). Its commander was none other than Colonel De Bruyne who for a while had combined the command of both Dutch Secret Services. In early 1942 BVT met representatives of SOE Dutch Section to discuss the question of co-operation. SOE, like MI6, would not hear of equal status and insisted on having overall control. As before, the British only required the Dutch to recruit reliable agents and help evaluate important information. In protest the Dutch Government instructed De Bruyne not to supply SOE with any agents for the purposes of sabotage. Those supplied were to be used only for the 'Plan for Holland'. After several further meetings SOE agreed to compromise, to the extent of allowing De Bruyne to discuss operations and to receive, in paraphrased form, the messages sent from the Netherlands. There was no mention of security and identity checks; security would remain firmly in British hands.

Having come to terms, Dutch Section and De Bruyne set about working out the 'Plan for Holland', based on information from Gerard Dogger's report, made in February 1942, in which he described the OD's work in some detail. The basic plan was to contact the OD and, with its help, train an underground army.

The relationship between BVT (renamed MVT in July 1942) and SOE remained distinctly cool. The Dutch could contact the then head of Dutch Section, Blizzard, only via a War Office telephone number, and he rarely appeared elsewhere. In fact, De Bruyne was the only Dutchman allowed access to his office at all. Lieftinck, second-in-command at MVT, did not even know where Blizzard's office was.

It soon became clear to the Dutch that, despite the so-called concessions they had wrung out of SOE, they were still regarded as little more than a recruiting agency. In fact, Dutch Section's attitude was such that one can hardly talk of co-operation. De Bruyne was informed of an agent's impending departure only a couple of days before the drop, leaving him with no time to study that agent's orders and make objections to anything he might not like.

How did this failure of communication affect the *Englandspiel*? It is easy to speculate. The Dutch might well have been more security conscious, given that their own nationals' lives were at risk. They would undoubtedly have been more aware of the problems in the Netherlands that an agent would face. They would have been more aware of an agent's likely reactions, the way he would see a problem and deal with it. They would also have had an advantage over Dutch Section in the analysis of information coming in from the Netherlands and in the collection of safe addresses. In short, who better to understand the Netherlands and the 'national psyche' than the Dutch? Dutch Section's arrogance led it into areas better understood by others. Had these potential advantages not been ignored, the *Englandspiel* might well have been avoided.

Blizzard's departure in February 1943 led to a thaw in relations. Seymour Bingham was much more approachable to the Dutch and even shared a flat with Lieftinck. However, these improvements did not extend beyond the personal level. The ice did not melt sufficiently to change things at an operational level. Until March 1944 MVT remained very definitely Dutch Section's understudy.

In the aftermath of the *Englandspiel* MVT was disbanded in March 1944, tainted with a failure for which it could hardly be held responsible. It was replaced by the Bureau Bijzondere Opdrachten, BBO, (Bureau for Special Missions) which continued with MVT's brief. The creation of the BBO also saw the official rehabilitation of former GS III employees, including its commander, General Van Oorschot. His firm dealings with the Dutch Section led to a better period of Anglo-Dutch relations. By that time, too, there was a precedent for true co-operation.

BI, the Bureau Inlichtingen (Bureau for Information), successor to CID, had managed in November 1942 to obtain an almost equal footing with MI6. The matter had been discussed with Churchill himself, and the Dutch had succeeded in holding out for conditions which would have been unthinkable two years before. The BI was allowed to brief agents with their own missions, separate from anything MI6 might give them to do. In addition MI6 undertook not to maintain contacts in the Netherlands without informing the BI and would in future employ only officers who had lived in the Netherlands and who understood the Dutch way of thinking. The advantages of this were obvious. The agents themselves spoke in general little or no English; now they could be briefed in a way and a language they understood. The Dutch were also able to supply these agents with their own security checks, usually in the form of test questions which, had they been efficiently used by SOE Dutch Section, would have made 'North Pole' impossible.

MI6, for its part, retained control of training, transport and radio communications. The codes were also kept from the Dutch, though they did receive copies of the original messages and could ask whether the security checks were present.

Relations between MI6 and BI at a personal level were also good, and this was reflected in the results achieved. In total forty-three MI6/BI agents were dispatched between the summer of 1943 and the end of the war, of whom about half were still operating when the Netherlands were finally liberated. It was one of these agents who sent the first official warning about the *Englandspiel* in June 1943.

With this precedent to follow, Dutch Section was able to make a better showing in its dealings with the BBO. SOE, humbled by the disaster in the Netherlands, about which the Dutch were understandably very angry, were in no position to resist Dutch demands for more say in actual operations. The final conditions closely resembled those under which MI6/BI operated: Dutch officers were allowed to monitor training courses and were informed of the precise orders given to the agents; furthermore, all messages received from the Netherlands were passed on in their entirety, including mention of security checks.

Although there were still many disagreements ahead, the basis of this agreement was such that Dutch Section was able to achieve the results it had so disastrously failed to achieve earlier in the war. Between March 1944 and May 1945 about a hundred SOE/BBO agents were dropped into the Netherlands, of whom some ninety per cent arrived safely, along with large quantities of arms and explosives.

By September 1944 things had progressed to the stage where joint meetings were being held by all four Secret

Services involved in the Netherlands – MI6, BI, SOE and BBO – in order to try to co-ordinate activities.

The earlier problems experienced by both CID and BVT/MVT with their British counterparts stemmed from British reluctance to trust the Dutch. At the time there was no certainty that all German agents in Britain had been rounded up, and the Dutch were likely candidates for German penetration. Despite the excellent relations between Churchill and Queen Wilhelmina, little was done in the first part of the war to remedy this situation. It is entirely understandable that the Dutch were annoyed – in the same way as General de Gaulle was annoyed – that the British should conduct operations in their respective countries behind their backs. In the Dutch case there was the added ignominy that the British were withholding information from an *official* Government in exile, a status de Gaulle could not legally claim.

The early years were also marred by a series of personality clashes. Neither Derksema or De Bruyne could adapt himself to Rabagliatti's methods. The latter was not given to straight dealing and was a product of a professional Secret Service. De Bruyne and Derksema were not. Both were Dutch marines, trained to fight a straightforward battle, in which orders were unquestionably obeyed and contracts kept. As such they were probably unsuited to the running of a wartime Secret Service. Nevertheless they were infinitely preferable to the men who ran Dutch Section.

Had SOE co-operated with the Dutch in 1942, as they were forced to in 1944, the *Englandspiel* might well have been avoided. The suspicion remains that, had the Dutch been told that Lauwers' or Jordaan's or Van Hemert's security checks were missing, they would have drawn the obvious conclusions.

22 Reactions to the *Englandspiel*

During the first post-war years the legacy of the *Englandspiel* was felt most in the Netherlands. Whilst the Dutch Parliamentary Inquiry busied itself questioning all the survivors it could find, the press had a field day trying to pre-empt its conclusions. Most of the speculation involved a conspiracy theory of some sort, in which a number of agents had been deliberately sacrificed for a variety of reasons. The evidence was at best fragmentary and depended on leaks from individuals with some connection with the *Englandspiel* and from the many war-crime trials being held. At worst these theories were twisted to settle old vendettas – for example, one distinguished Dutch author claimed that Major Bingham had been a sadistic homosexual who enjoyed the idea of sending young men to their deaths.

Fortunately for posterity, the Parliamentary Inquiry conducted a very thorough investigation, refusing to be intimidated by wild stories in the newspapers. Officially its brief was to examine the conduct of the Dutch Government in exile, and as such the *Englandspiel* was only part of its investigation. Nevertheless, it took up a significant amount of the Commission's time. Between 18 May 1948 and 30 May 1950 some 224 people were questioned under oath, including all the leading participants who had survived on the Dutch and German sides. These interviews produced several thousand pages of transcripts and represent a gold-mine to the modern historian.

There was only one major omission, and that was sadly unavoidable. The only British officer officially questioned was Major Laming, and then only to explain the intricacies of the Official Secrets Act. Unofficially the Commission was invited to talk, off the record, to some former SOE and MI6 officers and would add to British discomfort by publishing a résumé of what these men said. That the press speculation in the Netherlands had proved a severe embarrassment to the British Government there is no doubt. This was witnessed by the statement the Foreign Office produced on 14 December 1949 – a seriously flawed document, as we shall see.

When the Inquiry finally published its findings in late 1950, its conclusions were almost inevitably an anticlimax. There had been no treachery, no conspiracy; no one had been a sadistic homosexual or had deliberately kept quiet about the matter. The main conclusion was that the whole affair had been due to 'errors of judgement' and that no serious evidence existed for any other possibility.   An interesting by-product of the final report was the evidence it provided, proving that the Foreign Office statement had been at best inaccurate and misleading. This warrants closer consideration.

STATEMENT FROM THE FOREIGN OFFICE FOR DR DONKER CHAIRMAN OF THE NETHERLANDS PARLIAMENTARY COMMISSION OF INQUIRY

1. During the last year enquiries have been received relating to the evidence put before the Netherlands Tribunal concerning the conduct of clandestine operations in Holland and the German penetration of resistance movements. The Foreign Office has, of course, no standing in relation to the tribunal. However, certain allegations have appeared in the Netherlands press and elsewhere, to the effect that the British military authorities, in so far as they were responsible for the conduct of these operations, had other ends in view than those which they declared to the Netherlands authorities. There is not a shred of truth in these allegations: in organizing sabotage in the Netherlands, and in supporting the Netherlands Resistance Movement, the British authorities were guided by one consideration only – to attack the enemy in those areas where the Allied forces were not in contact with the German army. In implementing this policy, with which the Netherlands Government in exile were in complete

agreement, the British authorities received the whole-hearted collaboration of the Netherlands authorities, and the devoted services of many gallant Dutchmen.

2. The suggestion that the British authorities departed from the objectives which they had agreed with their Dutch colleagues and in particular, the suggestion that the lives of Dutch patriots were deliberately sacrificed in the interest of other objectives in the Netherlands or elsewhere, are both repugnant to His Majesty's Government and the British people, and are entirely lacking in foundation. In order, therefore, to correct any false impression which the above mentioned allegations may have created, the Foreign Office wishes to place certain facts before the commission.

3. The organization concerned with all these matters in the United Kingdom was disbanded immediately after the war, and the bulk of its records destroyed: this has necessarily put serious obstacles in the way of the Inquiry. It is of particular importance to note that the actual wireless messages to and from the Netherlands dealing with the day to day conduct of the operations were destroyed with the other records. It is impossible now to give the exact number of these messages, but, bearing in mind that similar operations were taking place in other territories occupied by the enemy, there could not have been fewer than several hundred thousand of them.[1] However, it has been possible to check certain of the relevant dates, and the following facts emerge.

4. The resistance activities were regarded and conducted by both sides as joint operations based in the United Kingdom.[2]

5. Communications to and from the United Kingdom were naturally controlled by His Majesty's Government. This was the normal rule, although its rigidity was, to a certain extent, relaxed as the war developed.

6. At a crucial stage in the penetration of the SOE/MID[3] operations, that is, in March 1942, when the messages from the agent Lauwers, alias Ebenezer, began to arrive without the proper security checks,[4] the senior Netherlands officer, then Colonel De Bruyne, was not in a position to check the

texts of the signals received and dispatched.

7. The enquiry conducted at the time in Great Britain was necessarily incomplete because no evidence on the German side was then available. But it conclusively established that the original penetration was due solely to the operations of the German Counter-Intelligence; and that these produced a chain reaction owing to the system of reception committees, which were jointly considered necessary owing to conditions in Holland, especially in view of the highly restricted dropping areas.

8. The most important result of the penetration of these operations was that, as it took place at an early stage it led to complete German control. An important contributary cause of the penetration, and particularly of its continuance was that the omission of the security checks by certain W/T operators was ignored.

9. Investigations were held at various periods after the original penetration had begun, but in each case a decision was taken to continue the operations. These decisions were reached after taking into consideration the personalities and characters of the agents, and with the knowledge that the security checks had been proved to be inconclusive as a test.

10. It was later realized that the decision to continue the operation was mistaken.

11. The controlling headquarters in London were not unaware of these reasons, and made repeated efforts to obtain a cross-check from inside Holland, and to discover indications of enemy control in the messages received. All these efforts proved abortive.

12. At the crucial date which, as mentioned above, was disastrously early in the proceedings, Major Bingham was not in charge of the British side of the section and was not in a position to decide the policy. He himself was opposed to the system of reception committees, and as soon as he took charge (in March 1943) insisted on doing away with it, and adopted the more secure system of the 'blind drop'.[5] Major Bingham was also responsible for ensuring that Dutch officers should be able to examine actual texts of

telegrams where appropriate.

13. The various and searching enquiries held by His Majesty's Government into the failure of SOE operations in the Netherlands during 1942 and 1943, leaving aside such errors of judgement as may have occurred in the course of their conduct, have not revealed the slightest grounds for believing that there was treachery either on the British or on the Netherlands side.

14. The allegation that the British intelligence agents, about whose existence and activities the Netherlands authorities were unaware, were employed in the Netherlands, is completely without foundation.

15. For reasons of elementary security, the organizations in the field controlled respectively by SOE whose function was to organize sabotage and resistance, and by the intelligence service, whose function was restricted to the acquisition of intelligence, were kept entirely separate. Hence it follows that there was no collaboration between the headquarters of these organizations in the operational sphere[6] and only occasional collaboration in intelligence matters as was necessary to ensure that each received information of direct interest to itself. When the intelligence service received information that SOE/MID operations had been penetrated, SOE headquarters were immediately notified. Such information was not, however, received until May, 1943.[7]

16. It is the wish of His Majesty's Government that no facts should be concealed which could assist the commission in their enquiries. The Foreign Office, therefore, invited the British officers whose names appear below and who had been responsible for the conduct of clandestine operations in the Netherlands during the war, to meet the chairman of the commission in their capacity of private individuals and to discuss the subject with him. They accepted the invitation, and a series of conversations took place in London from the 3rd to the 10th October. These officers were invited to answer with complete frankness any questions put to them. They were, of course under no obligation either to appear at all, or make any statements or to answer any questions.

Mr Laming (SOE)
Major-General Sir Colin Gubbins (SOE)
Brigadier Mockler-Ferryman (SOE)
Colonel Brook (SOE)
Colonel Cordeaux (Intelligence Service)
Mr Senter (SOE)
Mr Miller (SOE)
Mr Seymour (Intelligence Service)
Mr Bingham (SOE)
Colonel Rabagliatti (Intelligence Service)[8]

There is no need here to recapitulate these conversations, or which the salient points are at the disposal of the commission.

Author's notes on the text of the Statement

1. This is misleading. The number of those messages relating to the *Englandspiel* was between 1,000 and 2,000. The correct figure is probably about 1,700.
2. This is misleading. Until 1944 the Dutch had no real say in SOE operations. To talk of joint operations and to suggest the Dutch regarded these operations as jointly carried out belies the facts.
3. MID was a subsection of the MVT and as such did not send any agents to the Netherlands. SOE co-operated with MVT as a whole.
4. Lauwers had only one security check.
5. This is simply not true. Major Bingham did take over in March 1943 but did not adopt a policy of 'blind drops'. The last nine agents were all sent by Bingham to pre-arranged reception committees. Not until September 1943 was the first Dutch Section agent dropped blind under Bingham's command.
6. This was not true, as the case of Van der Giessen shows. SOE sent him to the Netherlands with new papers and money for the MI6 agent Niermayer.
7. It is unclear as to when precisely in May this information

was received. On 21 May Dutch Section sent another three agents into the Netherlands. If the warning arrived before that date, it suggests more incompetence.

8. This list is noticeable for its omission of Major Charles Blizzard, former head of Dutch Section for most of the *Englandspiel* and undoubtedly the man who could have told the commission most about operations in the Netherlands. Apparently Blizzard declined to talk about his role.

The publication of the Dutch Parliamentary Inquiry in 1950 caused little stir in Britain, though no doubt the Government were relieved at its conclusions. However, the affair refused to die completely and in 1953 a new controversy arose with the publication in English of Giskes' book, entitled *London Calling North Pole*. The account, written from Giskes' own experiences, seemed to suggest that Lauwers had co-operated willingly with the Abwehr; this was, after all, how it had appeared to Giskes. Lauwers himself added an afterword, mentioning that he had left out his security checks and had inserted several warnings into his messages.

The matter was taken up by Arthur Lewis MP who during February and March 1953 plied the Foreign Secretary with requests for information. Lauwers suffered the indignity of being accused in the House of Commons of treachery by Lewis, who had either failed to read Lauwers' postscript or did not believe it. It was left to Anthony Eden to clear Lauwers' name. Lewis then insisted on an enquiry by Select Committee, which the Government refused to allow. Thus rebuffed, Lewis's next ploy was to ask if the Foreign Secretary would meet a deputation, consisting of himself, a representative of the Dutch underground and the publisher Mr Kimber. The answer was an unequivocal no.

Despite these setbacks, Lewis refused to give up. In a written question on 13 February 1953 he asked for a list giving the official positions of a number of MI6 officers during the *Englandspiel* and for a report on conversations between British officers and the Dutch Inquiry. Again the Foreign Office refused to comply, but it did compromise to the extent of placing a copy of the statement given to the Dutch in 1949 in the House of Commons library. This did not satisfy Lewis, who continued with his questions. The Government's irritation became more and more evident, and no doubt they were relieved when, in March 1953, Lewis turned his mind to other matters. The only official questioning about the *Englandspiel* in the Commons had come to an end.

Later in 1953, a further book was added to the growing literature on the subject when Dourlein published his war-time memoirs. It proved far less contentious than *London Calling North Pole* and did not reveal anything new, at least as far as the Dutch were concerned. The first British account of the *Englandspiel* appeared in 1958, when E.H. Cookridge included a chapter on the subject in his book *Inside SOE*.

In 1967 the Dutch historian Louis De Jong, having seen that the British Government had allowed M.R.D. Foot to write an official history of SOE in France, applied to do likewise, using Dutch Section's records. Unfortunately a legal action brought against Foot's book had dampened the Government's enthusiasm for more revelations, and De Jong's request was turned down.

De Jong himself had spent the war in London before returning to the Netherlands in 1945, the sole survivor of his family. During the following years he dedicated his life's work to recording the entire history of the Netherlands in World War II, and in 1977 he decided to try again to record Dutch Section's work. This time the British Government was more forthcoming. Though still denying De Jong access to the files, it invited him to send a list of questions which would be answered as far as was possible. In November 1978 De Jong travelled to London to have talks with the former SOE officer Colonel Boxshall about Dutch Section's surviving papers. According to Boxshall, Dutch Section had failed to maintain a proper war diary, and very few files on the agents themselves seemed to have survived. In 1945 the Section had written an official history but this had been before the interrogations of Giskes and Schreieder and was therefore incomplete. The files had, in fact, been so poorly kept that it had been impossible to say anything about Dutch Section's operations in the official SOE history. One surviving memo had characterized the fragmentary files as a 'nightmarish mess'. Time has clearly done little to improve Dutch Section's reputation.

Interest in the *Englandspiel* was briefly rekindled in 1984, after a BBC documentary series about SOE. One of the episodes was devoted entirely to the Netherlands and presented testimony from Leo Marks in which he told of his role in unmasking the *Englandspiel*. This led to several newspaper articles and a few indignant letters to *The Times* but, as always, the matter petered out.

With time, as the war years recede, the issue of the *Englandspiel* becomes less emotional and controversial. One day, perhaps, the few surviving files will be released by the British Government. By then, no doubt, there will be no survivors of the events which took place between 1940 and 1944. And by then, too, whatever might be revealed will be no more than a historical curiosity.

Afterword

It is now over forty years since 'Operation North Pole', or *Englandspiel*, took place, and in the intervening years much has been learnt about SOE.

It has become clear, for instance, that the mistakes made by Dutch Section were also made by other country sections and differed only in degree. It has also become obvious that SOE greatly under-estimated the ability of its counterparts in the Abwehr and SIPO. There was nothing inevitable about 'North Pole': both Schreieder and Giskes proved highly capable counter-espionage experts, seizing the few opportunities which came their way and making excellent use of them. Yet even this would not have been sufficient without the services of their V-men Ridderhof and Van der Waals. It was Ridderhof who gained that all-important first entry into Lauwers' organization, which set the ball rolling. Schreieder was also able to track down Andringa, De Haas, Sebes, Klooss, Ras and Jordaan by the skilful use of his V-men. A slip-up at any one of these delicate stages would have led to Dutch Section's being warned by the Jordaan link. As it was, 'North Pole' continued.

Nor was the Germans' success assured after the start of the 'Plan for Holland'. Giskes and Schreieder were continually presented with problems which required all their cunning and ingenuity to solve – for example, the evasion of sabotage orders, and the non-return of the 'Plan for Holland' leaders. In addition, there was the continuous threat that the OD might learn of what was going on and that they were supposed to have been contacted by Jambroes. Also the problem of drop-zone security was always a problem for the Germans, and there remained the possibility – probability, in German eyes – that Dutch Section might drop control agents unannounced. Also, a continuous supply of 'chickenfeed' had to be obtained from a German High Command understandably reluctant to hand over any item of importance. That this was achieved says as much for Giskes and Schreieder as it does for Dutch Section.

However, the *Englandspiel* had little effect on the outcome of the war. The Dutch sector was only a minor part of SOE's total effort, and in any event Dutch Section under new leadership was able to play a significant role in the Netherlands during the last year of the war. The invasion, when it came, was in Normandy not the Netherlands, so that German hopes of learning about it were misplaced.

Nevertheless, the *Englandspiel* was a tragedy for the people who were manipulated by both SOE and the German Secret Services. It adds to our understanding of human nature and of the way in which individuals can be used and treated in times of war. In the *Englandspiel* human hopes and ideals were shattered, leaving those who survived with a sense of bewilderment and cynicism. The treatment handed out by SOE to Dourlein and Ubbink after their escape from the Netherlands was not only completely insensitive but also unnecessary. If they were under suspicion, they could easily have been confined somewhere more appropriate than a cell in Brixton prison. Nor did the Dutch authorities help the matter by their petty demotion of both men, through a strict adherence to regulations. If anyone put an end to the *Englandspiel*, it was Dourlein and Ubbink, whose miraculous escape from Haaren in August 1943 allowed SOE to learn the entire story. Their courage and optimism were among the few bright points of the *Englandspiel*, yet they too were eventually crushed.

Lauwers was also poorly treated by his fellow-countrymen after the war. He was never officially honoured for his work, though his courageous attempts to warn Dutch Section would have led to a death sentence had he been caught by the Germans. Ironically, his post-war marriage to Wout Teller's widow, whom at the time he had saved from a concentration camp, was the one happy postscript to his story.

It is clear that on one important point SOE was less than candid with its agents. They were constantly assured before their mission that, if anything went wrong, they would be picked up. This never happened, even after agents asked for help because the difficulties were too great to be overcome. Quite simply, once an agent was in the Netherlands, he was on his own. There was no glamour or romance attached to working for SOE for the controller, anonymous in his office, there was only responsibility, uncertainty and worry. For the agent in the field there was merely frustration, fear, torture and death.

Appendix: A. Agents Connected with the *Englandspiel*

Name	Organization	Dropped	Code-name	Arrested	Fate
Van Hamel	(MI6)	27.8.40	Van Dalen	14.10.40	Executed
Zomer	(MI6)	13.6.41	Van Zetten	31.8.41	Executed
Schrage	(MI6)	13.6.41	Visser		Drowned
Alblas	(MI6)	4.7.41	De Waard	16.7.42	Executed
Homburg	(SOE)	6.9.41		–	Killed in Action
Sporre	(SOE)	6.9.41	–	–	Drowned
Terlaak	(MI6)	1.10.41	Vermeulen	13.2.42	Executed
Tazelaar	(MI6)	2.11.41	Pieterman	–	Survived war
Lauwers	(SOE)	7.11.41	Ebenhaezer	6.3.42	Survived war
Taconis	(SOE)	7.11.41	Catarrh	9.3.42	Executed
Van der Reyden	(MI6)	9.12.41	Schoete	13.2.42	Survived war
Dessing	(SOE)	27.2.42	George	–	Survived war
De Jonge	(MI6)	23.2.42	Van der Plas	22.5.42	Executed
Baatsen	(SOE)	27.3.42	Watercress	27.3.42	Executed
Ras	(SOE)	28.3.42	Lettuce	1.5.42	Executed
Jordaan	(SOE)	28.3.42.	Trumpet (M)	3.5.42	Died 1945 Mauthausen
Andringa	(SOE)	28.3.42	Turnip	28.4.42	Executed
Molenaar	(SOE)	28.3.42	–	–	Killed on landing
Niermayer	(MI6)	29.3.42	Napier	16.10.42	Executed

Name	Organization	Dropped	Code-name	Arrested	Fate
Klooss	(SOE)	5.4.42	Leek (M)	1.5.42	Executed
Sebes	(SOE)	5.4.42	Leek	9.5.42	Executed
De Haas	(SOE)	9.4.42	Potato	9.4.42	Executed
Parlevliet	(SOE)	29.5.42	Beetroot	29.5.42	Executed
Van Steen	(SOE)	29.5.42	Beetroot	29.5.42	Executed
Van Rietschoten	(SOE)	22.6.42	Parsnip	22.6.42	Executed
Buizer	(SOE)	22.6.42	Spinach	22.6.42	Executed
Van Hemert	(SOE)	23.7.42	Leek	23.7.42	Executed
Jambroes	(SOE/MVT)	26.6.42	Marrow (M)	26.6.42	Executed
Bukkens	(SOE/MVT)	26.6.42	Marrow	26.6.42	Executed
Beukemaar Toe Water	(SOE/MVT)	24.9.42	Kale	24.9.42	Executed
Drooglever Fortuyn	(SOE/MVT)	24.9.42	Mangold	24.9.42	Executed
Jongelie	(SOE/MVT)	24.9.42	Parsley	24.9.42	Executed
Mooy	(SOE/MVT)	24.9.42	Cauliflower	24.9.42	Executed
Van der Giessen	(SOE/MVT)	1.10.42	Cabbage	1.10.42	Executed
Kamphorst	(SOE/MVT)	21.10.42	Tomato A	21.10.42	Executed
Koolstra	(SOE/MVT)	21.10.42	Celery A	21.10.42	Executed
Pals	(SOE/MVT)	21.10.42	Pumpkin	21.10.42	Executed
Hofstede	(SOE/MVT)	24.10.42	Tomato B	24.10.42	Executed
Steeksma	(SOE/MVT)	24.10.42	Celery B	24.10.42	Executed
Macare	(SOE/MVT)	24.10.42	Celery C	24.10.42	Executed
Pouwels	(SOE/MVT)	24.10.42	Tomato C	24.10.42	Executed
Dane	(SOE/MVT)	27.10.42	Cucumber A	27.10.42	Executed
Bakker	(SOE/MVT)	27.10.42	Cucumber B	27.10.42	Executed

Name	Organization	Dropped	Code-name	Arrested	Fate
De Kruyff	(SOE/MVT)	28.11.42	Mustard	28.11.42	Executed
Ruseler	(SOE/MVT)	28.11.42	Broccoli	28.11.42	Executed
Ubbink	(SOE/MVT)	29.11.42	Chives	29.11.42	Survived war
Overes	(SOE/MVT)	29.11.42	Cress	29.11.42	Executed
Terwindt	(MI9)	13.2.43	Chicory	13.2.43	Survived war
Van der Bor	(SOE/MVT)	16.2.43	Endive	16.2.43	Executed
Braggaar	(SOE/MVT)	16.2.43	Parsley A	16.2.43	Executed
Hulsteyn	(SOE/MVT)	16.2.43	Radish	16.2.43	Executed
Van Os	(SOE/MVT)	18.2.43	Broadbean	18.2.43	Executed
Van der Wilden	(SOE/MVT)	18.2.43	Tennis	18.2.43	Executed
Kist	(SOE/MVT)	18.2.43	Golf	18.2.43	Executed
Arendse	(SOE/MVT)	19.3.43	Seakale	9.3.43	Executed
Boogaert	(SOE/MVT)	9.3.43	Kohlrabi	9.3.43	Executed
Dourlein	(SOE/MVT)	9.3.43	Sprout	9.3.43	Survived war
Van Uytvank	(SOE/MVT)	21.4.43	Gherkin	21.4.43	Executed
Wegener	(SOE/MVT)	21.4.43	Lacrosse	21.4.43	Executed
Rouwerd	(SOE/MVT)	21.4.43	Netball	21.4.43	Executed
De Brey	(SOE/MVT)	21.5.43	Croquet	21.5.43	Executed
Mink	(SOE/MVT)	21.5.43	Polo	21.5.43	Executed
Punt	(SOE/MVT)	21.5.43	Squash	21.5.43	Executed
Zembsch Schreve	(SOE/MVT)	22.7.43	–	20.3.44	Survived war
Cnoops	(SOE/MVT)	23.9.43	–	–	Survived war
Van Schelle	(SOE/MVT)	18.10.43	Badminton	–	Survived war
Grun	(SOE/MVT)	18.10.43	Rugger	–	Survived war

Author's note:
This list is by no means a complete list of the agents sent to the Netherlands during this period, and represents merely those who are mentioned in this book.

Appendix B: The Plan for Holland: Contemporary Orders

MOST SECRET.

00182.

The Plan for Holland

Copy No.2

1. *Foreword*

When the time comes for the invasion of *Western Europe* by the United Nations, a vital contribution to victory can be made in *Holland* by the concerned action of numerous small bodies of resolute men. This action, to be effective, must conform in time, place and extent with the requirements of the invading armies. It must be carefully planned and the personnel to be used must be organised, properly instructed and adequately equipped for their work.

It is known that resolute men, ready to volunteer for any task, are available in their thousands. The number required for really vital action is not, however, very large and it should therefore be possible to employ specially selected men only for such purposes.

A plan has been drawn up and elaborated in some detail. Its essence is given in the following pages but it is fully recognised that many amendments may have to be made before this plan can be transferred from the plane of theory to that of practice. In particular, the study of local conditions and the judicious use of information not available in *London* will dictate the course to be followed in effecting modifications. The greatest possible latitude and the fullest possible freedom of action must be left to those directing operations on the spot, provided that the essential objectives are duly reached.

The Plan is not directly concerned with the numerous bodies

of men who, from their own resources, will undoubtedly be active in impeding the enemy and causing confusion in the rear areas – giving false information, spreading false rumours, causing isolated incidents and similar fifth-column activities; nor does it relate to any direct armed support for the forces of the United Nations which may have effected a landing.

00181.
2. *Object.*

The object of the Plan is, briefly, so to organise, instruct and equip *specially selected bodies* from the patriot forces in *Holland* that they will be in a position to create maximum and vital disruption in rear of the enemy and thereby prevent the movement of re-inforcements and reserves, *when the time is ripe to do so.*

3.*Objectives.*

No matter where the scene of actual invasion may be, the object will best be served by disrupting all lines of communication between *Germany* and *Holland* and between *Belgium* and *Holland*, such disruption to be made effective for the longest possible period, with a minimum of 72 hours.

It is considered that the objectives for attack should be, in order of priority:–

a) Railway communications.
b) Road communications.
c) Telecommunications.
d) Aerodromes; fuel and stores for aircraft and motor transport.

Maps have been prepared to illustrate the Plan. One map shows the railways and the main secondary roads in the frontier districts, which must be attacked, and indicates the various points which would appear to be the most vulnerable. On this map are also marked the 22 aerodromes which it is believed are used by German fighter aircraft. A second map shows the lay-out of telecommunications and, incidentally, power trans-mission lines, although attacks on the latter are not envisaged and must not be made unless specific instructions to that effect are given.

a) Railway Communications.

There are altogether 20 sections of railway which should be

blocked. Possible points of obstruction have been selected at bends, cuttings, embankments and switch-points. It must, however, be borne in mind that a section should be interfered with, if possible, at three or more points; for instance at a point indicated and at a point in each side not less than one kilometre distant. If the enemy is able to clear a line and use it again, the operation should be repeated at the same spot or at another suitable spot on the same section.

It is estimated that 10 men will be needed per section to be blocked. Some of these would be suitably armed to act as covering parties for the remainder engaged on the actual work of obstruction. The total number of men required for attacking railways would, on this basis, be 10 × 20 = 200.

b)   Road Communications.

It is estimated that by obstructing 51 road sections it will be difficult for the enemy to maintain road communications.

To obstruct these roads over a long period would be a very difficult matter. However, vulnerable points – where roads pass over or under bridges or through cuttings – can be found. It will be necessary to select a suitable section on each road and to arrange for interference all along that section. Although, through an arranged traffic accident, a road might be temporarily blocked at a certain point, it might well be essential to block it again at a different spot some hours later.

Some methods of obstruction will need the use of imported stores; in other cases, improvised methods such as the stretching of wires or the demolishing of a track or lorry, may suffice.

10 resolute men per road will be the minimum required. The total number will therefore be about *500 men.*

Untrained men who are only selected at the last minute can cause considerable confusion to the enemy, and thereby do useful work; for instance by changing road signs, misdirecting traffic, spreading rumours and causing the enemy to make mistakes. Any amount of men can be used for this purpose and they are not included in the total of *trained men* to be employed for the operation indicated in this Plan.

c) Telecommunications.

Both overhead and underground cables which were in existence before the invasion of *Holland* will be of use to the enemy. In addition to these he may have installed special lines of which there is no definite knowledge in this country.

Underground cables usually follow roads or railways, and

manholes placed 1800 metres apart give access to these cables. If it is possible to find a Post Office engineer who is fully informed in regard to the pre-war network, it would be well to discover from him at once where these manholes can be found and how they can be identified; also whether or not a special key is required to lift the manhole cover. A few hand-grenades dropped into the manholes will effectively destroy a line of cable, but to make location of the breakdown difficult, it is wise to attack three manholes in such a way between each of them there will remain two manholes untouched.

Where overhead lines are concerned, three pylons on each stretch should be demolished, again in such a manner that two pylons remain intact between each one brought down. This increases the difficulty of repairs.

It may also be possible to raid repeater stations.

It is estimated that *150 men* will be required for these operations.

d)   *Aerodromes etc.*

It is, of course, of the greatest importance to keep German fighter aircraft on the ground. There are several avenues by which this problem can be approached, but, short of armed raids, the most effective one will probably be to attack aircraft standing in the dispersal areas with hand-grenades.

Two men, one to act as armed cover and the other to throw the hand-grenades, would form an attacking party which the guards would have difficulty in intercepting. Four to six such pairs per aerodrome could perform a thorough task.

There are 22 aerodromes which are being used for German fighter planes, so that *220 men* might be needed as a minimum for these operations.

The destruction of fuel stocks is, obviously, best done by burning, although in some cases the piercing of tanks may be sufficient if the quantities stored are small. It is considered that little advance planning can be done but, when the time comes, untrained men belonging to the organisation might well receive a general order to do their utmost in this respect.

The number of men who might be used for such work is *not* included in the total.

4.   *Transport of stores.*

According to the figures given above, the minimum number of men required is *1,070*. It is estimated that the average weight of stores and arms needed by these men is 14 Kgs. per head, making a total of 14,980 Kgs. All these stores and arms will have to be transported by air and dropped by parachute to Reception Committees. The average weight which can be dropped conveniently by an aircraft is 590 Kgs. Therefore 25-26 sorties will be necessary to transport these goods to *Holland*. Some of the stores may fall into enemy hands and therefore a surplus is desirable.

It will be readily appreciated that, if weight can be saved by using hidden stores now in *Holland*, it would be possible either to use the aircraft for other purposes or to accumulate more stores than would otherwise be the case. It would therefore be well to investigate the possibilities of using such hidden stocks. In this connection it is wise to remember that some of them have deteriorated to such an extent as to be quite useless now.

5. *Organisation.*

For the purposes of the Plan, *Holland* has been divided into 17 zones. The exact boundaries of each zone will, of course, depend on the manner in which sub-organisations are distributed.

Each zone has been allotted a code name which will be used in all messages. A table giving these names is attached as an appendix. Furthermore, this table shows the minimum number of men which it is considered should be recruited in each zone, while a separate column indicates the total weight of stores which these recruits will need.

6. *Security.*

It will be appreciated that the maximum secrecy must be preserved with respect to this Plan. No one, not actively concerned, should know of its existence nor of the preparations being made to carry it into effect. Acquaintance with the details must be confined within very prescribed limits; for instance, an organiser in *South Limburg* should know nothing of the Plan as it applies to, say, *Overijssel*, nor, if possible, even that it does apply to that Province at all; similarly the men who will actually make an attack, although they must know in advance what will be required of them, need not *all* know, until the time has arrived, just where the attack is to be delivered. Precautions on these lines are essential and will readily suggest themselves to capable organisers.

The men recruited for this work must lead very careful lives until such time as they are needed. Participation in other underground activities must be rigorously excluded.

Other men, not these, must be used for the reception, transport and custody of stores.

7. *Warning for action.*

It must be clearly recognised that *no advance warning of any kind* can be given that the time is approaching when action will be required. It is fully anticipated that the knowledge that the United Nations have started their invasion will spread through *Holland* in a very few hours, no matter where that invasion takes place. Even so, it will be necessary to ensure in some very positive manner that action is not taken prematurely as a result of incorrect information or false rumours (which the Germans themselves may very well decide to spread in order to trap secret organisations into disclosure) or because a commando raid, and not invasion, has taken place. The method by which orders to act will be given, or the sign which is to be interpreted as orders to act, will be communicated in due course.

8. *Allied assistance.*

It is recognised that aid can hardly be expected from the inhabitants of a country unless some active support and encouragement is afforded by the United Nations. If *Holland* itself were the scene of invasion, these would obviously be forthcoming. If, on the other hand, the main battle were being waged elsewhere, it is improbable that fighter aircraft would be detailed for any important tasks, other than the interception of hostile aircraft operating from Dutch aerodromes. Bombers would, however, provide an intruder force operating over *Holland* throughout the 2d hours, engaged principally in attacks on centres of communication, aerodromes, etc. and thereby incidentally affording valuable cover for sabotage activities. The last mentioned would not be so readily detectable and much of the damage caused could reasonably be attributed to bombing.

12th June 1942.

Distribution:

Copy No. 1. Lieut. *Jurgens.*
Copy No. 2. Het Wnd. Hoofd C.I.D.
Copy No. 3. Lieut. Colonel K.
Copy No. 4. File.

Appendix

00175.

No.	Area	Code name	Men	Stores
1	Groningen	Savoy	30	420Kgs.
2	Drenthe	Ritz	40	560 Kgs.
3	N. Overijssel	Claridges	40	560 Kgs.
4	Z. Overijssel	Berkeley	130	1,820 Kgs.
5	N. Gelderland	Carlton	150	2,100 Kgs.
6	Z. Gelderland	Monico	80	1,120 Kgs.
7	N. Limburg	Kettners	160	2,240 Kgs.
8	Z. Limburg	Aperitif	90	1,260 Kgs.
9	Oost Brabant	Hungaria	60	840 Kgs.
10	Centraal Brabant	Crillon	80	1,120 Kgs.
11	West Brabant	Raffles	70	980 Kgs.
12	Zeeland	Shepherds	30	420 Kgs.
13	Z. Holland	Waldorf	30	420 Kgs.
14	Utrecht	Astoria	10	140 Kgs.
15	N. Holland	Miramar	50	700 Kgs.
16	Friesland	Splendide	10	140 Kgs.
17	Texel	Addon	10	140 Kgs.
			1,070	14,980 Kgs.

12th June 1942.

Operational Orders given to Jambroes before his departure for the Netherlands in June 1942.

MOST SECRET.

Operational orders Jurgens,
afkomstig van Departement van Marine.

00192
12.6.42
Copy No.2.

Orders for Jurgens

1.   You and *Boogaert* will be dropped together on the first favourable occasion from the night of 23/24 June onwards at a point .... (A) .... and to a Reception Committee, who will have made arrangements for the disposal of your parachutes and flying kit and for the safe housing of yourselves. From members of the Committee you will be able to obtain the latest information on rules and regulations affecting your safety

and on local topics generally. They will render you such assistance as may be required until you are ready to continue your journey but they should be told nothing whatsoever of your plans, nor should they know your destination when you leave them. You will be '*Jansen*' and Boogaert ' *Smit*' to them and they will report your safe arrival to us.

2. You should so order matters that you will be able to establish touch again with one or more of these men if, for any reason, you are unable to maintain wireless contact with us through *Boogaert* and wish to make use of the quick channel through which their leader communicates. No other link with the Committee should be preserved and its members should have no means of tracing you, once you have said 'good-bye'.

3. You will carry an identity card, a small number of food coupons for immediate use and the sum of Hfl. 5,000 in cash.

4. You are the leader of the party and, as such, have the final word in all matters of mutual concern. You will, however, leave *Boogaert* all reasonable liberty in the choice of locality or localities where he will establish himself for the purposes of wireless communication with Headquarters. The efficient maintenance of such communication, on your behalf and, in due course, on that of *Dubois*, is his sole duty in *Holland* and will normally include the enciphering and deciphering of messages. You will, however, have your own personal cipher, which will enable you to send and receive messages, (either through *Boogaert* or any other available channel) the contents of which will not be known to third parties. *All messages in your personal cipher will bear the prefix '(B)' en clair.*

5. You should separate from *Boogaert* as soon as possible after arrival, keeping touch with him only through intermediaries. It is preferable if neither of you knows where the other one is actually living. If it is necessary to meet at any time, do so as far away from your usual haunts as is reasonable in the interests of security.

6. To aid you in establishing yourself with every chance of safety, you will have, before you leave *England*, certain safe addresses where help will be forthcoming and know the method of approach which you should adopt towards each of them, as well as the code names to be used for them in the future.

7. You will carry out your mission in three stages, as follows:
(i) You will first of all make contact with leaders of the O.D. The procedure to be adopted in this connection is given in Appendix I. You will explain to these leaders that you have come from *London* with a joint mission from the Dutch Government and the British Authorities. You will tell them the

nature of the Plan which has been prepared, *and which you will have studied in all possible detail prior to your departure.* You will obtain their views in regard to it, but will make it quite clear that the Dutch Government in *London* expects them to give all possible help in executing the Plan, whatever those views may be. You will then discuss the best method of organising within the country those bodies of men which will be required to carry the plan into effect. You will report the substance of your conversations to *London*, through *Boogaert.*

(ii) After consultation with the leaders, and in the manner which they may think most appropriate to the circumstances, you will establish contact with members of the O.D. in the various districts in which the bodies of men will be required. As soon as you are satisfied that personnel is, or will shortly become, available in any given area, this will be reported to *London*, who will then arrange to despatch to that area at the earliest possible moment, a fully trained organiser-instructor, to perfect the organisation and prepare for the execution of the plan.

The personnel thus recruited with the help of the O.D. and almost certainly from amongst its members must thereafter devote themselves entirely to the Plan and engage no longer in normal O.D. activities. They will, in other words, be detached permanently from the O.D. and will form a separate organisation, controlled and directed from *London.*

As a guide it should be possible for one organiser-instructor to train and receive stores and equipment for from one hundred to two hundred men, according to the size and importance of the area in question and with the assistance of local organisers, and suborganisers. Thus, in some cases, two or more of the 17 zones into which Holland has been divided for the purposes of the Plan, may be grouped together under one organiser-instructor. The 17 zones and their code names, which will be used in all communications, and which you must learn by heart, are given in the Plan.

As far as may be possible each organiser-instructor will be provided with his own separate wireless operator.

(iii) You will endeavour to organise, with as little delay as possible and with the assistance of local partisans, not less than three and preferably four, Committees for the reception of stores and personnel in those parts of *Holland* which will be clearly indicated to you before your departure, and will explore the possibilities of transporting these stores within the country. It is of the utmost importance that explosives and other materials together with arms and ammunition shall be despatched from England without loss of time and distributed to secret dumps within the areas where they will be required for use.

The area organiser-instructors, acting in conjunction with *Dubois*, will ultimately be entrusted with this most essential task, but you must do all that is humanly possible in advance of their arrival to facilitate the speedy fulfilment of all preparations necessary for the successful execution of the Plan.

As a minimum you should organise within a few weeks one Committee to receive the organiser-instructors and a delivery of stores – up to six containers with a nett weight of stores of about 600 kg. – which can accompany each despatch of personnel.

Attached as Appendix II are important notes on the reception of personnel and stores by air. These must be carefully memorised.

Bear in mind that:–

a. The districts which are suitable for reception are, in most cases, a good distance from the scene of operations, so that the *transport of stores within Holland* must be organised with great care and thoroughness. This task alone will require the co-operation of a large number of men under expert direction.

b. The men used for reception and for transport must not be any of those recruited for the operations described in the Plan, nor, as far as this may be possible, should they know exactly what they are receiving and transporting or for what purpose it will be used.

8. During your conversations with the leaders of the O.D. you will ask them what they are prepared to do in the way of *direct* military support to an invading force, on what scale this support could be given and what arms and ammunition would be needed for the purpose. This problem will then be studied quite separately from the rest.

9. You will probably be asked what replies have been given by H.M. The Queen to certain questions put to her by '*Gerard*'. You will state that these questions, which are of a political nature, do not concern you and will be answered by another man, who will be despatched for the purpose. Her Majesty and Her Majesty's Government are, however, willing to afford all possible help of the nature known to the leaders.

10. It is understood that *Dubois* will follow you to Holland at an interval, if possible, of four to five weeks only; at any rate not later than about the middle of August. He will have had the fullest possible training in sabotage, demolitions and para-military activities. Moreover, he will know a great deal more about the details of the Plan than have been given to you and the

methods by which it can best be implemented. *Dubois* will act as your technical adviser and assistant and will take over your duties as soon as arrangements can be made for your return to *England*. The means by which *Dubois* will get into touch with you in *Holland* are discussed in Appendix III.

11. We intend to bring you back to this country as soon as possible after *Dubois'* arrival, in order that you may report to us verbally and discuss the future in greater detail than would otherwise be feasible. The alternative methods by which your return may be affected are dealt with in Appendix IV.

12. Should your normal channel of communication with us through *Boogaert* be interrupted, the following alternatives will be open to you:—

a. As indicated in paragraph 2 above. You could establish touch with another wireless operator by again making contact with a member of the Committee which received you. Messages sent or received by you through this channel should of course be in your own personal cipher and bear the prefix '(B)' en clair.

b. Through.................'(C)'....................................

It is believed that written messages or quite small packages can be sent through this intermediary up to about the end of November. Transit time is approximately one month. This channel of communication might, therefore, prove valuable for the despatch of a long report, even whilst wireless communication was being satisfactorily maintained. It has not, however, been tested yet and you should therefore consult us before actually making use of it, if you are able to do so.

Boogaert has also been informed about this intermediary and could encipher a report before transmission, if you did not wish to do so yourself.

Approach to ....'(C)'....................................

would be made by a 'cut-out' using the code word '*Katwijk*' In all messages referring to this channel, use the code word '*Hamburg*'.

c. The Man *Pyl*, who is referred to in the memorandum dealing with your return to *England*.

d. By letter, using your letter code, addressed to ....
'(D)' .... this must be considered very slow and uncertain route, to be employed only as a last resource.

N.B. The blank spaces at (A), (B), (C) and (D) will be filled in shortly before your departure.

Distribution.
Copy No. 1. Lieut. *Jurgens*
Copy No. 2. Het Wnd Hoofd C.I.D.
Copy No. 3. Lieut. Colonel K.
Copy No. 4. File

MOST SECRET.

00189

Copy No. 2.

Supplementary order for Jurgens

The I.D. It has been explained to you that the I.D. forms a separate branch of the Secret Organisation '*Oom Alexander*', and that it exists for the collection, arrangement and distribution of information regarding the enemy. Its functions are, in fact, those of a military intelligence service.

We intend to despatch a liaison officer with his own wireless operator to work exclusively with the I.D., so that the most important information collected may be made available to the Dutch Government and the British Authorities in *London* almost as quickly as it reaches the O.D. itself.

As soon as you are able to do so, you will inform the Leaders of the Secret Organisation of our intention and pave the way for the arrival of the liaison officer and his introduction to leaders of the I.D. We cannot say, at this moment, when he will be sent but it should not be later than about the third week in August.

Although you and the liaison officer will not work together and should not know each other, it should be possible for him to make contact with the persons awaiting him through one or other of the various addresses you have. You must make suitable arrangements for this on the spot.

In any messages concerning this matter use the code word 'Chalfont'.

1st June 1942.

Distribution:
Copy No. 1. Lieut. *Jurgens.*
Copy No. 2. Het Wnd. Hoofd C.I.D.
Copy No. 3. Lieut. Colonel K.
Copy No. 4. File.

00188

Copy No. 2.

APPENDIX I.

Methods by which contact can be made with the military branch (O.D.)
of the secret organisation 'Oom Alexander'.

1. The method which must be attempted first of all is through:–
Mevr. Ziegler–Cooymans, Van Meerkerkenstraat 14, Den Haag.
She should be able to bring you into contact with:–

    a.   The Centraal Bureau,
or b.   A provincial commander
or c.   The Chief of Staff.

If at all possible, do not go to Mevr. *Ziegler* yourself in the first
instance but send a suitable intermediary. This 'cut-out' (or you),
when meeting this lady should say:–

> 'I come from *Gerard*. In order to prove this I will add "alles
> sal rech kom" and tell you that the little picture of St.
> Christopher has done splendid work on its journey'.

Then ask Mevr. *Ziegler*:– 'Will you go to the Doctor for me and
ask him these questions?':–

> (i) Have *Gerard's* and *Ab's* friends still the same positions
> in the organisation and does he, the Doctor, know how
> they can be contacted?
> (ii) If he does not know how to establish this contact, can
> he say how one should get into touch with one of the
> provincial commanders (preferably the Commander of the
> *Betuwe* or the Commander of *Den Haag*)?
> (iii) If neither of these questions can be answered in the
> affirmative, can contact be established with the Chief of
> Staff?'

If one of these questions produces a satisfactory reply, Mevr.
Ziegler should then ask the Doctor to give her an introduction to
the person concerned. (N.B. The order of preference is that of
the questions themselves.) She should take this introduction
home and keep it in a safe place until you approach her in
person. If you have previously used an intermediary, arrange a
pass-word with him or her, which will tell Mevr. Ziegler at once
who you are.

You and the Doctor must not know each other and you must inform Mevr. Ziegler to this effect.

The code word for Mevr. *Ziegler* in messages is '*Tante Greet*'.

2. *Should Mevr. Ziegler* for any reason, be unable to assist, approach:

Frederik Jacob *Klyzing*, Inspecteur van Politie. Ooievaarlaan 12, Den Haag.

Details of the approach to this man appear in the instructions concerning 'safe addresses', which we have given you.

Klyzing could put you in touch quite easily with the Commander of *Den Haag*.

The code word for *Klyzing* is '*Casino*'.

3. If neither of these methods succeeds, you will establish touch with:–

either Ir. H.H. *Rieuwerts de Vries*, Bakenbergscheweg 160, *Arnhem*, (Reserve Commander of the *Betuwe*).

or Ir. L. O. *van Delden*, Arnhemsche Octrooibureau, van Heemstralaan 98, *Arnhem*

and ask to be put in touch with:–

Res. Maj. *Schotman*, Gewestalijke Commandant *Betuwe*. through whom you should able to establish contact with the leaders of the O.D.

The code words are:–

De Vries '*Eerste Ingenieur*',
Van Delden '*Tweede Ingenieur*',
Schotman, '*Majoor*'.

4. Should all these channels fail you, approach:–

Kees Wegerif, Van Somerenweg 16, Rotterdam.

Kees is the son of Ds. *Wegerif*, Ned. Herv. Predikant in *Rotterdam* and lives with his parents.

Should Kees not be available, ask his parents to put you in touch with Mik *Blauw*.

This channel should also bring you eventually into contact with the leaders of the O.D.

The code word for *Wegerif* is '*Kees*'; that for Mik *Blauw* is '*De vriend van Kees*'.

5. Lastly Dr *Bolle*, who is mentioned among the 'safe addresses' given you, could almost certainly put you in touch with the O.D.

The code word for Dr *Bolle* is '*Bloem*'.

Important note

If any of the persons whom you approach demand some further proof of your identity and bona fides, we will arrange for a message to be broadcast in the European News Service of the BBC. You must inform us by wireless what message is to be sent and on which days.

21st June 1942.

Distribution

Copy No. 1. Lieut. *Jurgens.*
Copy No. 2. Het Wnd. Hoofd. C.I.D.
Copy No. 3. Lieut. Colonel K.
Copy No. 4. File.

MOST SECRET.

00185.

21.6.42

Jurgens

In paragraph 6 of your Orders, reference is made to 'safe addresses'. We understand that you have a number of your own, which you will use for preference; these are recorded in Appendix III. We give you, however, the following which have been checked fairly recently and are believed still to be quite safe. The decision as to whether you use them or not is in your hands. *You must notify us, in due course, whether or not you have approached these persons.*

1. Frederik Jacob *Klyzing*, Ooievaarlaan 12, Den Haag.

This is the same man as is mentioned in Appendix I, and there is no objection to your approaching him for assistance, *whether you use him to get in touch with the O.D. or not.*

You may use your own method of approach, or the following:– Send a 'cut-out' with a message to the effect that a friend of his 'brother-in-law' wants to meet him. When you see *Klyzing*, say: 'I have an introduction to you, *Dogger*, alias *van Schaik*, told me in *London* that you had two pseudonyms, namely "*Strik*" and "*Stork*". *Dogger* had supper with you last New Year, when you listened to Radio Oranje, using a chair and wire.'

The code word for *Klyzing* in messages is '*Casino*'.

2. Dr, *K. Bolle*, Arts, Stationsstraat 29, Pijnacker.

First of all find out where and when Dr. *Bolle* sees patients. Go to him then, as though you were a patient, and tell him that you heard in *London* from *Broekman* that Dr. *Bolle* knew Freddie *De*

Jong who went to the U.S.A. via *England*. He sailed to *England* with the party *Schilp-Broekman*. Dr. *Bolle* had conferences, before their departure, with *De Jong*, *Schilp* and *Broekman* in the 'Sectiebureau Stadsreiniging Amsterdam'; his wife was also present. After the arrival in *England*, Radio Oranje broadcasted the following message: '*Mop Penta Johnson schitterend geslaagd*'. You should then say to Dr. *Bolle*: 'This is my introduction'.

Dr. *Bolle* will be able to give you suitable addresses in *Den Haag*.

The code word for Dr. *Bolle* is '*Bloem*'.

MOST SECRET.

00184.
Copy No. 2.

APPENDIX III

Methods by which Dubois may contact you in due course.

You have given us three addresses, at which *Dubois* may be able to get in touch with you. It is understood that you will reconnoitre these addresses on arrival in the field and notify us as to which *Dubois* should use.

A code word has been assigned to each address and *Dubois* will be told how he can identify himself to the persons concerned.

The details are as follows:–

1. Mrs. *Van der Voort van der Kamp*, Lagevuurscheweg 1, Laren.
Code word: *Zwager*.

Recognition sentence: '*Ik kom met berichten van uw zwager Weiselberg*'.

(It is understood that *Weiselberg* is an Austrian emigrant now serving in the British Army.)

2. Mrs. *Eskens Crabbe*, Burcht Apotheek, Zuiddijk, Zaandam. Code word: *Apotheek*.

Recognition sentence: '*Ik kom van een ouden vriend die al anderhalf jaar weg is*'.

3.Miss Toni *Van't Hoff*, Onderwijzeres, Kamerlingh Onnesweg 469, Hilversum. Code word: *Wijzer*.

Recognition sentence: '*Ik kom van den leeraar die bij u gelogeerd heeft*'.(It is understood that if this lady is not at home, the members of her family can be trusted.)

Alternative addresses, which may be used, are those of *Klyzing* and *Bolle* –see Appendix I.

Finally, should none of these addresses prove suitable and you wish to give us another one for *Dubois*, for which no code word has been fixed, approach *Pyl* through *Pors* – see Appendix IV. *Pyl* has a means of coding names and addresses *before enciphering*, which gives additional security.

Distribution:
Copy No. 1. Lieut. *Jurgens*.
Copy No. 2. Het Wnd. Hoofd C.I.D.
Copy No. 3. Lieut. Colonel K.
Copy No. 4. File.

21st June 1942.

MOST SECRET.

00183.

Copy No.2.

APPENDIX IV.

*Methods in which you may be brought back
to England in due course*

The alternatives are: by air, by sea, overland to the South and thence by air or sea.

By Air. It is decided to employ this means, all arrangements will be made by *Dubois*, who will have been specially instructed to that effect.

By Sea (a) You approach Mr. and Mrs. *Pors*, Zilkenduinweg, *De Zilk, Hillegom*, preferably through a 'cut-out' in the first instance. You call yourself *Johannes* and ask to be put in touch with Mr. *Pyl* of the Firm *Pyl Van den Berg*. When you see *Pyl* you show a desire to meet *Charles* and describe Major *Blunt* to him.

Pyl will make all the arrangements and you should follow his instructions. In messages refer to *Pyl* as '*Jantje*'.

(b) You might, although this seems unlikely at the moment, be able to escape through the channel mentioned in paragraph 12 (b) of your orders – code word '*Hamburg*'.

If this proved to be the case, we would give you the necessary instructions through *Boogaert*.

Overland. This method would be slow and is not to be recommended unless all others have failed.

It is not possible at this stage to give you any indication as to how it could be arranged.

15th June 1942.

Distribution:

Copy No. 1. Lieut. *Jurgens.*
Copy No. 2. Het Wnd. Hoofd. C.I.D.
Copy No. 3. Lieut. Colonel K.
Copy No. 4. File.

Bibliography

By far the most important source of this book was the Dutch Parliamentary Inquiry, with its thousands of pages of testimony and reports. What remains is mostly background reading, although there are some important personal accounts.

J. Beevor, *SOE, Recollections and Reflections 1940-45* (The Bodley Head, 1981)

A. Brissaud, *The Nazi Secret Service* (The Bodley Head 1974)

C. Cruickshank, *SOE in Scandinavia* (Oxford University Press, 1986)

R. Deacon, *A History of the British Secret Service* (Granada, 1980)

P. Dourlein, *Inside North Pole* (William Kimber, 1953) – Dourlein's own story of his war-time adventures, which has few equals. He provides a detailed account of his escape from Haaren.

M.R.D. Foot, *SOE, The Special Operations Executive 1940-46* BBC, (1984) – By far the most important British source on SOE, both readable and detailed.

M.R.D. Foot, *Resistance* (Eyre Methuen, 1976). More interesting background material.

M.R.D. Foot and J.M. Langley, *MI9 Escape and Evasion* (Futura, 1980) Excellent background reading.

H. Giskes, *London Calling North Pole* (William Kimber, 1953) – Giskes' own account of 'Operation North Pole' and the first to appear in the English language. Readable and interesting, with a remarkable preface written by his old adversary, Lauwers.

J. Haestrup, *European Resistance Movements 1939-45* (Meckler, 1981)

Philip Johns, *Within Two Cloaks* (Kimber, 1979). Useful background reading by a senior intelligence officer who commanded Dutch Section in the aftermath of the *Englandspiel*.

R.V. Jones, *Most Secret War* (Hamish Hamilton, 1978)

Ronald Lewin, *Ultra Goes to War* (Hutchinson, 1978)

J. Masterman, *The Double-Cross System in the War 1939-45* (Yale University Press, 1972)

Erik Hazelhoff Roelfzema, *Soldier of Orange* (Sphere, 1982). Roelfzema provides an action-packed and mostly accurate account of some of the most spectacular secret operations of the war.

D. Stafford, *Britain and European Resistance 1940-45* (Oxford University Press, 1980) Textbook analysis of some of the wider issues of European Resistance. Very academic.

G. Welchman, *The Hut Six Story* (Allen Lane, 1982)

Nigel West, *MI5* (Granada, 1983)

Nigel West, *MI6* (Grafton, 1985) Contains a somewhat inaccurate account of MI6's operations during the period of the *Englandspiel*.

D. Wheatley, *The Deception Planners* (Hutchinson, 1980)

European Resistance Movements Proceedings of the 2nd International Conference, Milan 26-29 March 1961: L. De Jong, 'The Dutch Resistance Movement and the Allies 1940-45'.

L. De Jong, *De Duitse Invasie: Fragmenten uit Het Koninkrijk der Nederlanden in de Tweede Wereld oorlog,* (Staatsuitgeverij, S-Gravenshage, 1977)

L. De Jong, *Het Begin van 'Het Englandspiel'* (Staatsdrukkerij, The Hague, 1978)

L. De Jong, *Het Koninkrijk der Nederlanden in de Tweede Wereldoorlog deel 9* (Staatsuitgeverij, S-Gravenshage, 1979). A classic account of the *Englandspiel* by the foremost Dutch military historian.

Gerard Dogger, *De vierkante maan* (Sijthoff, Amsterdam,1985)

J. Rep, *Het Englandspiel* (Van Holkema en Warendorf NV, Bussem, 1978). Notable for a very detailed account of Lauwers' capture and interrogations.

J. Schreieder, *Het Englandspiel* (Van Holkema en Warendorf NV, Amsterdam, 1949). Schreieder's own account of the *Englandspiel* written shortly after the war. Factual but rather dry.

J. Somer, *Man in Oorlog, De dagboeken van Majoor dr J.M. Somer. Hoofd Bureau Inlichtingen te London, 13 Maart 1942 - 22 September 1943* (Bosch & Keuning nv, Baarn, 1981). The diaries of the Dutch Intelligence Officer who sorted out the *Englandspiel* from the Dutch side. Provides a very human insight into the pressures of running a Secret Service.

De Parlementaire Enquete Commisie 1940-45, delen 4a, 4b, en 4c, de Nederlandse geheime dienst te London en de verbinding met het bezette gebied (verslagen en verhoren) (Staatsdrukkerij, The Hague, 1950) As already mentioned, the major source of this book.

Index